REFUSALS AND REINVENTIONS

REFUSALS AND REINVENTIONS

ENGENDERING NEW INDIGENOUS AND BLACK LIFE ACROSS THE AMERICAS

Daniel Ìgbín'bí Coleman

THE OHIO STATE UNIVERSITY PRESS
COLUMBUS

Library of Congress Cataloging-in-Publication Data
Names: Coleman, Daniel B., author.
Title: Refusals and reinventions : engendering new Indigenous and Black life across the
    Americas / Daniel Ìgbín'bí Coleman.
Description: Columbus : The Ohio State University Press, [2024] | Includes bibliographical
    references and index. | Summary: "Uses the theoretical and methodological frameworks
    of decolonial pedagogies and lineages of Black, decolonial, and trans feminisms to
    demonstrate how creative insurgent labor in southern Mexico and the southern United
    States exist in and/or carve open access to the pluriverse"—Provided by publisher.
Identifiers: LCCN 2023052051 | ISBN 9780814215647 (hardback) | ISBN 0814215645
    (hardback) | ISBN 9780814283400 (ebook) | ISBN 0814283403 (ebook)
Subjects: LCSH: Intersectionality (Sociology)—Mexico. | Intersectionality (Sociology)—
    Southern States. | Indigenous peoples—Mexico—Social conditions. | Indigenous
    peoples—Southern States—Social conditions. | Black people—Southern States—Social
    conditions. | Black people—Southern States—Social conditions. | Decolonization. |
    Gender nonconformity. | Feminism.
Classification: LCC HM488.5 .C654 2024 | DDC 306.76/8097—dc23/eng/20240205
LC record available at https://lccn.loc.gov/2023052051

Other identifiers: ISBN 9780814259047 (paperback) | ISBN 0814259049 (paperback)

Cover design by adam bohannon
Text design by Juliet Williams
Type set in Adobe Minion Pro

For us: works-in-progress trying to get free

CONTENTS

ILLUSTRATIONS

ACKNOWLEDGMENTS

In the spirit of this book and the collective work that it is based on, *Refusals and Reinventions* would not have been possible without a village of support including community members; colleagues; friends; blood, chosen, and spiritual family; and partners over a decade of life. This is for you; this is for us.

Maferefun Gbogbo Orisha! Maferefun Gbogbo Egun!

My editor at The Ohio State University Press, Ana Maria Jimenez-Moreno, has been the most gracious and encouraging guide. Thank you for believing in this work from inception to completion and the many iterations in between. I have greatly enjoyed our fruitful collaboration.

Three anonymous reviewers provided critically generous, thorough, and thoughtful feedback on this work. Thank you for the time and care you took with my manuscript, which ultimately allowed me to listen to the spirit of the book and what it was asking me to bring forth.

Institutional support has also sustained the production of this book. I express my gratitude to my first institutional home—the University of North Carolina at Greensboro's program in Women's, Gender, and Sexuality Studies—who enthusiastically encouraged the birthing process of this book in its early iterations. I am very grateful to my former directors, Dr. Mark Rifkin and Dr. Lisa Levenstein, for guiding me in getting this work funded, for seeing its promise, and for supporting the beginning of my scholarly career. I am also grateful to Dr. Sarah Jane Cervenak and her colleague Dr. J. Cameron

Carter for reading early excerpts of the work and providing important feedback that helped the book to take new shape and shift direction. I would also like to thank the Faculty First Award through the Office of Research and Engagement for their summer 2019 grant funding, which allowed me to spend deep time back in Chiapas. My thanks also to Linda Arnold Carlisle for the funding I received through the Linda Arnold Carlisle Grant of the WGSS program in 2020 and for the Kohler Grant through the College of Arts and Sciences in 2021. I would also like to thank my former colleagues Dr. Danielle Bouchard and Dr. Derek Krueger, the extended WGSS body at UNC Greensboro, and Anthony Verdino and Dr. Jason L. Herndon for unwaveringly supporting and advocating for my scholarship, teaching, and artistic production in big and small ways.

To my colleague and friend Dr. Neelofer Qadir, who saw me through the latter half of my time at UNC Greensboro in our micro faculty members of color tea-drinking and treats support system. Thank you also for providing such encouragement on my early and unpolished chapter drafts. And to two amazing scholar friends who overlapped with me during my time at UNC Greensboro, Dr. Tara T. Green and Dr. Claudia Cabello-Hutt, thank you for your mentorship and friendship during such formative years of my scholarly career.

I'd also like to thank my marvelous undergraduate and graduate students, whose brilliance has impacted this work. I'd like to give special shout-outs to graduate students whose thinking and generosity have informed my approach to teaching and mentorship and are also part of the spirit of this work: MK Garcia, Jaimie Corey, Emmy Vaught, Dr. Kendra Bryant, Rosalinda Kowalczewski, Kelton Hollister, Farimah Bayat, Anna Elliott, and Kemisa Kassa.

To my second institutional home, Georgia State University's Institute for Women's, Gender, and Sexuality Studies, thank you for being a soft landing. I am grateful to have another very supportive director, Dr. Jennie Burnet, who welcomed me with open arms and made the space and time for me to see this book to completion. Thank you. To my colleagues of the Writing In Network program, Dr. Cirleen DeBlaere and my cohort, Dr. Rosita Scerbo, Dr. Tiffany A. Player, and Dr. Michelle Zoss, for the gorgeous supportive space we held for one another's writing processes. I'm grateful to have completed my major revision in the company of you all. To Dr. Stephanie Y. Evans, thank you for being the senior scholar friend I've longed for and for your reciprocity, genuine kindness, and wisdom. To Dr. Sonny Nordmarken for such sweet, easeful friendship as we each come into Atlanta. To the rest of my colleagues in WGSS at Georgia State, thank you for the blessing of a simple and collaborative workplace that opens great spaciousness for authentic teaching, abundant writing, and a life outside of those walls. Thank you also to the Africana Studies Department at GSU for the warm welcome and affiliation and for being such a grounding force for a young Black scholar.

My phenomenal students at GSU, graduate and undergraduate, have deepened my love for teaching and mentoring and renewed my conviction that critical thought is crucial to bringing the pluriverse into existence.

To Global Exchange and the Hemispheric Institute for Performance and Politics in the Americas, thank you for providing meaningful and ethical opportunities for learning and traveling. A special thanks to Dr. Diana Taylor for creating the space to come back to Chiapas on terms that were in alignment with my political and ethical values.

To the Elsewhere Museum and the Constellations Fellows Residency, which provided me a space to come back into performance practice and take artistic risks, thank you for trusting me with whatever I brought to you. A special thank-you to George Scheer, Gui Villaba Portel, and Emily Ensminger.

Maritea Dæhlin and her performance residency platform La Trenza Negra provided the housing and studio space to be with the mountains and forest of San Cristóbal de las Casas in the summer of 2019 to reflect on my movements through its worlds. Thank you, sweet friend.

To the community of photographers whose images grace the chapters of this book, you deserve acknowledgments beyond the credits. In order of appearance: Moysés Zuñiga Santiago, photojournalist extraordinaire and friend and colleague who has accompanied me in many a vulnerable performance moment. *¡Gracias por este corazón tan grande y tierno que llevas dentro!* Kelly Creedon—I have fond memories of being alongside you and our Durham family during our organizing events and interventions. Thank you for gracing us with your talent. Nelly Cubillos, your joy and levity in times of great political turmoil in Mexico and the world was always such a balm and a blessing. *¡Gracias por estar, querida amiga!* And Daliri Lopez Oropeza—*me conmueve profundamente el compromiso que tienes al periodismo y fotoperiodismo, especialmente en México donde es un peligro contar la realidad de los pueblos. Gracias por tu generosidad en compartir tus imágenes conmigo/con nosotrxs y por confiar en mis palabras.*

To my long-term mentors and dear friends from my graduate education, Dr. Shannon Rose Riley, Dr. Della Pollock, and Dr. Catherine Walsh, the minds, hearts, and spirits of each of you inspire me in ways unending. Shannon, thank you for teaching me how to articulate my performance-making as a methodological approach to research, informing the pages here and elsewhere, and for inviting me to write about it. Della, thank you for seeing me in all that I am and for holding me with such grace. Cathy, *qué te puedo decir. Este libro es fruto de haberte conocido y de verme reflejado en tí de multiples maneras. Gracias por ser quien eres y moverte come te mueves entre los mundos. Tus maneras de caminar, pensando han sido un faro de luz para este trabajo y vida.*

My loveship and political-artistic partnership with Doris Difarnecio constituted a bedrock upon which worlds were formed. To my community, friends, and other connections formed in Chiapas, Mexico, whose work, friendship, love, and collaboration have had tremendous influence over my organizing, artistic work, and scholarship: Dr. Tito Mitjans Alayón, Magno Morales, Yolanda Castro Apreza, K'inal Antsetik, Drx. Marisa Ruiz Trejo, Berenice Vera, Dra. Patricia Chandomí, Mari Santiz Collazo, Juan Santiz, Arturo Gomez, Jesi Gomez, Monica Gomez, Dra. Xochitl Leyva Solano, Dra. María Teresa Garzón, Dra. Ines Castro Apreza, Dra. Rosalba Icaza, Xun Sero, Maricarmen de la Encarnación Petate, Rosas Rojas, Gely Pacheco, Gio Gomez Leal, Vere, Montse Mwezi, Sandy Gomez, Pía Qu, Ruperta Bautista, Medhin Tewolde, Cristina Díaz, Lore, Favricio Huerta, and Beto and *cuates* from El Paliacate.

To my community, friends, connections, and other mentors (largely those formed in the Southern US) that have influenced this work: Joseph Megel, Dr. Renée Alexander Craft, Dr. Walter Mignolo, Dr. Hannah Gill, Dr. Ali Na, Dr. Marie Alyssa Garlock, Dr. Miranda Dottie Olzman, Dr. Raul Moarquech Ferrera-Balanquet, Dr. Mab Segrest, Mary Hooks, Jade Brooks, Dr. Alexis Pauline Gumbs, Dr. Wayne Erik Ryšavý, Dr. Grover Wehman, Joie Lou Shakur, Ash Williams, Beth Brockman, Isaac Villegas, Dr. Cole Rizki, Monet Marshall, Cherizar Crippen, Holden Sessions, CJ Suitt, Dr. Fatimah Salleh and Eric Sorensen, Damien Pascal-Domenack, Florence Siman, Glo Merriweather, T. Grace Nichols, Jessica Moss, and Spirit McIntyre. I owe special expressions of gratitude to three people in particular. Emanuel Highlander Brown, thank you for our soul Black trans siblinghood, filled with deep affection and mutual respect and appreciation. Dr. Serena Sebring, thank you for your beautiful heart and guiding light in my own sojourns in activism. Thank you especially for saying, "We need you to write!" gina Breedlove, thank you for being a friend to my soul. I am grateful for the ways we reflect one another's light back to each other as we each journey forward.

Also, to Nina Otis Haft, Roberto Gutierrez Varea, Violeta Luna, Erica Mott, and Roberto Sifuentes—all artist-teachers with such tremendous integrity.

Lia García, thank you for your commitment to our siblinghood as a site of trans sanctuary. *Te amo sirenita linda.*

Saba Taj, thank you for gracing us with your gorgeous image for this cover. Thank you for collaborating with me and for helping make my vision come to life!

Two invitations, one to Mexico and one to Madrid, helped shape the course of this book and the many audiences and iterations the work requires. Dr. Sayak Valencia and her invitation to keynote the event "El regimen live: Extrañamiento visual, género, y feminismos en la economía de la Muerte" ("The Live Regime: Visual Estrangement, Gender, and Feminisms in the Economy of Death") at the Encuentro Nacional de Investigación Sobre Fotografía (National Reseach Gathering for Photography) in Mexico City, Mexico, in September 2018 helped me continue to think about the intersections of necropolitics and gendered violence in the Mexican context. The second invitation was by Migrantes Transgresorxs to Madrid, Spain, in February 2019 for a residency as part of the POPS (Programme Oriented towards Subaltern Practices) in their trans epistemologies track at Matadero Madrid's Centre for Artists in Residence. I would especially like to thank Alex Aguirre, Iki Yos, and Leticia Rojas Miranda and all of the workshop participants for thinking with me about the potentials of trans pedagogy for people of color.

My loveship with Ignacio Hutia Xeiti Rivera over a significant portion of this writing sustained and nurtured important thought-heart intellectual percolations about our many worlds. I would also like to thank my relationship with Dani d'Emilia and our Proyecto Inmiscuir, which further refined how I think about art and life conversing. My unclassifiable connection with Amber Khoi was a co-construction of expanded perception when differently constituted minds come together. Elizabeth Atwood Nelson's love held the birth of this work with nothing but affirmation and encouragement. Additionally, beloveds to thank include Dr. Karma R. Chávez, Dr. Meagan Solomon, Dr. Rolando Vasquez, Dr. Louis Yako, Dr. Claudia Sofía Garriga Lopez, Dr. Isis Sadek, Cara Hagan, Guillermo Gómez-Peña, Michele Ceballos Michot, Dra. Liliana Perreira Braga, Micheal Mpyangu, and Dr. Shannon Wong Lerner. J. Mase III and Lady Dane Figueroa Edidi were indispensable to my decision to engage in spiritual activism in secular academia.

To my godfamily, especially my elders Nicole Carr, Deborah Davis, Dr. Yvette Thomas, Oba Oriate Willie Ramos, and Alaje Thomas; my godsiblings and cousins Hezekiah Williams III, María Cherry Omírelekún Galette Rangel, Devonta Thomas, Brion Taylor, Rin Dakai, Kerrion Dean, Lynn Zolicoffer, Dr. Elizabeth Pérez, and Lakesha Crawford, I would not be where I am today in life and with this work without the love and support of every one of you. I love you to life!

Tina Louise Vasquez and Jud Esty-Kendall, your priesthoods and part-nership were my first example of what was possible for my life on the other side. Thank you for the good things that you poured into my early spiritual development and alignment—what allowed me to shift how I take care of my energy in performance work and, therefore, my very way of being an artist and in the world.

Mom and Dad, I could not have learned to integrate scholarship and art-istry the way I do today had you not endlessly encouraged both my artistic and intellectual self throughout my childhood. Thank you for loving me and supporting my dreams. I love you both, dearly.

To each of my four siblings, Michelle, Matteo, Nichole, and Michael, for being my inspirations and reminders that we all have our own paths to walk.

Finally, thank you to my fuzzy familiars, Xiqi and Gaza—whom I honor here as the glorious sentient beings that they are—for being the spirit pups who have seen me and my beloveds through the last decade of our lives with so much individual and communal joy, healing, affection, silliness, and sweetness.

Por/Para la Vida (For Life)

By Means of Introduction

The book in your hands or on your screen is a listening practice from several creative portals of entry. Through these portals, we will gain insights into ways of being/becoming[1] and creating knowledge (thinking/doing) made possible only by acknowledging our many worlds. The book adds its voice to the scholarship aimed at challenging the modern world's "algorithms of completion," the carefully calculated manipulations of congealed notions of human-made hierarchies and meanings for the purposes of modernity's own perpetuation, controlling who we are allowed to be and what we are allowed to know (Garrison Institute, 2021). Said differently, *Refusals and Reinventions* is an exercise in all that can be learned and gained by decentering some of the dominant, absented, and Euro-ethnocentric modern humanist delusions about superior and singular ways of being and knowing. We live for something else.

In *Refusals and Reinventions,* when I refer to the many worlds within this one, I am referring to the concept of the "pluriverse," offering my scholarship to the endeavors of other decolonial thinkers. I understand the conceptual work of the pluriversal way of seeing to be one of presencing and

---

1. I will elaborate more on the "why" of the slash between being and becoming in future chapters. As an introductory moment, you need to know that I see offering pluriversal takes on ontology as part of being and becoming on an ever-transformative continuum.

documenting some of the ongoing existences of our many worlds and their knowledge-life practices around the globe. As a form of practice, the pluriverse refers to "heterogeneous worldings coming together as a political ecology of practices, negotiating their difficult being together in heterogeneity" (De la Cadena & Blaser, 2018, p. 5). Through pluriversal thinking and the pluriverse, we can re-envision being/becoming and thinking/doing in the face of the collapsing and endlessly mutating modern/colonial global neoliberal capitalist world order.[2]

One of the originating conceptual frameworks for the pluriverse—relevant to this work—comes from the Zapatista motto "un mundo donde quepan muchos mundos" or "a world in which many worlds fit" (see De la Cadena & Blaser [2018] and Escobar [2020]).[3] I think of the pluriverse, within the parameters of this book, as a framework for thinking about being/becoming and thinking/doing that recognizes the *epistemological* "fact" that "people believe different things about reality" and the *ontological* "fact" that "there are different realities being done in different practices" all within and beyond what we, as a species, tend to loosely call "the" world (Law, 2015, p. 127, after De la Cadena and Blaser [2018] and Escobar [2021]). For the sake of clarity throughout the book, when I use "thinking/doing," I am referring to epistemology, and when I use "being/becoming," I am referring to ontology (I will unravel some of the nuances and reappropriations I move with for each of these Western terms in forthcoming chapters).

A central question guides the selection of four creative "case studies" that we will use to address the more abstract philosophical conundrums of this pluriversal book: What are some examples of political and creative projects that demonstrate, on the ground, how we can practice something other than what is given to us within the enclosures of "the" world—the purported singular totality that manages the operations of the present modern/colonial[4] global neoliberal capitalist world order—for people not situated at the primary axes of power?

The fictional singular totality that maintains and controls what I am naming the modern/colonial global neoliberal capitalist world order is something

---

2. I understand myself to be situated within and living from a pluriversal consciousness.

3. All translations from Spanish are my own unless otherwise noted.

4. As will be elaborated in the endnotes that follow, this slash between modern and colonial is important to decolonial epistemological and ontological projects because, as Mignolo (2011) articulates, "the interpretative mechanism of the rhetoric of modernity" participates in the "concealment of coloniality" (p. 52). Introducing the slash to keep modernity and coloniality in constant relation is meant to undo that concealment—"there is no modernity without coloniality" (Mignolo & Walsh, 2018, p. 4). My citational practice with this phrase is meant to invoke the genealogies of its emergence and the longevity of historical arcs and revisions it allows us to see. Hence, my work here engages in a constant assessment of the colonial designs glaringly present in modernity.

you will also see me refer to as the OWW, or "one-world world." The OWW is a concept of John Law's (2015) and refers to "a world that has granted itself the right to assimilate all other worlds, and, by presenting itself as exclusive, cancels possibilities for what lies beyond its limits" (John Law cited in De la Cadena and Blaser, 2018, p. 3).[5] The OWW is a dynamic that has convinced itself and others that it is all there is. In the context of the Western Hemisphere, I see the framework of the OWW as a way of naming the operations of coloniality or "the monopoly of modernity over the representation and appropriation of the real" (Icaza & Vasquez, 2013, p. 696). It has an epistemological and ontological stranglehold over our notions of what is "real."

We will be borrowing from Nelson Maldonado-Torres's (2007) definition of coloniality in this book. It is worth listening, for a moment, to Maldonado-Torres for what his work clarifies, while remaining in the purview of what the OWW maintains:

> Coloniality is different from colonialism. Colonialism denotes a political and economic relationship in which the sovereignty of a nation or a people rests on the power of another nation, which makes such a nation an empire. Coloniality, instead, refers to long-standing patterns of power that emerged as a result of colonialism, but that define culture, labor, intersubjective relations, and knowledge production well beyond the strict limits of colonial administrations. . . . As modern subjects we breath[e] coloniality all the time and every day. (p. 243)

What is important about this definition of coloniality is not only that it is distinct from colonialism but that it is directed at the area that has come to be known as "the Americas." Maldonado-Torres (2007) elaborates, "Coloniality is not simply the aftermath or the residual form of any given form of colonial relation. Coloniality emerges in a particular socio-historical setting, that of the discovery and conquest of the Americas" (p. 243).

The language of the OWW helps us make a macrotheoretical critique of hegemonically reproduced and often cisheterosexist, racist, xenophobic, classist, ableist, homophobic and transphobic, neofascist supremacies throughout the hemisphere and the world. False totalities are not always as glaringly obvious as when coming from fascist actors. The OWW's coloniality sneakily operates by posing as a set of tantalizing symbols of "modernity" and "progress," training citizen-subjects as the OWW's army. The goal is to make everyone manipulable and hell-bent on policing singular or totalizing views of a world, humanity, and hierarchies. We must ensure that the will of the modern/

5. In some places I will use "modern/colonial civilizing project" and in others, "modern/colonial global neoliberal capitalist world order," depending on the context.

colonial world order is not internalized to the point of enacting colonial operations on each other, a consequence of abandoning the pluriverse. To echo Emil Keme (2018), "a confrontation with the hegemonic system must begin with an assessment and confrontation with ourselves" (p. 45). This perspective is baked into the work of this book.

In light of the grammar of pluriversality representing a departure from dangerous singularities, three additional subquestions arise: (1) How do forms of insurgency seen as creative refusals,[6] rebellions, and reinventions (henceforth referred to as "creative insurgency/ies"), like the case studies we will think with, transform how we create knowledge (our thinking/doing) about our being/becoming (perspectives on our existence) under the duress of the totalizing presence of a modern/colonial global neoliberal capitalist world order? Here, insurgency refers to "the permanent continuum of struggle and change" (Walsh, 2023, p. 54).[7] (2) How do these creative insurgent practices give us access to our humanity to better be, become, feel, think, and do, together, the various forms of labor required to call in, access, and exist inside of and among a plurality of worlds? And (3) What do praxis and engaged witnessing have to teach us about what worlds from the pluriverse hold?

Before continuing, a note on who "we" are. "We," settled on for the purposes of maintaining an appropriate scope, is addressed to Black/Afro-descendant people and Native/Indigenous[8] people of all genders, located in the Western Hemisphere. Our "we" includes racially and ethnically mixed people, in our desire to avoid replicating essentializing or reactionary exclusions. The "we" I invoke here is one that needs no convincing about the significance of

---

6. I use the term "refusals" throughout the text, following the work of Native/Indigenous scholar Audra Simpson. Simpson (2014) speaks of "ethnographic refusal," which I understand to mean a refusal of ethnographic and ethnological accounts of Native and Indigenous peoples that are about "representing" difference—a politics that implies an absented universal colonial Human that is the norm, to which Native and Indigenous people are the Others of.

I also find the term fitting for Black refusal. I consider the work of Kevin Quashie (2012) to be naming what Black refusal can be or look like. I am inspired by his use of "quiet" as an antidote to "resistance" so that we are not constructing Black people and subjectivity solely through the lens of resistance and expressive life. It behooves us, Black people especially, to not consider Black struggles for liberation in an unfree "world" only as resistance because of how this locks Blackness and Black people in a dialectic relationship to whiteness. One way to do this is through refusing to play the game.

7. Further, Walsh argues that "insurgency" does not refer only to revolutionary turning-over but exists in a long horizon of ongoing and unending struggle (Walsh, 2023, p. 54).

8. I introduce a slash between "Black" and "Afro-descendant" and between "Native" and "Indigenous" to account for just some of the hemispheric variations of these categorical partitions, thought together.

cisgender women, transgender people, and *otroas*[9] in spiritual-political stewardship roles trying to get us all freer. Our "we" is endlessly plural, majestically nuanced, full of its own contradictions, and not always in alignment. Still, I refuse to give up on the role of collectivity for those of us with radical hope.[10] We will critically read the impacts of refusal from the embodied perspectives of women, trans people, and otroas involved in struggle. We will read these racialized gender perspectives for the collective opportunity they create to invoke more capacious forms of consciousness and action, perspectives that mythologize no one.

"We" is meant for those of us who, due to the ostracizing effects of coloniality, can only understand our lives as deeply relational. Therefore, we will relate to one another through an anticapitalist ethic that recognizes that there is room for *all* of humanity on a planet whose greatest destiny is one that contains many worlds.[11] We are also the descendants of those for whom "the" world ended a long time ago.[12] We will be encouraged by the death of the Anthropocene as an opportunity for a new pluriversal emergence. With all of this in mind, a final note of caution about romanticizing community or collectivity.

We is possible here through coalitionally grounded connections and shared affinities based on what Sylvia Wynter (1995) has called "conspecific relation"[13] (or accepting the collectivities made possible through reappropriat-

---

9. The term "otroas" will be addressed more completely in chapter 4. By way of entry, "otroas" is a term that emerged from Zapatista territory as a way of naming genders and sexualities in Indigenous community that cannot be subsumed under Euro-North American systems of classification.

10. I think of radical hope, following Gustavo Esteva, in the following manner: "not the conviction that something will happen in a certain way, but the conviction that something makes sense, no matter what happens" (Gustavo Esteva in conversation with Arturo Escobar in Escobar [2021, p. 119]).

11. In the modern/colonial world system we find ourselves in, it is common to experience fraught relationships, especially between cisgender women and transgender people. I have experienced this firsthand, particularly in organizing and in interpersonal spaces. In this book, rather than center these conflicts, largely present because of the fear of there not being enough room for all of us, my book assumes that cisgender women and transgender people can honor one another's truths as relational.

12. The idea that "the" world ended a long time ago for some of us is a sentiment shared by many (see Hoppe [2020, p. 126], Wynter [1995, p. 17], and Yusoff [2018, p. xiii]).

13. Sylvia Wynter's (1995) term "conspecific relation" is incredibly important, because it points out how terms like "Black" and "Native/Indigenous" are umbrella terms for a vast population, in the hemispheric Americas and around the globe, who have different languages, cultures, histories, values, cosmological intricacies, etc. These terms are inherently coalitional, then, but do not necessarily describe political affiliation or shared values. For this reason, what follows (affinity-based coalitions as defined by Bailey) is wonderfully important for this book.

ing the modern/colonial world's taxonomic categorizations) and what Moya
Bailey (2021) has described as "affinity-based coalitions," which are predicated
on ideological alignments that do not assume that shared identitarian categories alone are enough to engage in shared struggle (Wynter, 1995, p. 11; Bailey,
2022, 76).[14] An illustration of conspecific relation with an affinity-based coalition can be found in the words of Fausto Reinaga, who said, "I am not Indian,
damnit, but you have made me Indian and as an Indian I am going to liberate
myself" (Reinaga cited in Mignolo, 2008, p. 325). Here, we are to understand
the "you" to mean the "criollo" (Spanish descendants born in the colony)
elites in Bolivia. In other words, when Black/Afro-descendant and Native/
Indigenous peoples working together in conspecific relation and in affinity-
based coalitions reappropriate categories (like "Indian") used to oppress them,
colonization crumbles from within, having been denied the power to determine the meanings of overly simplistic and archaic categorizations designed
to differentiate an "us" and a "them." Such exercises in crumbling are part of
the collective sentiment of our gathering together.

Refusals and Reinventions challenges us to engage a more nuanced and
even fraught "we," probing the depths of the plurality among us, even or
maybe especially for those of us who claim deep affinities. I want my readers
to question assumed coherence within their and our senses of "we" because of
how "we're complicit, implicated, and tied in to things we abjure" due to the
sheer reach of the modern/colonial global neoliberal capitalist world order's
tentacles (Shotwell, 2016, p. 7). As painful as this also is to admit, *we* are also
the problem. How can we, following the words of Diana Taylor (2020), "challenge the colonialist imperative that others speak our language and the fantasy
that we understand each other" under such relentless conditions of duress (p.
79)? The enemy we are addressing from without here is an invitation to attend
the places where this enemy hides within and among us. What does it look
like to honor one another in "who we be[15] / become" through what we think/
do, despite the ways the enemy also lurks within? Let us start here.

Now that we have situated our "we," a tertiary level of questioning arises.
Refusals and Reinventions asks not only how we move through the forces of
hegemony at work in this purported singular "world" but how the work of
tirelessly creating, maintaining, and existing in the pluriverse of worlds moves
us toward other ways of being/becoming and thinking/doing. These lessons

14. About the latter, Moya Bailey (2021), in her work on digital activism and the power
of the hashtag #GirlsLikeUs, notes how this tag helped to create an online network of trans
women with shared leftist political imperatives, not simply an apolitical catch-all space for all
trans women regardless of political commitments (p. 76).

15. I intentionally use "be" here as an AAE (African American English) play on words. "Be"
here is meant to invoke the desire to simply exist (in plentiful being/becoming) without fear of
violence for the mere fact of your existence and the historical meanings projected onto it.

only become available to us by bridging spiritual-cosmological listening to historical-social-political realities. This is the labor of this book.

Refusals and Reinventions engages in a listening practice with four creative case studies selected as part of a decolonial pedagogical praxis of living and doing (more on what "decolonial pedagogical" means below). We will think principally from North Carolina and Chiapas, forging and establishing a North-South and South-South dialogue in the creation of transborder and pluriversal knowledge and conversations. The case studies we will think with demonstrate how creative insurgent political work, through its poetic provocations and doings, creates worlds, sustains worlds, and provides access to those very worlds, despite the dominant order's ongoing attempts at assimilating, subsuming, and eradicating our peoples, our cosmologies, and our entire ways of existence—our worlds.[16]

Refusals and Reinventions is meant as a reminder that there were worlds that held us before modern/colonial global neoliberal capitalism, that those worlds are with us now, and that we have the divine right to recover, reinvent, and practice what we can of our worlds. I am talking about an other-side-of-capitalism kind of abundance that can only come from being/becoming and thinking/doing from a pluriversal space of wholeness. I invite us to think with one another from sites of struggle, to be with the openings found in the discomforting mess that is our navigation of these worlds in the face of the centripetal force of the modern/colonial civilizing project and its racialized gender grammars.

I bring Greensboro and surrounding regions in North Carolina (US) and San Cristóbal de las Casas and surrounding autonomous regions in Chiapas (Mexico) into unexpected relationality for two interrelated reasons: (1) For the place each of these locations holds on the global map of justice movements: African American civil rights and abolition and Native/Indigenous autonomy and decolonization, respectively. In 1960 attention on the actions

16. I consider this work to be aligned with what Walter Mignolo (2011) calls "epistemic disobedience," building on the work of Aníbal Quijano (2007). He says,

> Epistemic disobedience leads us to decolonial options as a set of projects that have in common the effects experienced by all the inhabitants of the globe that were at the receiving end of global designs to colonize the economy (appropriation of land and natural resources), authority (management by the Monarch, the State, or the Church), and police and military enforcement (coloniality of power), to colonize knowledges (languages, categories of thoughts, belief systems, etc.) and beings (subjectivity). (Mignolo, 2011, p. 45)

By aligning with this understanding of how the colonial project affected every aspect of life in the hemisphere, I understand the creative refusals, rebellions, and reinventions or "creative insurgency" that I share here to be doing the work of turning toward life and away from the modern/colonial order's deathly grasp.

in Greensboro catapulted sit-ins into the national civil rights imaginary as a primary tactic. In 1994 San Cristóbal de las Casas became the epicenter of the public declaration of the Zapatista uprising, ultimately symbolizing successful Native/Indigenous autonomous stewardship of ancestral lands worldwide. And (2) my intentional movements and lives in each of these locations: the studies used in *Refusals and Reinventions* will focus on a five-year period (2014–2019) where the life I lived and the struggles I engaged in at each of these locations brought me alongside of and into perspectives and practices from the pluriverse. Allow me to expand upon my positionality—the sociopolitical followed by the geopolitical—prior to more fully articulating the historical significance of making these connections.

Grounding Positionality and Intentionality

Some of the sociopolitical categories that situate me are Black mixed-race from the US, or "afronorteamericano"[17] in Chiapas; lightly melanated; AFaB (assigned female at birth); transmasculine nonbinary; queer; bilingual in English and Spanish (nonnative, acquired); formally educated / middle class;[18] and more recently, the first transgender ordained Lukumí priest in my direct spiritual lineage.[19] I name these positions with their implications of privilege and

17. "Afronorteamericano" is the designation my friend Dr. Tito Mitjans Alayón (an Afro-Cuban Black feminist transmasculine scholar) uses in the context of our friendship and work together in San Cristóbal de las Casas.

18. Here I am not trying to conflate formal education and class by introducing the slash. Instead, the slash exists here because my middle-class status has been based on what my educational attainment has afforded me access to. Still, it has always been a slippery slope. Class and education do not necessarily (or even typically) have the direct correlation they used to have, given the reality of the capitalist dystopia that is the United States.

19. Lukumí is an Afro-diasporic religious and spiritual tradition whose cosmological precepts and spiritual understandings originated predominantly from people who came from what we now refer to as "Nigeria" and the former kingdom of Dahomey (what we now know as Southern Benin). It is a tradition whose practices, rituals, protocols, and ordinations were developed in Cuba due to the coming together of different West African people in the colony during the Transatlantic Slave Trade. Therefore, Lukumí theology and traditions reflect West African diasporic and Black Caribbean diasporic developments, grounded in the worship of the Orisha. Due to Cuban refugeeism, migration, and immigration, the tradition made its way to the United States in the twentieth century. Lukumí has spread around the globe and is now practiced by people of all races, even if it remains a traditionally Black/Afro-diasporic and Caribbean tradition. I come from a Black American lineage that is joined with an early Cuban lineage through our elders. Those of us who get formally ordained into the priesthood of the tradition—we are initiated Omo Orisha, or children of the Orisha—have been initiated into the mysteries of the Orisha or the sacred deities and guardians of our consciousness. These mysteries are not for public consumption and meant to be sacredly stewarded by those who are spiritually sanctioned, via divination, to do so.

oppression because of the way position comes to bear on our perspectives and analyses. Some of the nuances of the multitudes I contain and am contained by are worth storying a bit more for the sake of the work. I relay that below, followed by some unraveling of the connection between positionality,[20] lived experience, and study and their impact on my approach to this work.

Mainstream identity politics in the US might categorize people like me as biracial, especially because I have a white, or Euro-descendant, matrilineal line. However, my socialization and training as a light-skinned mixed-Black girl in strict, white supremacist, Eurocentric ballet institutions during a professional childhood career marked and shaped my body as always-already Black and determined my treatment. For this reason, I find that the clean cut the term "biracial" reaches for falls apart at its encounter with socio-historical-political life in the modern/colonial global neoliberal capitalist world order. My racialized and gendered body was framed as the stumbling block to my athletic and artistic aspirations. The lightness of my skin color did not protect me from the unrelenting and daily anti-Black racism hurled at me from teachers and choreographers. They failed to successfully groom me into anti-Blackness and internalized misogynoir,[21] resulting in my departure from the professional dance world on the eve of my adulthood and my turn toward other expressive and politically oriented art forms that celebrated a vast array of bodies and identities.

Though institutional and dance spaces have not been my only experiences with anti-Blackness and misogynoir, I name the embodied experience of my childhood because of how healing from it continues to shape my relationship to Blackness, gender, and creative work: namely, my conviction that Blackness, all forms of gender expression, and creativity will be sites of great joy and world-making in anything that I am a part of. The intersectional nature of the

---

20. I spend this time on my positionality to evidence the subjectivity of my thinking and to remain accountable to the sociopolitical realities of the OWW systems that we operate in. At the same time, in pluriversal, collective, and interrelational thought, I remain wary of positionality-as-apologetics, or positionality used for the purposes of a reductionist or essentialist exercise to justify the value (or lack thereof) of the work purely based on reductive and essentialist ideas about categories that are made in the OWW (Alcoff, 1991–1992, p. 16). This approach creates paralysis and forecloses on solidarity as well as coalitional and transnational labor. It also assumes that these locations are static, individually created, and not existing in a dynamic pluriverse (containing worlds in which their meaning falls away or transmutes altogether). Also, because "we live in compromised times," we are all implicated in the mess that we are in, a mess I choose to be with (Shotwell, 2016, p. 8).

21. "Misogynoir" is a term coined by Moya Bailey (2021) in 2008 and "is a portmanteau of 'misogyny,' or the hatred of women, and 'noir,' the French word for black which also carries a specific meaning in film and other media" (Bailey, 2021, p. 1). Further, Bailey (2021) explains, "Misogynoir describes the uniquely co-constitutive racialized and sexist violence that befalls Black women as a result of their simultaneous and interlocking oppression at the intersection of racial and gender marginalization" (p. 1).

race and gender politics of my material and embodied experiences over time has also meant, for me, that my trans personhood comes not from a re-storied childhood within transnormative frameworks (i.e., misrecognized boyhood)[22] but instead stands on the unerasable experiences, positive and negative, of being a mixed-Black girl and young woman. Building on this landscape, my experiences as a racialized trans and gender nonconforming person over the last decade, coupled with intellectual and community-based study of gender and queerness, inspired the deep time I have spent researching, studying, and thinking about the centrality of sexuality, gender, race and ethnicity, and Christian religion to this purported singular world's hegemonic control. For this reason, the analyses in the following chapters are grounded in racialized gender theorizations coming out of historical-material-political conditions that shape existence by denying the pluriverse. The Black, trans, and decolonial feminist investments that carry the forthcoming analyses, then, have been shaped by the trajectory of my lived experiences and embodied transformations, collective emergence contingent upon geopolitical realities, and courses of study to contextualize and expand upon my learnings, all thought in the context of a pluriverse.

Since my departure from professional dance worlds and my politicization as a historical actor existing in communities traversing many worlds, I have turned to various forms of art-, dance-, and performance-making as important mediums for responding to the horrific conditions the singular world creates. I am particularly invested in art whose goal is to create affirmations and transformation in its publics that are intellectual, psycho-emotional, cultural, spiritual, or all of these. Art can be one of the very vehicles through which we transform our existences and invite others to do the same. Making this kind of art took me around the world and back, forever changing how I exist in my body and the collectivities that shape it. For this reason, in this book I center the role of performance and other creative work to help guide us into other worlds.

One additional nuance is needed prior to continuing. In the long-standing colonial and imperial dynamics between the United States and Latin America, scholarly production has been part and parcel of these tensions. I will henceforth use Abya Yala South slash Améfrica Ladina to refer to the area otherwise known as Latin America (including the Caribbean countries that

---

22. I want to be very clear that I do not imply a hierarchy of normative versus nonnormative transness. What I am critical of is coercing trans people into adopting legible narratives when they face the pressures of acceptance and access to basic resources. The claim that one has been "born in the wrong body" can be manipulated for the mainstream in ways that make it palatable and assimilable into otherwise conservative and still binaristic logics.

get lumped in with this modern/colonial geopolitical categorization). Abya Yala has become an important substitution for Latin America, meant to refuse naming that represents the Spanish and Portuguese colonization of the continent. Allow me to explain why I have chosen these names and configurations.

Abya Yala (sometimes Abiayala) is a term in the Native/Indigenous Guna language that means "land in full maturity" or "saved territory" (Keme, 2018, p. 42; Walsh, 2017, p. 18, footnote 3). The Guna or "Guna Yala" are one of eight Native/Indigenous populations in Panama (Keme, 2018, p. 42). Keme (2018) also notes that Abiayala appears to be the only term that has been created from an Indigenous language in the continent that contemplates the entire hemisphere as an "Indigenous collective project" and that for this reason its usage was favored by the Guna and, more recently, by transnational Indigenous and non-Indigenous peoples in the hemisphere (p. 49). Keme (2018) also tells the story of Aymara leader Tupaj Manami ("one of the founders of the Tupaj Katari Indigenous rights movement in Bolivia"), who traveled to Panama after hearing of the Guna Yala's conflict with US imperialism in their territory in the late 1970s. Since Manami was able to travel, the Guna asked him to spread the message and significance of using Abiayala to other Indigenous nations—a "first step towards epistemic decolonization and the establishment of Indigenous peoples' autonomy and self-determination" (Keme, 2018, p. 43). Joining with the Guna and Manami initiatives, Keme (2018) proposes using Abiayala to signify a transhemispheric Indigenous bridge, bringing together alliances between Indigenous and non-Indigenous peoples to create a "historical bloc that opposes ideas and civilizational Eurocentric projects like 'Latin (America)'" (p. 43). Since the Guna, Keme, and Manami's "Abya Yala" includes the entirety of the Americas, and many who use the term do not include the US and Canada, I have opted for "Abya Yala South" to both acknowledge the original geopolitical meaning of the term and its disidentification from modern/colonially designed geopolitical borders, while still focusing on the geopolitical portion of the hemisphere south of the US border when referring to Abya Yala because of the political significance of this separation: transnational but not conflated.

Walsh (2017) notes that "Abya Yala" as a term runs the risk of erasing the Afro-descendancy of "Abya Yala South," even if the spirit of a historical bloc would not exclude Black people. For this reason, and in the vein of the hemispheric and Black-Indigenous transnational bridge being made here, I introduce the phrase "Améfrica Ladina" after "Abya Yala South," following the work of its creator, Brazilian scholar M. D. Magno (1980) ("Améfrica Latina" in its original form) and the late Black Brazilian feminist Lélia Gonzalez's theorization of it as "Améfrica Ladina" (Alvarez & Caldwell, 2016; Cardoso, 2014, 2019;

Henson, 2021; Magno, 1980; Rios, 2019; UCPA, 2018). Gonzalez built upon Magno's original formulation of "Améfrica Latina" as a counter-terminology to "Latin America" when asked to speak about conditions that pertained to Brazil as "Latin America," in ways that could account for its uniqueness as the only country colonized by the Portuguese and for its tremendous Black/Afro-descendant population (see Magno [1980]).

Born Leila de Almeida to a Black father and Indigenous mother in 1942 in Belo Horizonte, Minas Gerais, Brazil, Gonzalez was one of eighteen children in a working-class family and spent most of her upbringing in Rio de Janeiro (Henson, 2021, p. 349). Gonzalez, a scholar and political organizer for Black people in Brazil, adopted "Améfrica Ladina" and theorized her own terminology based on this geopolitical reconfiguration—what she called "amefricanidade"—to unite Black people throughout the Americas through a shared sense of "displacement, colonialism, slavery, and ongoing structures of white supremacy" (Henson, 2021, p. 351). Henson further explains,

> She does this by refusing how nationality takes primacy as the noun in one's identity, reducing the "Afro" as an adjective. Instead of "Afro-Brazilian" or "Afro American," Gonzalez flips it. She utilizes the term Amefrican via the following formula: American + African = Amefrican. It signals Black people as first and foremost "African," thus the root or base of Black people's identity. The American, truncated as "Ame-," is illustrative of Black people's routes to and within the Americas. This is why the Ame- is an adjective identity that acknowledges the routes as well as transformations of Black people in the Americas, thus altering but not replacing their African root identity. (p. 351)

The Améfrica of Améfrica Ladina and amefricanidade, while of a Black transnational diasporic sensibility, is, additionally, careful to not reinforce US hegemony. Of note, Brazil is the second largest Black country in the world, meaning far more Black people were brought to Brazil during the Transatlantic Slave Trade than anywhere else in the Americas (Alvarez & Caldwell, 2016, p. vii). These conceptual frameworks were used by community members and scholar-activists like Gonzalez in the postmilitary dictatorship period of Brazil (1964–1985) to articulate "black women's experiences, identities, and struggles" (p. vii). And, in alignment with what this book argues later on in the introduction (with respect to Wynter and Black civil rights in the US), "though Afro-descendant Brazilian feminists were aware of developments in the U.S., in its origins, it was largely 'homegrown,' less directly influenced by black feminisms in the U.S. or elsewhere in the diaspora" (vii).

Also of note, amefricanidade's critique of the intersections of colonialism and its attendant racism and cisheteropatriarchy also encompasses Indigenous women as part of this shared analysis, betraying the modern/colonial civilizing project's modes of operation, classification, and segregation across the massive geopolitical landscape known as "the Americas." Though the meaning of "ladino" shifts with geopolitical lines in Abya Yala South / Améfrica Ladina, for Gonzalez it means a "transitory and insurgent connection of a subject in movement and transformation, that recolonizes from within, and as a strategy of subversion, the colonial structures of Latin America" (Gonzalez quoted in Henson, 2021, p. 355). Subversion from within, as we will trace throughout, is a dynamic I see as a key component of pluriversal being/becoming and thinking/doing.

As stated above, it was Gonzalez that changed Magno's term "Améfrica Latina" to "Améfrica Ladina." She did this to decenter Europeanness and Latinness and appreciate Black/Afro-descendant, Native/Indigenous, and mixed-descent peoples who center their Blackness, their Indigeneity, or both (Gonzalez cited in Henson, 2021, p. 355). Gonzalez's work cuts through Brazil's infamous "racial democracy"—a Brazilian brand of the melting pot theory— and the whitening project of *mestiçagem* (miscegenation) (p. 354).

For these reasons and others, I bring a Black/Afro-diasporic naming sensibility and a Native/Indigenous naming sensibility together—Abya Yala South / Améfrica Ladina—to critically name the southern half of the continent.

Continuing these nuances of geopolitical grammars, taking after the thought of Ramón Grosfoguel (2006), my work fully comprehends that "*no one* escapes the class, sexual, gender, spiritual, linguistic, geographical, and racial hierarchies of the Euro/North American capitalist/patriarchal modern/ colonial world system," even as we critique the very construction of these partitions (p. 21; emphasis mine). I acknowledge the impossibility of fully transcending the present world order at the level of the sociopolitical, while also practicing the co-constitution of critical subjectivity in relational webs of care and struggle that are meant to honor and account for many worlds. My privileges of skin color, nationality, educational attainment / class, and institutional employment are privileges I intentionally mobilize. I am propelled by the knowledge I carry in my body-mind-spirit from firsthand experiences with oppression and the epigenetic, atemporal memories of the suffering of my ancestors; by the lessons learned in the work of caring for and struggling alongside communities outside of and intersecting my own in an ecological consciousness of interrelation; and by participating in transnational networks of thinkers, makers, and doers who know that a softer experience of human and more-than-human life is the birthright of all. I mobilize what I am able, existing in intentional community (never assumed or forced), in the service of collective liberation praxes, some of which are explored here. With this aspect of my positionality articulated, I can now share my geopolitical situatedness in each location.

I am a transplant to the US South from the infamous "Left Coast," motivated by the profound spiritual tether I have to my Black ancestry, which could not be satisfied if perpetually geopolitically and historically dislocated. Navigating my life project, in part, by building my home in the geopolitical region that once housed my ancestors' enslavement on both sides of my paternal lineage is part of my own refusal to surrender to singular notions of these Southern geographies while honoring the pull of my spirit to dwell in the insurgence of an-other family legacy. It was in the South where I learned how to move in the direction of this refusal.

My ticket home was the pursuance of a scholarly career in the South. I chose Southern-based scholars who believed in the path of knowledge production as central to any process of transforming socio-political-spiritual consciousness, where life and thinking are integrated pieces of one another, not a detached "career." Concomitantly, then, I became involved in the political movement work of the region, particularly with multiracial LGBTQ+ organizations like SONG (Southerners On New Ground) who believe that issues that are vital to the South are also vital to the rest of the United States. Said differently, I worked alongside radical organizing hearts from or based in the South who understand that the South is a place where all the major issues facing the nation play out. Rather than see the region as an extremist exception to an otherwise liberal nation a (worn-out mythos about the region and the nation), what Southern organizers fight for is the right to remain and make life here by honoring, protecting, and defending the many worlds that are ours, in contradistinction to the racist, xenophobic, homicidal, and terroristic actors and policies who stand in proud synch with slavery and genocide. It is powerful to exist and fight alongside people who will never let the South be fully turned over to its Confederate children. Then, you find that you are also one of the people carrying that torch of refusal forward.

Some of the issues and campaigns I have been involved with in Southern organizing have included how to intervene in and stop ICE raids on undocumented Latinx communities, comprehensive immigration reform with a queer and feminist political lens,[23] and prison abolition as part of the long-term

---

23. In particular, the campaign I worked on took political framing and inspiration from the 2010 zine "Undoing Borders: A Queer Manifesto" by the California-based organization HAVOQ (Horizontal Alliance for Very Organized Queers). The zine is an excellent resource for defining political terms related to the impacts of neoliberalism on undocumented immigration on the US-Mexico border. It also unpacks, with great nuance, why anyone working

and unfinished project of Black liberation. Sometimes political organizing in the South looks like political education and relationship-building, involving movement elders and newbies alike, over Southern potluck meals in peoples' homes.

The South is also where I first was called to Afro-diasporic spiritual community and initiation, where I first engaged in what is now being called "healing justice"[24] work, and where I continue[25] to make artistic/artivist[26] work to respond to various forms of political oppression leveraged against women, queer and trans folks, and Black people and other people of color. In the process, not only did I find home and transformation through relationships and struggle, but I have actively participated in the shaping of a richly diverse and joyously defiant Southern cultural-political life.

My political, ethical, and relational commitments in the *Mexican* South began in 2007 through a "reality tour" with the organization Global Exchange. Global Exchange describes itself as "an international human rights organization dedicated to promoting social, economic and environmental justice around the world."[27] The limiting language of human rights and the necessary critiques of it might distract from the beauty of their work. Their "reality tours" invite individuals (often students) to apply to participate in a delegation to select locations, typically in Abya Yala South / América Ladina. The local site is experienced through learning alongside collectives, organizations, and movements combatting the major issues negatively impacting the region. The course uses a course reader, with contributions from an array of authors with aligned critiques of neoliberalism, to supplement work in the community. During my tour, we also had daily scheduled conversations to process what we were learning through witnessing and reading; we used these sessions to develop critical thought needed to more completely analyze how forces like colonialism, imperialism, neoliberalism, and capitalism have led to or otherwise contributed to the issues that communities face. We also learned about our individual and collective roles in global problems and how to exist responsibly locally and internationally.

---

on issues relating to borders and immigration can benefit from thinking of them through a queer lens (not just the queer border crossers). The zine is still available online here: https://undoingborders.wordpress.com/.

24. For an account of healing justice work that demonstrates the centrality of the South, I recommend Page & Woodland (2023).

25. Though artistic production ebbs and flows like so much else, I remain an active performing artist with much forthcoming work in the South.

26. I introduce a slash between "artistic" and "artivist" work because not all artistic work serves an artivist function. Mine does. Artivism refers to politically activated artwork meant to serve an activist purpose.

27. Quoted from Global Exchange's webpage: https://globalexchange.org/.

A solid portion of my 2007 reality tour took place deep in the jungle inside Zapatista territory. Our job as delegates was to interview Zapatista men and women in Caracól Morelia[28] about the most recent threats, attempted coercion, and methods of intimidation being leveraged against them by the Mexican military. (We had been briefed about some of the issues we might hear about by another of our political guides local to the region.) After documenting the experiences of the *compas*,[29] we filed written reports with the principal human rights center in Chiapas, El Centro de Derechos Humanos Fray Bartolomé de las Casas (Friar Bartolomé de las Casas Center for Human Rights). My justice-centered experience in San Cristóbal left within me a commitment to return, under the proper circumstances.

In the summer of 2013, after the first year of my doctoral program in North Carolina and grounding in the US South, I found myself back in San Cristóbal de las Casas, Chiapas, for an Art and Activism summer seminar with Diana Taylor, Lorie Novak, Jesusa Rodríguez, and Jacques Servin of the Yes Men[30] through the Hemispheric Institute for Performance and Politics in the Americas, New York University. I joined an international contingent of graduate students, artists, community members, and thinkers who had applied to participate. The course bridged scholarship, activism, and performance

28. The Zapatistas have been organizing their territories into autonomous municipalities called Municipios Autónomos Rebeldes Zapatistas (Rebel Zapatista Autonomous Municipalities), or MAREZ, since 2003. These zones are named after and organized around the symbol of the *caracol* (plural: *caracoles*), or "snail." Of the significance of this symbol, and in tracing the Zapatista oral histories about the snail and its presence in the communities, Diana Taylor (2020) says,

> The caracol, as a social formation, enacts the system of equivalences. The snail, for the Maya, was the glyph for zero. It symbolized birth, rebirth, and fertility, as well as confinement coming from the womb and female sexual organs [sic]. Snails move directly through the earth, epitomizing rearguard theory, the knowledge that "flies at low altitude . . . stuck to the body." Zapatistas honor the slow and steady pace of the snail, the patience and expenditure required for all doing. Snails carry their homes with them; their paintings and sayings encapsulate an entire worldview. The snail shell serves as the design layout for their communal lands that spiral open from the tight administrative centers. The snail both encloses and exposes—it's both a door and a window that enable and regulate contact with the outside world. (p. 97)

The snail, as we can see from this passage, is at the heart of Zapatista cosmology. There are five Zapatista caracoles: La Realidad, Roberto Barrios, La Garrucha, Oventic, and Morelia.

29. "Compas" is a term used in Zapatista communities to refer to those who are intracommunity members and sympathizers. It is short for what is now "compañeroas," a gender-neutral term for "those who accompany me." It also approximates a Spanish neologism for "comrades," harkening back to the early days of Zapatista political organizing and the influences of socialism and communism on this movement's thinking.

30. For a more extended conversation about who the Yes Men are, see Taylor (2020).

through seminars and reading assignments, working with local organizations, cyber art-hactivism, and public performance intervention. Of the pedagogical approach to the course, Taylor (2020) says, "We have to see and do to be able to know, but . . . we also need to know to be able to see and do" (p. 80).[31] We spent time reading important literature to support our learning about the region and the present impacts of modern/colonial global neoliberal capitalist extraction. Like in my 2007 trip, we continued to study the impacts of colonization and coloniality in the region, including de- and anticolonial struggles (Taylor, 2020, p. 80).

As a group project, we were tasked with using art and computer hacking as environmental activism (directed by Jacques Servin and inspired by his work as one of the Yes Men) to create a real-world intervention into the extractive machine of Monsanto in the region. Monsanto (as a company focused on genetically modified crops) was threatening the livelihood of corn and the lives sustained by it—a crop that is at the heart of much of Native/Indigenous cosmology, cuisine, and ecological life. Mesoamericans spent ten thousand years participating in the evolution of corn and call themselves "the people of the corn" (Taylor, 2020, p. 230).

At the time of the course, Mexico had petitioned the Mexican Secretariat of Agriculture (SEGARPA) to approve of expanding the reach of genetically modified corn in Mexico, and the public was anxiously waiting to see what the government would say (Taylor, 2020, p. 290). On a designated day and time,

---

31. Diana Taylor (2020), in the endnotes of her text, describes this very summer school course in 2013:

> Art and Resistance, the course description read, "explores the many ways in which artists and activists use art (performance, mural paintings, graffiti, writing, music) to make a social intervention in the Americas. The theoretical part of the course remains in active conversation with the practice-based-research component of the course. Jesusa Rodríguez will lead an intensive one-week performance workshop that will culminate in a public action as part of the course. Jacques Servin of The Yes Men will also participate, offering a lecture and a lab. Lorie Novak will lead the digital media component of the course. Performances, video screenings, guest lectures, and visits to FOMMA, Chiapas Media Project, a Zapatista community, and other activist projects will provide an additional dimension to the questions raised by the theoretical readings and discussions. Students will be encouraged to explore possibilities for practice-based research, develop their own sites of investigation, and share their work in a final presentation." See Hemispheric Institute of Performance and Politics, Courses: Summer 2013: Art and Resistance: https://hemisphericinstitute.org/en/courses/summer-2013-intro-art-and-resistance-in-san-cristobal-de-las-casas-mexico.html (pp. 269–271).

This course believes in decolonial pedagogical praxis (if not in name, in practice) and situated work as a place from which to participate in local-global political life.

we impersonated the Monsanto server. On a fake website that people would be redirected to when they visited Monsanto's company website, we issued a fictitious official announcement from SEGARPA that GMO corn would be planted by Monsanto. We kept it cheeky, also saying we were going to put measures in place to combat critics of what this would do to the diversity of the corn: a seed vault and a digital archive called "Codex Mexico" for the preservation of Mexican culture (Taylor, 2020, p. 237). Monsanto was not happy,[32] but our little prank demonstrated the power of the intersection of art, education, and ethical intervention into the modern/colonial global neoliberal capitalist world order.

A great portion of my undergraduate training had focused on the impacts of US imperialism and global neoliberalism on populations deemed less than human in Abya Yala South / Américaca Ladina. For this reason, I sought out opportunities like these to ground my ongoing education in community-based knowledge coming from the people most impacted by extractivist and imperialist neoliberal capitalist economic systems and their attendant sociopolitical dynamics. Through my global and transnational justice- and art-based educational training and exchanges, I came to understand my role—as a publicly engaged college-educated person and politicized Black American learning from peoples experiencing various forms of modern/colonial violence in other nations—to be one of theorizing with and from, rather than studying about (Walsh, 2014). My ongoing sojourn with thinkers who see knowledge as part of the practice of living inspired a recognition of the agency of my response-ability[33] to mobilize the privilege of my positions (like US citizenship) to engage in local, international, and diasporic local-global political allyship and principled struggle[34] as people in intentional relation. My

---

32. For more on the impact of the hack and the full response, see chapter 9 of Taylor (2020).

33. "Response-ability" is a term that has re-presented itself time and again in feminist studies as "a post-anthropocentric feminist ethics" with other humans and more-than-humans on a deeply relational and entangled planet (Hoppe, 2020, pp. 126–127). The shifts from responsibility to response-ability, or our ability to respond, "share the idea that there is a need to go beyond individualizing notions of responsibility in addressing the multiple, never fully graspable interdependencies of the present condition" (Hoppe, 2020, p. 127). I appreciate Hoppe's approach, because she builds on some of the primary returns to response-ability, forwarding an "etho-ecological practice of *responding as composing* with otherness" (Hoppe, 2020, p. 127).

34. "Principled struggle" is a phrase coined by N'Tanya Lee of LeftRoots. I first encountered the term during organizing strategy sessions and retreats with Southerners On New Ground (SONG). Principled struggle is meant as "a more productive approach to managing internal differences." Further, principled struggle is "grounded in a shared power analysis, north star, and commitment to a political project" so that people moving in struggle together can "maintain focus on the larger constituencies we're accountable to" (Mitchell, 2022).

responses to injustices outside my country of origin are grounded in moments of prolonged relocation and in long-term commitments to people and place—including invitations to be alongside—as part of a global network of rebellious thinkers, artists, and doers, seeking after life.

From the nature of the depth of my reencounter with San Cristóbal in 2013 and the commitments that unfolded within and adjacent to the Art and Activism course, I established a secondary political home in Chiapas, which also served as a locus of enunciation for four years, through my local-global loyalty to collaboration in our interwoven struggles. I will elaborate more on this in the next chapter. I take time with this positionality because although it is my story or itinerary that moves us through these places, it is never mine alone. My life is meant as a testament to cosmologies of collectivity that displace the individual as a solitary, nonporous unit of one. Let us now return to the question of the historical significance of forging this transnational bridge.

Historical Significance

I ask us to appreciate how these unexpected interlocutors (North Carolina and Chiapas) demonstrate how de- and anticolonial movements, particularly in the era after the Bandung Conference of 1955,[35] have continued to proliferate around the globe. These movements are attempting to maintain, or at least partially and imperfectly rescue, entire ways of living and being of little to no value to the homogenous conglomerate of modern/colonial global neoliberal capitalism. Sylvia Wynter (1995) makes similar connections between distinct groups of peoples of the global majority[36] working in different parts of the world during specific time periods. Referring to the era just after Bandung, she calls these interrelated local-global movements the "general upheaval" of 1950s and 1960s de- and anticolonial struggles (Wynter, 1995, p. 41). Wynter

35. Haddad-Fonda (2017) rightly argues that the Bandung Conference should not be mythologized nor historically decontextualized. It was a meeting of twenty-nine Asian and African countries to talk about their political futures as former colonies. There were observers present as well, including Black Americans from the US. What is important about this conference, and the reason I mention it here, is the role it played in anticolonial sentiment and critiques of Western imperialism and colonialism, influencing social movements and the formation of critical global organizations, like the World Social Forum, around the planet.
   For a brief but useful overview of the Bandung Conference, for those unfamiliar, please see Haddad-Fonda (2017).
36. I shift to the term "global majority" when referring to most of the world's populations in concert with others of similar sentiment who wish to decenter hegemonic conceptions of "minoritized" people who are actually the global population's majority. In decentering singular notions of a "world," the term "global majority" is most apropos.

describes discontentment around the globe during this era as a form of "collective refusal." Wynter signals Black civil rights in the US as an example of a movement that, though a response to a specific set of US historical and political circumstances, is responsible for "triggering" rebellions elsewhere, including those of Native/Indigenous peoples of the Americas (p. 41). It is true that Black civil rights in the US has been an inspiration for some global movements, partially because of some of its critiques of US imperialism and state terror, an opening for transnational solidarity. Groups like the Dalit Panthers in India are exemplary of such inspiration. Still, in this book I choose not to sustain a claim like Wynter's (1995) that Native/Indigenous struggle in Abya Yala South / Améfrica Ladina had Black civil rights in the US South as their primary inspiration; such thinking today repeats the geopolitical supremacy of Blackness in the US.

Instead, I am curious about the *retroalimentación* (or feedback loop) of *ongoing* Black civil rights and abolitionist struggle and Native/Indigenous sovereignty and decolonial movements, intra- and transnationally. My book emphasizes transnational[37] conversations between Blackness and Indigeneity across national borders, without doing so at the expense of the *intra*-relations between Blackness and Indigeneity in each location. The creative insurgent refusal work I engage with and in includes artivist political interventions and performances whose spiritual-political energies are infused with the unending nature of the struggles for Black/Afro-descendant civil rights and abolition and Native/Indigenous sovereignty and decolonization. We will also listen for how Black civil rights and abolition are also held by Native/Indigenous historical-spiritual presence and how Native/Indigenous sovereignty and decolonization are held by Black/Afro-descendant historical-spiritual presence.

To think Blackness and Indigeneity together in a Western Hemispheric American context, we must reckon with the ongoing suture between them created by the continuous reality of conquest. We do this by understanding how the oppressive forces that draw our histories together do so, in part, by absenting our worlds through the ongoing force of coloniality and racialization. We can choose, instead, to turn our backs on the notion of a singular world.

To engage in the theoretical work of thinking Blackness and Indigeneity alongside one another, I follow the scholarship of Tiffany Lethabo King (2019) for the language she offers for the task. For example, she names hemispheric colonial actors "conquistador-settlers"—part of her project of "pull[ing] settler

---

37. "Transnational" here refers to hemispheric conversations that move across Blackness and Indigeneity, not just across borders.

colonial studies offshore . . . to make it contend with Black thought"[38]—to describe the actants of "conquest" (King, 2019, p. 19). Here, conquest refers to the *ongoing* colonial conditions and relations that structure coloniality's impact in the hemisphere. The language of conquest, as a conceptual choice, allows us to hold genocide and enslavement together, connecting Blackness and Indigeneity through "both the violence enacted on the Indigenous and Black body and the possession of land" (pp. xi, 212). After King (2019), I use both terms, "conquistador-settlers" and "conquest," to make present the ongoing colonial conditions for Blackness and Indigeneity in each location as part of a relational historical-structural analysis.

What I hope is becoming clear to my readers by now is that this work is born of the process of living critically in our many worlds, always-already in relation. In this way of living, thought is not separate from the practice of living but is in service of it, just as any given individual is inseparable from the collectivities we are constituted by and that we co-create, thus destabilizing the modern mythos of individuality. As a next point of entry, I will outline the decolonial pedagogical and spiritual web that describes and delineates the process for reading the work that has already unfolded and that is to come in the listening practice and analyses ahead.

Decolonial Pedagogical and Spiritual Performance Praxes of Living-Writing-Doing-Making

Since it is intentional living and a hemispheric approach to the longevity of modern/colonial violence that brought this work together, this research

---

38. Part of King's (2019) project in *The Black Shoals,* which I aim to follow in praxis here, tests the limitations of settler colonial studies' discursive frameworks. Marking the crux of her critique of the analytical approach by calling it *"White* settler colonial studies," King (2019) calls in the white usurpation of analyses of Indigeneity through the new field of settler colonial studies, established 2005–2006 (p. 62). She also sets the history's lineage straight. "Settler colonial/ism" was first coined by the Native/Indigenous feminist Haunani-Kay Trask—a history largely occluded by white male scholars of Indigeneity (King, 2019, pp. 55–58). King (2019) also very importantly signals what was going on prior to "settler colonial studies": "robust yet imperfect discussions were occurring between Black and Indigenous communities" (p. 62). I align with King's approach in my scholarship here as well because I find that some of the foundational arguments that mark settler colonialism as a different process than colonization simply do not work so neatly in countries like the United States or Mexico. For example, Wolfe's popularly cited claim that settler colonial invasion "is a structure, not an event" created clear boundaries around what countries get most named settler colonial states—the United States, Australia, and South Africa among a small handful of other examples—leaving out conditions of settler colonialism in countries like Mexico (a country whose history could also be classified under the framework of colonization).

is situated in a method of being/becoming and thinking/doing that can be referred to within the framework of the decolonial pedagogical.[39] I think, write, and live in the lineage of Catherine Walsh's work on the topic (2013, 2014, 2017, 2023)[40] alongside her global interlocutors; a cohort of which I am a part.[41] Walsh develops this method from the geopolitical location of Abya Yala South / Améric Ladina, significant because Abya Yala South / América Ladina constitutes the part of the Western Hemisphere whose ways of being/becoming and thinking/doing have been obfuscated not only by the elites of this part of the hemisphere but also by the hegemonies of the "Global North." My use of decolonial pedagogy as a method of being/becoming and thinking/

---

39. The framework of "decolonial pedagogy" as an approach to being/becoming and thinking/doing provided me with the lens to name my approach to scholarship (in its imbrication with artistic creation as well as organizing/activist and spiritual work).

40. I am part of a generation of scholars trained by those who composed the original working group and collective of scholars working at Duke University and UNC Chapel Hill called the "modernity/coloniality project" (the legacy of which has been more recently referred to as the modernity/coloniality/de-coloniality paradigm). I note this to honor the lineage of thought that introduced me to other ways of thinking and existing academically. I also want to note that none of those who composed the original working group feel comfortable with their work being considered part of a "canon." By citing them here, my point is not to reproduce a canon but to acknowledge and honor the academic lineage that allowed me to get to this work. I work with arguments that I see genuine use value in, for understanding the dizzying chaos that is our many worlds.

The modernity/coloniality working group gathered throughout the early 2000s around a series of themes. The collective met in various locations and ended up "mapping" decoloniality as the organizing principle around which coloniality as constitutive of modernity was articulated. They used Aníbal Quijano's (1992) foundational text "Colonialidad y modernidad/racionalidad [Coloniality and modernity/rationality]" as a cornerstone for their development of the problem with centering Europe in modern epistemes. What was significant about this group was that it brought together critical thinkers largely invested in Abya Yala South / Améric frica Ladina / the Americas, located in multiple locations, willing to debate, contest, and offer other ways of thinking about the multiplicity of worlds that we exist in and the epistemic justice required to address them. What is very important to clarify about this working group (and the critiques it has faced because of its geopolitical location and the race of some of the scholars in it) is that none of the scholars are arguing that their working group was the beginning of decolonial thought; rather, the working group marked an epistemic shift in European, North American, Abya Yala South / América Ladina (predominately) academic spaces so that knowledges from those who have always been refusing colonization could and would be appropriately centered. For more on an example of the thematic questions that arose in these collective beginnings in 2004, and the scholarship that precedes my work here, see Escobar (2003) and Mignolo (2011).

I owe my introduction to decolonial thought to this lineage of scholars, particularly given my mentorship by Catherine Walsh and Walter Mignolo between 2014 and 2017.

41. To clarify: I am of the global interlocutors that have been expanding upon decolonial pedagogies with Walsh. I was an invited contributor to the second edition of her text *Pedagogías decoloniales: Prácticas insurgentes de resistir, (re)existir, y revivir* [Decolonial pedagogies: Insurgent practices of resistance, (re)existence, and re-life].

doing locates itself in the pluriverse of a flow between two Souths—where relational realities of worlds that cannot be contained by the modern/colonial geopolitical order's singular universe and its borders get to commingle and intertwine.

To get to the meaning of "decolonial pedagogy," we first need a shared definition of the decolonial for this work. Let us listen[42] to Walsh's (2014) explication of "the decolonial," as a definitional alignment and point of departure,

> The decolonial comes not from above, but below, from the margins and borders, from the people, communities, movements, collectives who challenge, interrupt, and transgress the matrices of colonial power in their practices of being, action, existence, creation, and thought. The decolonial, in this sense, is not a fixed state, status, or condition; nor does it denote a point of arrival. It is a dynamic process always in the making and re-making given the permanence and capacity of reconfiguration of the coloniality of power. It is a process of struggle not just against, but also more importantly for—for the possibility of an otherwise. A process that begets movement, invites alliance, connectivity, articulation, and interrelation, and strives for invention, creation, and intervention, for radically distinct sentiments, meanings, and horizons. (note 5)

To this definition, I would add that decolonization here takes seriously the restoration of Indigenous and Black relationships to land and sea as a necessary part of any decolonial process. Tuning in with this articulation of "the decolonial" as "a dynamic process always in the making and re-making" that is "for the possibility of an otherwise," the creative practices that we will dwell with share what we could call a "decolonial sentiment" of being "por la vida" or "for life." Here, life is the "otherwise."

I am borrowing this use of "por la vida" from Víctor M. Toledo's (2015) writing about ecocide in Mexico. He says, "La batalla final es por la vida" (the final battle is for life) because, he argues, the last battleground that we are facing, due to the planetary-level ecocidal crises, is for the life of the human and more-than-human inhabitants of this planet (Toledo, 2015, p. 15). I would add a slight modification for our purposes, as the title of this introduction does, to say "por/para la vida"—distinctions not translatable at the level of the preposition in English. If "para" refers to a destination, a goal, or a purpose,

---

42. I borrow "let us listen" from Arturo Escobar (2020), who uses the phrase as an invitation to relate to extensive citation moments differently throughout his book *Pluriversal Politics: The Real and the Possible*. I appreciate this invitational modality for and with the reader, as it shares the approach I take with my audience, with you.

then *para la vida* (for life) means that the purpose is to be always moving in the direction of life. "Por" is a preposition that can be used to express the cause or reason of an occurrence or with time and prices. In this case, *por la vida* (for life) means we move for the purpose of life. What I like about each of these expressions is that when placed before "life," they can each denote the decolonial process with a horizon, where the "arrival" is to be inside the practice of life. The fact that the current system is killing all of us, albeit in different ways,[43] is not enough for those perpetuating the killing to change course. The purpose, then, of creative insurgency is to invite others into keeping our many worlds alive—being inside of life, with us—and sharing our channels of access and the lessons we learn from them. Whether we can always feel it or not, every movement into the pluriverse weakens something in the modern/colonial global neoliberal capitalist world order and its solipsistic and delusional OWW universality.

Being on behalf of and striving *por* or *para la vida* means being on the side of learning, beyond the limitations of its conceptualization in institutionalized school systems. For this reason, the point where the pedagogical and the decolonial meet is of utmost importance here.

The pedagogical of the "decolonial pedagogical" is where we "critically read the world" by foregrounding the inseparability between the political, the pedagogical, and the spiritual. This inseparability of life spheres creates forms of being/becoming, thinking/doing, based in the struggle to subvert the modern/colonial order of things that dehumanizes (and, by default, deontologizes) people and whose intention is to eradicate the cosmological, epistemic, and embodied knowledges beyond its OWW bounds (Walsh and Freire as cited in Walsh, 2013, p. 38). Decolonial pedagogy is a form of critical pedagogy and practice-based knowledge. It is birthed and reborn through political-pedagogical-spiritual struggles that not only subvert the power of modern/colonial global neoliberal capitalist order and OWW civilizing logics but also revalorize, remix, and create political, ontological, epistemic, spiritual, and existential modes of existence, otherwise, from a pluriverse of worlds (Walsh, 2013, p. 32). What we learn through the struggle to revalorize, remix, and create is the pedagogical in the decolonial. We write this down to share our visions for the possibilities of this labor, together.

Considering what makes it possible to bring the decolonial and the pedagogical together, we must be wary of storying movements from the perspective

---

43. Here, I am riffing on Catherine E. Walsh (2023). She says (describing the reason for her more recent "cries"), "It is a cry against the capitalist-extractivist-heteropatriarchal-racist-modern/colonial system that is killing us, though not necessarily all in the same way" (Walsh, 2023, p. 25).

of hegemonic society, where their emergence tends to be framed as reactions and "resistances" to modern/colonial global neoliberal capitalist violence as well as to "industrialization, failed social revolution and incomplete democratization" (Icaza & Vásquez, 2013, pp. 688–690). I agree with Icaza and Vásquez (2013) that when we read social movements against these forces solely as "resistance," we lose the "eventfulness," creativity, and world-making of these movements (pp. 686–691). To this I would add that we lose the pluriversal perspectives and openings that come from the forms of lifework that can happen in insurgency and refusal. For this reason, you will note that I choose not to use the word "resistance" in this study (unless quoting others), because I am invested in seeing how all the work that we dwell with moves *for* something else altogether. The classroom is the practice of living—of being human as praxis,[44] if you will—in ever-evolving relation.

In this decolonial pedagogical matrix, I must introduce a second-to-last pedagogical interplay for our Black/Afro-descendant and Native/Indigenous coming together: where the pedagogical meets the cosmological-spiritual. Like Walsh (2017, 2023), I converse with M. Jacqui Alexander's (2005) practice-based spiritual and Caribbean feminist thinking for its role in the construction of (and for our future readings of) being/becoming and thinking/doing otherwise. Alexander's (2005) contributions to the Sacred/spiritual are crucial, because they allow us to situate diasporic praxes as pedagogical examples of praxes that invite new perspectives on the value of pluriversal creations that evade(d) capture;[45] bridging old worlds and new. By this I mean that the specificity of The Crossing as a pluriversal Sacred site of knowledge—as the beginning of Blackness—does not disinvite contemplations with Native/Indigenous Sacred cosmological knowledge founded in praxis. Instead, I argue that these diasporic/epistemic openings invite us to be curious about

---

44. The phrase "on being Human as praxis" comes from the organizing theme of a collection from Sylvia Wynter's oeuvre, edited by Katherine McKittrick (2015) and called *Sylvia Wynter: On Being Human as Praxis*. In chapter 1, McKittrick (2015) explains the Wynterian logic behind this organizing theme, saying,

> Being human is a praxis of humanness that does not dwell on the static empiricism of the unfittest and the downtrodden and situate the most marginalized within the incarcerated colonial categorization of oppression; being human as praxis is, to borrow from Maturana and Varela, "the realization of the living." (pp. 3–4)

The realization of the living is the labor it takes for those alive and those no longer in human form to sustain and re/create our many worlds. Being human as praxis makes "human" a verb that "challenge[s] the profitable brutalities that attend the realization of Man-as-human" (McKittrick, 2015, p. 7).

45. Here I am riffing on M. Jacqui Alexander (2005), p. 289.

and to listen to Native/Indigenous cosmological understandings about existence. I make this connection because diasporic practices resulted from a stripped indigeneity, demonstrating our species's creativity to reinvent ourselves to keep alive, in the face of the modern/colonial world order's attempts at obliteration. I draw from my Afro-diasporic spiritual, epistemological, and ontological praxis and praxes resembling those of Alexander (2005), to honor cosmology's role in pluriversal knowledge production.

Alexander's (2005) invocation of the Sacred gives us a pedagogical opening to think with and through other connections between Black/Afro-descendant and Native/Indigenous cosmologies as well. Her notion of the Sacred, which I share, asks us to engage with peoples whose cosmologies include precious and holy ecological networks of cosmological systems founded in notions of continuity and reciprocity between the human, nonhuman, and more-than-human life forms on this planet. Additionally, truly practicing and sitting with Black/Afro-descendant and Native/Indigenous cosmologies—that a secularized-Christian, and what Iyko Day (2021) calls a "romantic anticapitalist,"[46] relationship to Nature cannot even begin to apprehend—puts you in touch with forces far greater than the OWW, forces that are something other than the modern/colonial world's conception of Nature.

In the book, I will analyze how these cosmologies shape how people come to be/become and think/do, through various forms of refusal. Ecological and spiritual cosmologies not recognized, but also demonized and threatened, by the modern/colonial global neoliberal capitalist world are part of what allows dysselected[47] humans to understand themselves as manifestations of the Divine, in turn garnering the strength to locate their being/becoming and thinking/doing from an ancestrally present elsewhere. I will creatively think with Black/Afro-diasporic/Afro-Caribbean and Native/Indigenous cosmological/ecological/spiritual knowledge, respectively, when analyzing the

---

46. "Romantic anti-capitalism" is a term coined by Iyko Day (2016) meaning "an ideological framework for settler colonialism to respond to economic and technological crises by imagining whiteness through indigenizing tropes of purity and organic connection to land that function to distort and deflect responsibility for capitalist modernity" (pp. 36–37). Day (2016)—drawing connections between settler colonialism's impacts on Native/Indigenous people and the racialization and exploitation of Asian immigrants to the US and Canada—uses her ideological framework of "romantic anticapitalism" to analyze the rationalization of terra nullius and the genocidal approach to Native/Indigenous people while subsequently producing a "spatial alienation" for an exploited and racialized Asian labor force, "the embodiment of the abstract evils of capitalism" (p. 34).

47. "Dysselected" is Wynter (2003) citing Darwin's "'dysselected by Evolution until proven otherwise' descriptive statement" where, based on the observations and geographic and religious beliefs of the conquistador settlers, Native/Indigenous people and Black people were considered "dysselected" by God and Man (the overrepresentation of Man as human) (p. 267).

labor of Black/Afro-descendant Native/Indigenous pluriversal creative insurgencies, inspired by Alexander's (2005) openings into other worlds.

To reiterate an important point, our engagements with Native/Indigenous-led and -centered creative insurgency consider the category of Native/Indigenous, like Black/Afro-descendant, to be one of conspecific relation (also recall Reinaga from earlier in this introduction). According to Arvin's (2015) useful definition, "indigeneity . . . refers to the historical and contemporary effects of colonial and anticolonial demands and desires related to a certain land or territory and the various displacements of that place's original or longtime inhabitants" (p. 121). Indigeneity here is not just an identity like it is used in modern/colonial global neoliberal capitalist world order—meant to flatten Indigenous worlds into "a category determined by racism and colonialism"—but rather a category that signifies "the knowledge and praxis of indigenous peoples" (Arvin, 2015, p. 121). Here, Indigeneity is "in *articulation* with raciality and coloniality rather than a category that refers directly back to these other categories" (p. 121; emphasis mine). Restated, Indigeneity is not defined by the racial and colonial oppression that has severely impacted Indigenous land and lives in the hemisphere but rather gets articulated *with* these oppressions while also focusing on Indigenous worlds and the lives and knowledges therein. This brings us to an "analytics of indigeneity" (Arvin, 2015).

In an "analytics of indigeneity," Indigenous people are not idealized, allowing an acknowledgment that "indigenous knowledge and practice can either be anticolonial or participatory in colonialism, . . . in racism" (p. 121). We are invited to be wary of a romantic origin story, so we do not replicate the sanitizing logics of modern/colonial notions of purity;[48] there is no idyllic return to what once was, nor to a utopian future. Though we have already established that we will engage in Native/Indigenous work and thinking that has been invested in sovereignty and decolonization (and is therefore anticolonial in its approach to colonialism and racism), it is important to ground an "analytics of indigeneity" (like Blackness as part of the African diaspora) in the understanding of Indigeneity as a term that is inherently nuanced, complex, and plural by virtue of the diversity it is meant to "represent."

---

48. A commitment to *impurity* is crucial here, because the very modern/colonial construction of purity, as Alexis Shotwell (2016) so poignantly articulates, "is a racialized concept" stemming, in part, from the debates about whether humans came from monogenetic lines (from a single gene line) or from polygenetic lines (from multiple gene lines), the latter of which has been used to justify and authorize practices of enslavement and terra nullius doctrines, upholding genocide as righteous on the basis of seeing some people as being "made" for obliteration due to historical, social, and political dysselection (Shotwell, 2016, p. 15; Wynter, 2003, p. 267).

An "analytics of indigeneity," thinking with Arvin (2015), "should enable both a critique of how indigenous peoples are always seen as vanishing as well as opening up the boundaries of indigenous identity, culture, politics, and futures, to new productive possibilities" (p. 126). This way of thinking Indigeneity as an analytic considers the ongoing struggles against colonialism and Indigenous racialization as something Indigenous people must continuously confront, but it does not define them as people. An "analytics of indigeneity" is another layer for holding Indigeneity as a nuanced and complex category of conspecific and affinity-based coalitional relation amongst different groups of people from many different worlds that get called "Indigenous." Exercising this analytic, we will spend the necessary time with the historical-social-political scenes that Indigeneity is up against, specific to the chosen site. We will then engage in pluriversal listening practices with Native/Indigenous cosmological understandings of being/becoming and thinking/doing appropriate to the region.

Finally, because the case studies we will think with are, in a multitude of ways, challenging forms of racialized gender violence that help sustain the hegemony of the modern/colonial global neoliberal capitalist cisheteropatriarchal[49] world order, I need a plurality of feminisms to analyze the place of race, racialization, Blackness, and Indigeneity, at their intersections with gender, in these practices of creative insurgency.

Transfeminist, Black feminist, and decolonial feminist thought direct my analyses throughout this study, beginning from specific veins of thought within them. I take these forms of thought as necessarily and wonderfully overlapping, crossing a complex but cohesive span of historical emergences, geopolitical locations, and prerogatives for knowledge and existence that I will interweave here.

---

49. In this way, I am agreeing with Arturo Escobar (2014) in his preface to the monumental decolonial feminist collection *Tejiendo de otro modo: Feminismo, epistemología y apuestas descoloniales en Abya Yala* [Weaving another way: Feminism, epistemology, and decolonial commitments in Abya Yala]. In the preface, Escobar (2014) affirms the significance of this collection (some of which I will cite in this book) in highlighting how decolonial feminisms assert that decoloniality cannot exist without de-patriarchalizing life (p. 11). As an extension of the work of the modernity/coloniality/decoloniality paradigm/working group (see footnote 39), he affirms (following the work of these feminists from Abya Yala South / Améfrica Ladina) that "struggles against capitalism, racism, homophobia, and all forms of domination related to the modern/colonial world system must incorporate strategies of de-patriarchalization [*sic*] as a central element" (Escobar, 2014, p. 11). He continues just after, "For this reason, I dare to affirm that the reflection propitiated in this volume, at the intersection of feminisms and decolonial thought, is one of the most important and advanced proposals in the theoretical-political debates in the continent" (p. 12).

The transfeminist thought that I use finds its greatest allegiance with the activism and scholarship of Sayak Valencia (I am firmly grounded in but not limited to her interventions). We will understand transfeminisms always in the plural when confronting the extraordinary violence of neoliberalism, late capitalism, and globalization. For our purposes, we will understand transfeminism principally as two things: (1) a lens of analysis that bridges multiple forms of feminist practice through expanding the subjectivities and corporealities of who feminism attends to, one that begins by centering the livelihood of racialized transgender women (after Koyama, 2001);[50] and (2) as "non identitarian networks of care and transnational dialogue, where the historic memory of the minoritarian becomings [*sic*] intersects with strategies of resistance and social transformation to build communities of emotional support and survival in a necroliberal context" (Valencia, 2019, p. 181).[51] To be clear, "nonidentitarian" here does not signal a postidentitarian turn like we see in Euro-centered academic practice (see King, 2017). Instead, "nonidentitarian" exists in the purview of Sylvia Wynter's notion of the "human-as-Man," which challenges the liberal humanist criterion for and requirement of categorization-as-inclusion into a modern/colonial world order (Wynter, 1995).

Transfeminisms, in this regard, allow us to open the interpretative frameworks brought to bear on being/becoming and thinking/doing in racialized and gendered OWW realities. This is important in the context of a pluriversal study, because identity is wrought under conditions of hegemony, whereas subjectivity attends to the struggle toward agency as a member of the species (Wynter, 1995). Transfeminist thought brings us to "life and sustainability politics against this binary, heteropatriarchal, and necroliberal *cis-tem*"[52] (cis-tem*s* in the plural for our purposes) (Valencia, 2019, p. 181). We will

50. Emi Koyama's (2001) "Transfeminist Manifesto" (as an early transfeminist text) understood transfeminism to mean "a movement by and for trans women who view their liberation to be intrinsically linked to the liberation of all women and beyond. It is also open to other queers, intersex people, trans men, non-trans women, non-trans men and others who are sympathetic toward needs of trans women and consider their alliance with trans women to be essential for their own liberation." While the definition that I am operating with here is in concert with the many iterations that transfeminisms have undergone, it is the element of the liberation of trans women as central to transfeminist politics and analysis that I will hold onto through the book.

51. Valencia (2019) uses Achille Mbembe's (2012) concept of necropolitics "as a reference point to talk about violence as a link between the colonial and the contemporary project of modernity though the systematic and continuous elimination of dissenting populations" (p. 184).

52. For my readers who may not be familiar with the term "cisgender," it refers to people whose gender identification matches the sex they were designated at birth. "Cis-tem," then, is a play on words, understanding that the hegemonic systems we move within are figured by and for cisgender people.

continuously query the role of the colonial/modern racialized gender system in maintaining the agendas of the modern/colonial civilizing project that is the OWW.

Transfeminist and Black feminist thought exist on a continuum in this book, because transfeminism, in its capacious intersectionality and attention to institutionalized and interpersonal power, owes much of its genealogical emergence to Black feminism. The forms of Black feminist thought I move with here—particularly because we will spend more time focusing on the population of Black Americans, whose ancestors were enslaved in the US South (not to the exclusion of Afro-descendants in Mexico, nor African and Afro-diasporic refugees, migrants, and immigrants in any of these regions)—are those lineages of Black feminism who place their origin in the displacement of the subject of "Black/woman" under the modern/colonial civilizing project and the geopolitical specificity of its manifestations in its nation-states, like the US. I will think with Black feminist interlocutors like Spillers (1987), Roberts (1997/2016), Snorton (2017), Cooper Owens (2017), and Gumbs (2016) to underline the significance of continuing to attend to how the Transatlantic Slave Trade reconfigured race and gender for enslaved people vis-à-vis the location of the Black woman, challenging conquistador-settlers' rigid enclosures around race and gender (among other fixed categories).

Racialized un/gendered formations in the plantation economy were further complicated by the legal constraints of *partus sequitur ventrem,* or "that which is born follows the womb," that juridically marked the child of an enslaved woman with her legal status. This legal doctrine existed alongside the economic need for enslaved women "breeders" to keep the plantation economy prospering after the importation of newly enslaved people was banned in 1808 (Cooper Owens, 2017). *Refusals and Reinventions* joins a lineage of Black feminists establishing historical continuities of the colonial/modern gender system for Black women (and, by design, for Black people). Remaining with the particularity of this Black geopolitical legacy, this study then also follows Black queer feminist formulations. We will understand that if Black women are free, it will necessitate the freedom of all people, because it would require the downfall of modern/colonial conditions that structure unfreedom (Combahee River Collective, 1977).

Decolonial feminisms are the final layer of this transnational feminist continuum, abundant enough to hold elements of both transfeminisms and Black feminisms. Decolonial feminisms are indispensable to decolonial thought's investments in other ways of being/becoming and thinking/doing.[53] The

---

53. For an excellent critique of what happens when decolonial thought does not center decolonial feminisms, I recommend Breny Mendoza (2014).

decolonial feminisms we will concern ourselves with here emerge from thinkers from Abya Yala South / América Ladina theorizing from geopolitical territories in the US and in Abya Yala South / América Ladina, addressing the impact of the colonial/modern gender system on Black/Afro-descendant and Native/Indigenous peoples.

The framework of decolonial feminisms that is important for our purposes is María Lugones's (2007, 2010) introductory contribution to the concept. Thinking hemispherically, we will understand from Lugones (2007, 2010) how the "colonial/modern gender system" was upheld, in large part, because "turning the colonized into human beings was not a colonial goal" (p. 744). Lugones (2010) called decolonial feminism "the possibility of overcoming the coloniality of gender," or a form of feminism that was not reliant on subjectivity formation through the colonial/modern racialized gender system's violence (p. 747). I remain with these aspects of the foundational work of Lugones (2007, 2010),[54] even though decolonial feminisms have grown exponentially, because it is Lugones's inaugural articulation that set the discursive conditions for continuing to challenge the "semantic consequence of the coloniality of gender" (p. 745). Or in other words, her work gives us the language and analysis to discuss what the conquistador settlers made meaning of (in this case related to gender) and how the meanings attached to colonized gender formations continue to shape so many of our lives. Through this, we might understand how categorizations of colonized peoples into always-already racialized and gendered nonbeings, part of what conquistador-settlers do, perpetually reinstantiate the colonial difference. It is for this reason that we will be with creative insurgent work that challenges oppressive modern/colonial violences upheld by racialized and gendered frameworks from the idea of OWW.

A Final Note for My Readers

In addition to the specificities that construct the "we" that has already been named, it is important to be transparent about the constraints of this book. The reality of this book being situated with a university press in the US

---

54. Though it is outside of the purview of the current study to explain at length what I see as the limitations of Lugones's work, part of what I find limiting is some of what I also find limiting about Oyěwùmí's (1997) work, who Lugones uses as a primary referent. That is: though there are certainly important cases to be made about how prior to the colonial encounter, Native/Indigenous and Indigenous African cultures did not organize their entire societies around a visuality-focused and genitalia-obsessed construction of gender, there is perhaps too much of a negation of gender at work overall in ways that J. Lorand Matory (2005), for example, addresses with respect to Oyěwùmí (1997).

academy comes with institutional, linguistic, and geopolitical limitations that I do not believe I can fully transcend within this text alone. I invite you to engage with future and concomitant lives of this work across modalities, venues, and languages, variations required for pluriversal audiences.

For the sake of scope and to be true to the specificity of the pedagogical lessons and movements here, I do not cover anything about Asian presence in the Western Hemisphere in this text (though it is implicated by addressing peoples of mixed racial or ethnic descent and those who have been impacted by colonialism, imperialism, racialization, and cisheteropatriarchy). This limitation is not meant to foreclose upon other dialogues and conversations with more of our pluriversal worlds. Still, it is important to signal that significant connections can be made between Blackness, Indigeneity, and Asianness—speaking to the United States for a moment. In the racialized framework that Iyko Day (2016) elaborates, "the primary relationship between settler colonizers and Indigenous populations is land, in the case of African slaves[55] transported to the United States it is *labor*" (p. 27; emphasis in original). African Americans are made into "aliens" post-Emancipation because formerly enslaved people were sutured to Blackness, and since they were not immigrants, they could not be sent "back" anywhere; they were an "*undisposable* alien labor population" (p. 29; emphasis in original). Then, African Americans and Asians came to figure into this picture, "shar[ing] an alien status in a triangular framework," on Indigenous territory, in order to make the white population wealthy (p. 31). Finally, after waves of Asian labor migration and immigration followed the decline in plantation economies and the rise in industrialization, Asians were racialized as hyperefficient workers whose labor—read from the Marxian framework of abstract labor—was increasingly devalued and exploited as surplus values increased (p. 47). This modern/colonial extractive practice is yet another form of colonial relations in territories of conquest.[56]

Chapter Breakdown

This decolonial pedagogical project and these ways of being/becoming and thinking/doing might also be described as research-cum-lived-experience. For

---

55. Following the conventions established by P. Gabrielle Foreman and other senior slavery scholars of color, unless citing the language choice of other authors, it is most appropriate and humanizing to use "enslaved (as an adjective) rather than 'slave' as a noun" because "['slave'] disaggregates the condition of being enslaved with the status of 'being' a slave. People weren't slaves. They were enslaved" (Foreman et al., n.d.).

56. For more on this, see Day (2016).

this reason, the writing will continue to shape-shift in form: weaving between personal narrative, story, theory, history, language, images, performance, and cosmopolitics. I invite you to follow the creative and serpentine journey of each chapter and to create connections of your own.

Refusals and Reinventions has four chapters followed by a coda. Chapters 1 and 2 begin with creative performance entries from my residencies in San Cristóbal de las Casas, Chiapas, and Greensboro, North Carolina, US, respectively. I open with these performance moments because I used the residency periods between 2018 and 2019 to reflect on some of the lessons learned by living and moving in each location. In chapters 1 and 2, the highlighted performance and residency moments at the start of the chapter then lead to a geopolitical and historical mapping of more details about each location—situating the Native/Indigenous and Black civil rights histories, accordingly. The creative performance entries serve as memory exercises that recall decolonial pedagogical and pluriversal lessons gleaned from my participation in specific creative insurgencies in favor of Native/Indigenous and Black/Afro-descendant life in each location (again, respectively). Subsequently, chapters 1 and 2 spend time theorizing the intersection of the cosmological-spiritual-political work of countering racialized gender formations in the OWW, by demonstrating openings these creative insurgent practices make in the pluriverse.

The second section of the book, chapters 3 and 4, centers creative insurgent actions I have been adjacent to in each of these locations, each read for their value as performance work that has effects in our worlds. Chapters 3 and 4 participate in bridging the geopolitical locations of the US and Mexico, and Mexico and Spain, respectively, demonstrating the power creative praxis holds to transform the limitations of the borders of nation-states that help to solidify the modern/colonial civilizing project's singular conceptions of existence. Each chapter begins by setting the reason behind these two creative insurgent choices and readings, followed by the geopolitical and onto-epistemic suturing that they portend, culminating in readings of the onto-epistemic poetry of each of the actions and their implications for pluriversal thought and practice.

Chapter 1 takes us to San Cristóbal de las Casas, Chiapas, Mexico, to think and move with the lessons gleaned from creative artivist work against femicide/feminicide and other forms of state violence in the region. Thinking against the site where neoliberalism and necropolitics meet, I dwell with the creative insurgent practice of metaphor and mourning and its connection to Native/Indigenous grief in the region. We will use regionally specific Tseltal cosmological understandings of the self to pluriversally feel into some of the "all" that has been lost.

Chapter 2 takes us to Greensboro and Durham, North Carolina, the United States, to think through abolitionist work and tactics in the long struggle for

Black civil rights, refusing the ongoing subordination of Black women (cis and trans), mothers, and caregivers in the many afterlives of enslavement. Learning from the power of political work that hacks the judicial system, we will listen for the re-writes in Black motherhood—through a Black queer Caribbean feminist theoretical sensibility—made possible through the actions of decolonial pedagogical abolitionist refusal as spiritual and pluriversal rewriting.

Chapter 3 reads the performance work of one interlocutor, "Lia La Novia Sirena," for its invitation into what I am calling the "trans break," as a lens through which to query absolutist ontological assertions of Black nonontology and suspend a hierarchization between Black/Afro-descendant and Native/ Indigenous ontologies in the hemisphere. We will practice how the break allows us entrance into other worlds' Afro-diasporic and Indigenous cosmological-spiritual-political formations otherwise by opening up the metaphors made available in the transfeminist and decolonial pedagogical artistic work of Lia García.

Chapter 4 imagines the Zapatista journey of Squadron 421 and the details of its performance as an invitation to read the entanglement of Black/Afro-descendant and Native/Indigenous connections between land, sea, and gender fluidity as forms of coalitional Sacred accompaniment. Troubling the ongoing ways that Blackness gets conflated with the sea and Indigeneity gets conflated with water, I conjure the Atlantic spiritual encounters we can envision during the voyage. Additionally, I read the role of the otroa aboard, Marijose, and the directives for their arrival on Spanish soil as indicative of the knowledge Native/Indigenous people from the highlands of Chiapas hold about the Sacred place of people with "other" genders and sexualities.

The book concludes with a coda that engages us in a final pluriversal reading practice with one another; an exercise in probing the depths of our many worlds and what it might look like to be open to experiencing pluriversal perception.

Now, into the pluriverse.

CHAPTER 1

A Full-Dignified-Just Life

Insurgent Grief

It is the summer of 2019, and I am back in San Cristóbal to spend two months dwelling in site in an artist residency predicated on making decolonial pedagogical reflections on the pluriversal lessons I have learned by being/becoming, thinking/doing in this place. The intention of this summer's practice is to reckon with how we shape place, how we are simultaneously shaped *by* place by our movements through them, and what there is to learn through this co-constitution. In one performance exercise, I spend an afternoon engaging in a walking practice in one neighborhood in San Cristóbal de las Casas, accompanied by a crew of friends and colleagues who recorded my movements and the surrounding environment's sights and sounds on video.[1] Figure 1.1 shows a still taken from the video in which I am pictured from behind while walking through one street of the neighborhood known as El Cerrillo. Partially inspired by, though geopolitically distinct from, Michel de Certeau's (1984) "Walking in the City," based on a walking tour he took in New York City, I stroll through one of San Cristóbal's historically emblematic Afro-descendant neighborhoods.[2] I choose the neighborhood of El Cerrillo because of my commitment to keeping Blackness and Indigeneity in relational

---

1. See Coleman (2020).

2. El Cerrillo's status as emblematic of the existence of Afro-descendant people and their history in San Cristóbal de las Casas is not necessarily common knowledge, given that it is a place still plagued with the presence of the OWW and its modern/colonial orders.

FIGURE 1.1. Still of the author walking in the Barrio El Cerrillo,
San Cristóbal de las Casas, Chiapas, Mexico.

entanglement as an intentional space-making practice, particularly because
previous studies on the histories of Blackness and Indigeneity in the region
taught me how San Cristóbal is just another town that can fulfill the Mexican
nationalist narrative "aquí no hay negros" (there are no Black people here).
It is micro spaces of forgotten geographies[3] and the palimpsestic layers that
emerge in social-historical-political absenting that put me in the imaginative place to engage with other otherwises. My walking practice this day is an
embodied meditation on place-making through performance that I use as a
form of embodied recollection.

I think of my walking performance as a mode of "site-particular"[4] creative entryway to decolonial pedagogical insights (Noé, 2009). Site particu-

3. Here, by using the term "forgotten geographies," I am riffing on Ruth Wilson Gilmore's (2008) conception of "forgotten places." Forgotten places refer to places that have been
abandoned as capitalist neoliberal greed chooses what places to invest in for its own benefit
(Gilmore, 2008, p. 31). San Cristóbal de las Casas is not a forgotten geography or place, but its
walk with Blackness *is* a geographical layer forgotten by the great majority of the public.

4. "Site-particular" is a term coined by Ilya Noé, moving away from the "battlefield" that
"site-specific" (when referring to performances and art) has turned into (2009, p. 149). Site-
specific has become contested terrain because of the types of relationships artists are "supposed" to or are expected to have with the environment they are moving and working in. Site-
specific performances and installations are known for responding to more codified ideas or
realities about a specific place, thereby making work that can respond to hegemonic impulses
or be more radical in approach. "Site-specific" is "used to describe work that is determined by
and physically bound to its environmental context" where "*site* is defined as the actual material
location" (p. 149). Additionally, a major issue with site-specificity is its modernist approach,
where there's an assumption of a neutral space that is being viewed by a universal subject. Even
as "site" has been expanded to think about things like the social and the political, what "site"
names remains too nebulous. The limitations here lie in the types of codifications that already
exist or that are put in place about "site," alongside a lack of clarity about what is being congealed in the definition of site.

larity is "open to changing geographies," because sites are not imagined as simply preexisting "formally, conceptually, or ideologically" within given geographic constraints (pp. 149–150). Site particularity is an important perspective for the work engaged in this text because it allows site to be *constructed* in a dynamic relationship between the artist, the geography, and the audience. Let us listen to Ilya Noé's (2009) language here for articulating the relevance of this approach to site, for the work of this chapter and for the larger work. Site-particular "is an ongoing series of interrelational and open-ended processes: always partial, multiply layered, often contradictory and messy, and produced by active agents negotiating between all kinds of positions and working through all kinds of relationships" (p. 150). I love how site particularity allows for humanness, situated subjectivity, and plural possibilities for engagement with the geographies of place (human geographies) assisting our understanding of the unending angles and pluriversal realities any given site is made of.

Site particularity involves "becoming situated and valuing particularities" where there is no room for a given artwork or person to participate in the rigid codification of a site. It also does not assume that specific experiences can be universalized for these sites. To be clear: this does not mean that site particularity is yet another form of relativism or a mode of responding to universalist, modernist claims. Rather, neither static notions of local conditions nor the momentum of shifts and changes can fully determine what can be known about a place (Noé, 2009, p. 150). Site particularity, then, is not simply about "understanding" a site but rather about *a collaborative conversation with place,* where learning and unlearning, assessing and reassessing, listening and re-listening, and multiple forms of encounter and curious inquiry shape the relational engagement, teaching us to endlessly see and feel and be open to re-seeing and re-feeling a site.

As I walk to activate site-particular engagement in El Cerrillo, memories greet me as I gaze down the sloping street into the bustling center of San Cristóbal. No corner of the city is untouched. I hear the voices that have enunciated the names of murdered cisgender girls and women, time and again, in the face of impunity and selective amnesia.[5] The echoes of the names of cisgender girls and women—especially of Native/Indigenous peoples and

---

5. In the edit of the video performance, I insert feminist voices of chants from actions I participated in during summer 2017, following what I heard as I walked. You can hear and watch this in the video (Coleman, 2020) from minute 3:33 to minute 4:01: "Ni una menos, ni una menos, ni una menos, vivas nos queremos" (Not one more, not one more, not one more, we want us [feminine plural] alive).

peoples of mixed Indigenous descent[6]—are of those who have lost their lives to targeted, gratuitous, and collateral violence of the OWW. I am referring to what is called femicide/feminicide and to other forms of state-sanctioned violence baked into the fabric of the modern/colonial global neoliberal capitalist order's manifestations in Mexico. Walsh (2023) culls the distinctions between femicide and feminicide from scholars of these phenomena: "*Femicide* is the term usually used to refer to the deaths of women by men who kill them because they are women, while *feminicide* refers to all the violence committed against women and their self-determination, including state violence resulting from omission and negligence" (p. 29). I introduce a slash between femicide and feminicide because our concern here is with both interpersonal violence (femicide) and state violence (feminicide) as embodied manifestations of the OWW's racialized gender coloniality that can be enacted by anyone. The slash signifies, then, femicide's slippery relationship with feminicide, if we take feminicide to mean the violent regime or conditions of the colonial/modern gender system in this local and national context. It is important, then, to also emphasize that the impacts of the colonial/modern gender system in Mexico reach beyond cisgender girls and women.

I recall my participation in and co-curation of various creative actions and performances between 2013 and 2015, consolidated under a platform called Arte Acción. Arte Acción is a platform I formed alongside Doris Difarnecio based on work she was already doing. It uses performance, public interventions, and critical and creative pedagogy as a means of generating something other than the stultifying energy of impunity in the face of extreme forms of violence that take the lives cisgender girls and women, transgender people, cisgender boys and men, and people of other genders. Through the various forms of creative insurgency that Arte Acción engaged in, the platform also served as a container for accompanying the family members that must survive the brutality of losing (largely) women in their lives to this unfathomable violence. The platform serves as a form of public witnessing and collective grief. Before continuing, allow me to explain how I arrived at this work, so that we can trace a trajectory of meaning-making made possible from my direct participation in this local and national reality in the context of Mexico.

In summer of 2013, as noted in the introduction, I returned to San Cristóbal de las Casas for the first time since 2007 with the Art and Activism course out of the Hemispheric Institute for Performance and Politics (NYU). I was returning to Chiapas on the tail end of a two-month residency period in a

---

6. Here, I am using the term "mixed Indigenous descent" because the purpose is to engage with Indigeneity and not the Mexican whitening project of *mestizaje* that belittles the place of Indigeneity in shaping people's family histories.

small town called Mineral de Pozos in the state of Guanajuato, Mexico. My time in Mineral de Pozos was funded by UNC Chapel Hill's Institute for the Study of the Americas, where I was a doctoral student at the time. The connections of members of the Chapel Hill community to this small town were formed through transnational partnership with community members in Guanajuato who had experienced the impact of mass northern migration (largely to North Carolina) on their lives in Guanajuato. My purpose of being there, then, was to offer free workshops in movement and dance and in performance for cisgender women and children who remain in Mineral de Pozos—a largely abandoned but beautiful mining town that had been dramatically impacted by modern/colonial global neoliberal capitalist prerogatives.

During my time in Mineral de Pozos, a group of queer Mexican artists from San Miguel de Allende (one hour away by car) learned of my stay and came to visit me, inviting me into community for my personal well-being. At the time, I was identifying as a queer woman of color. After meeting these artist-friends, they drove down every weekend to bring me to San Miguel de Allende and back. During my weekends in San Miguel de Allende with these artists, the topic of the shocking recent rise in femicide rates in the state of Guanajuato became a regular point of conversation. As a socially engaged artist and queer woman of color, I felt compelled to use my art-making to invite further community dialogues about the increase in violence against women in the region. The night before boarding the plane from Guanajuato to Chiapas, I performed the first iteration of a solo piece entitled "De Eso No Se Habla," or "Of This We Do Not Speak," for a public audience on the terrace of an arts building in downtown San Miguel de Allende. I chose the name to mark the pervasive yet unspoken nature of femicide in the region.

This performance, utilizing feminist body art and ritual, served as a creative denunciation and ritual holding space where the women murdered in Guanajuato in 2013 were made present. I used my nude body in performance to politicize and spiritually contend with the colonial/modern gender systems' grip on women's lives in this context. During the performance, I poured hospital-donated women's blood over my body from a bucket and then utilized the blood as paste to plaster letter-sized sheets of paper showing the profile contours of women's faces and the names and ages of the murdered on them to the floor around me. Then, lit candles held by audience members and planted around the pages and my body marked the space as a ritual for refusing to forget. The soundscape that I used included splices of news clippings from media in Guanajuato speaking to these murders, the voices of public defenders who had worked on these cases, the discourse of regional feminist organizers, and ambient sounds. A community dialogue that followed the performance served the purpose I intended it for: an invested public in critical conversation about the disease of the colonial/modern gender system in Guanajuato and in Mexico, writ large.

The very next morning, I boarded my plane to Chiapas. With the memories of that ritual and dialogue fresh in my body, I needed to extend beyond the scope of the summer course in my commitment to reengaging with San Cristóbal and its people outside of institutionally designed constraints. I decided to hold a performance night with a colleague in the course who was from Brazil and also interested in sharing her political performance work with the local community. We chose a combined café and dive bar called "El Paliacate" and invited the public. I repeated the form of "De Eso No Se Habla" but created a new soundscape based on the voices of people addressing femicide in the context of San Cristóbal. At the performance was Doris Difarnecio, former employee of Hemispheric Institute and long-time resident of San Cristóbal with a deep history of working with Indigenous women in the region.

After the performance, Difarnecio invited me and others to accompany her and local family members in their monthly action against femicide, noting a shared commitment in our work. An activist living in the region, Difarnecio had begun a series of public demonstrations against femicide and other forms of state violence against women in 2012 after the brutal murder of Tseltal teenager Itzel Janeth Méndez Pérez on September 14, 2012. Following the public demonstration and outcry, which were met with absolute silence from the state, on the fourteenth day of most months Difarnecio creatively intervened in the Plaza de la Resistencia in the late afternoons alongside the family members of the murdered women—an opening that offered the family members the opportunity to be held and witnessed repeatedly by civil society in an iterative mourning practice. The actions also served as a creative and pedagogical denunciation of the utter impunity of the state. Activists across feminist organizations would also join at the plaza.

After visiting one of Difarnecio's actions in the summer of 2013, we organically evolved a partnership and collaboration, forming the loose street collaborative Arte Acción[7] in Chiapas, or Action Art in Chiapas. I returned to North Carolina at the end of the summer, finishing up my graduate coursework while flying to Chiapas every six weeks or so, pushing my finances to the limit. I finally uprooted my life and moved to Chiapas in May of 2014. I followed my commitment to immersing myself in my relationships and in work on the ground.

---

7. And one that Difarnecio now continues as an itinerant feminist performance and pedagogical space. For more see: https://www.facebook.com/arte.accion.5.

The purpose of this chapter, following this contextualization and entry point, is to engage in a deep reading of one action with Arte Acción in the fall of 2014 where I, once again, offered my body as a conduit for investigating the micro and macro operations of the colonial/modern gender system in the region. Following the site-particular walking performance that led us to the case study here, what ensues in this chapter considers how the brutal femicides of cisgender girls and women in the context of Chiapas is part of a larger national colonial/modern gender system/feminicide context that is part of the afterlives of colonization and the Mexican state's and conquistador settlers' ongoing attempt at Native/Indigenous genocide. I argue that insidious and normalized forms of violence like the kinds we will consider here are the modern/colonial world order and OWW's intention to "finish the job" of eradicating Native/Indigenous people. Part of the operation of power here works by obliterating a sense of self as conceived of by Indigenous worlds. From this perspective, the case study that we will dwell with uses public intervention and performance as an opportunity to listen to and with the compounding forms of state-sanctioned violence that plague Indigenous people in the context of Mexico. Because of the people the action and case study address, we will ultimately see how these dynamics impact Indigenous people of all genders due to the colonial/modern gender system's racializing logics.

Given the compounding nature of this violence, the latter half of this chapter zeroes in on the labor of collective grief as a pluriversal opportunity to learn from Native/Indigenous cosmological-spiritual relationships to being/becoming and thinking/doing in the region that get all but obliterated for far too many Native/Indigenous people. Here, "grief" is a portal analyzed through one performance action. Because of the depth of its sentiments, grief is envisioned as a pluriversal conduit to the cosmological contours of being/becoming, thinking/doing in a conspecific Indigenous context. We will imagine this creative insurgence, then, as an opening for a pluriversal existence despite the OWW's perpetual attempts at annihilation.

In what follows, I will first situate the history and significance of Zapatismo as a fraught and incomplete political-military-social-economic-cosmological-spiritual series of processes and one of the primary players that charges this landscape with the complexity of Native/Indigenous refusal. For the purposes of the limited scope of this chapter, here we will emphasize the multipronged Zapatista movement's origins, ending with the historical turn toward recuperating Native/Indigenous cosmologies, which helps us build an "analytic of indigeneity" for our subsequent reading. Following the work of significant Mexican scholars on the topic, it is necessary to acknowledge how Zapatismo helped the country's more contemporary Native/Indigenous worlds and ways of comprehending existence. I will then situate the decolonial and transfeminist frameworks for understanding the colonial/modern gender system and its racialized dynamics in the context of femicide/feminicide and other forms of state-sanctioned violence. Following, I will story us through the details of the specific action and case study and accompanying illustrations. The case study and ritual performance serve as a historical conversation about the depth and longevity of Native/Indigenous grief when read through the channel of the colonial/modern gender system's reach. We will contemplate how an iterative grief practice asks us to face the larger regional dynamics of what is being grieved: Native/Indigenous ancestral cosmological understandings of a dignified life and existence. We will be with this cosmological pluriversality grounded in Indigenous cosmologies through an "analytics of indigeneity" to understand the salience of creative insurgency as a means of accessing pluriversal ways of being/becoming and thinking/doing.

Unfinished Histories, Complex Designs

San Cristóbal de las Casas and Chiapas are known world-over for the Zapatista movement, which has been and continues to mean many different things. It is, following the arguments of Xochitl Leyva Solano (1999), an *ongoing process* of a series of political, military, ideological, social, economic, and cosmological-spiritual reckonings about the status of Native/Indigenous people and the conditions of their lives in Mexico and in the world (p. 56). It is also a movement that has helped Mexico move toward democratization. Zapatismo is a polysemic process that has stirred local, national, and transnational alliances with its "plan de once puntos" (eleven-point plan) emphasizing "the right to work, the land, the habitat, an adequate diet, health, education, autonomy, liberty, democracy, justice, and peace" (EZLN, 1994, cited in Leyva Solano, 1999, p. 61; Leyva Solano, 1999, p. 74). The latter foci have stirred lay people, activists and organizers, intellectuals, and artists worldwide who are sympathetic to the cause. Sympathizers also tend to be people who have a shared analysis of overly conservative leftist politics that stop short of challenging neoliberalism. It is important to understand Zapatismo not from a triumphant, romanticized, or decontextualized imaginary but from a sober reckoning of the complexity of its constituent elements, which have profoundly impacted the region and the world.

What we know as "Zapatismo" is not a monolithic cause. It is a many-pronged movement and ideological position that has included armed insurgence, rebellions, and massive theorizing and other intellectual production;

it also has both a social-political front that is military or armed (the EZLN [Ejército Zapatista de Liberación Nacional or the Zapatista Army of National Liberation]) and fractured loci of "civil society" sympathizers that are local, national, and now inter- and transnational. The social, political, and military or armed Zapatista front, and its accompanying EZLN military leaders, has been structured over several phases: 1983–1994, 1994–2005, 2005–2017, and 2017 to the present, all marked by a series of complex political processes and demands; a plurality of figures and leaders, stakeholders, audiences, and players; and a series of transformations (Rauch & Schachtel, 2020, p. 17).

Through the complexities of the birth of the EZLN and Zapatismo, a civilian arm developed to distinguish itself from the militarism of the EZLN. Leyva Solano (1999) and Leyva Solano and Sonnleitner (2000) articulate this civilian arm as the Nuevo Movimiento Zapatista, or NMZ (New Zapatista Movement), otherwise known as "neoZapatismo," or "a dynamic process constituted by a plurality of interests, wills, and identities, which inscribe it within a field of contradictions and unresolved tensions" (Leyva Solano, 1999, p. 58; Leyva Solano and Sonnleitner, 2000, p. 165). Following the theoretical framework of Leyva Solano (1999) and Leyva Solano and Sonnleitner (2000) as lenses through which to understand the various branches of Zapatismo, let us now look at what distinguishes these key aspects of the process (EZLN vs. NMZ) and the significance of these distinctions to the local, national, and transnational impacts of the work, ultimately locating the significance of this multipronged and ongoing movement for Native/Indigenous people of the region.

It is now well known that on January 1, 1994, a coalition of Native/ Indigenous people from Chiapas, accompanied by key mestizo allies, marched down from their homes in the forested highlands into San Cristóbal de las Casas, arriving at the Plaza de la Resistencia[8] to declare war on the Mexican government. This first arm of Zapatismo that launched the declaration, the EZLN, was of a clear political and militaristic character; a military that had been approved by the Zapatista Clandestine Indigenous Revolutionary Committee (General Command [CCRI-CG]), a crucial governing body in the territories (Leyva Solano & Sonnleitner, 2000, p. 170; Hansen, 2002, p. 11). Strategic in their communications and use of internet technology, the First Declaration of the Lacandona Jungle[9] that came with this declaration of war

---

8. This plaza came to be known as the "Plaza of Resistance" and then the "Plaza de la Paz" or "Plaza of Peace" after the takeover.

9. This record is available (as are the entire record of Zapatista communiques) in multiple languages here: https://enlaceZapatista.ezln.org.mx/1994/01/01/primera-declaracion-de-la-selva-Lacandona/.

(EZLN, 1994), marked the Zapatistas as savvy communicators in an era before the internet was widespread or accessible (especially in southern Mexico).

In the First Declaration of the Lacandona Jungle, the EZLN not only declared war against the Mexican government, but they also declared themselves the inheritors of Native/Indigenous struggles and peasant struggles and placed themselves in stark opposition to the 1992 celebration of five hundred years since the onset of colonization (EZLN, 1994, cited in Leyva Solano, 1999, p. 61). This First Declaration was also an invitation to Mexican citizens to join the Zapatistas in armed struggle and march on Mexico City to defeat the country's military. Their plan included permitting people-elected administrative authorities, entering summary judgments on all Mexican military and police officers who had been treasonous or oppressive, and creating new brigades with all Mexicans who respected and collaborated with EZLN leadership. At the end of their declaration was a call to end the extraction of resources in areas controlled by the EZLN.

The overly simplified history of this original moment that circulates in political lore conceives of it as a declaration of Native/Indigenous autonomy. Instead, the beginning of the movement was marked by militarism and juxtaposing interests. Arguably, then, agreeing with Leyva Solano (1999) and Leyva Solano and Sonnleitner (2000), it is perhaps only appropriate to look at the movement as one of polysemic composition. Let us remain for another moment with the complexity of this history.

The juxtaposing interests of the movement were the result of the racial and ethnic (and therefore class) differences of all those involved, as well the result of the differing educational and life experiences (due to the former) of those at the head of its leadership. There are key elements to note here. The EZLN was formed on November 17, 1983, by three mestizos and three Native/Indigenous "Chiapanecos" (Hansen, 2002, p. 10). The formation of this originally six-person EZLN began when Subcomandante Insurgente Marcos, a mestizo man from Mexico City born Rafael Sebastián Guillén Vicente, and fellow activists from the National Liberation Forces (FLN)[10] arrived in Chiapas from major cities. Given the presence of mestizo and Euro-descended Mexicans with formal and urban educations, however radical, there were European sociopolitical and economic ideologies present in the political articulations of the original founders of the EZLN. Their communications demonstrated their study of European and Caribbean political, economic, and ideological warfare,

---

10. The FLN was established as a clandestine organization in 1969 in Monterrey. The organization was composed of university students who served as "advisors, directors, and militants of unions, political parties, indigenous, urban, and rural movements" (Leyva Solano, 1999, p. 56).

inspired by European and Caribbean class-based revolutions of those regions, as the personal and political investments and visions being played out by the mestizos allying with the Native/Indigenous people in Chiapas.

For these reasons, the First Declaration was inspired by eleven years of a notably Marxist-Leninist-Guevarist "foco-centered protracted guerrilla war"[11] scheme led by these six initial EZLN leaders and their Native/Indigenous recruits (Genovese, 2016, p. 1; Leyva Solano, 1999). In the spirit of this scheme, Marcos, the infamous mestizo *vocero* or spokesperson of the EZLN between 1994 and 2004, became one of the mythological figures of the movement; recognized for his ski mask, pipe, army gear, and appearances on horseback. What activists in Mexico today would call a "Whitexican," Marcos's undergraduate training in philosophy at UNAM (National Autonomous University of Mexico) and his exposure to European theories and international political movements clearly played a major role in the initial structuring of the EZLN and some of its early prerogatives of "war." The formation of the EZLN put its militants and voceros in control of what Leyva Solano (1999) and Leyva Solano and Sonnleitner (2000) call the "official discourse" of Zapatismo—or the communiques published and permanently archived publicly on the Enlace Zapatista website (https://enlaceZapatista.ezln.org.mx/)—establishing them as the movement's "cultural brokers" (p. 65). This is noteworthy not only because it is questionable that Native/Indigenous people in Chiapas would conceive of their struggle as one that should be rooted in a Marxist-Leninist-Guevarist foco-centered approach but also because imbricated with this concern, we should not ignore that the great majority of Native/Indigenous people in communities in Chiapas were experiencing an "illiteracy" rate of around 30 percent (see Leyva Solano, 1999, p. 65, footnote 9). This reality and the political, economic, and ideological origins of European and Caribbean political movements simply did not mesh with the Native/Indigenous reality of Chiapas at the time (or even much of that reality to this day), marking an obvious multicultural root of Zapatismo that was not motivated or guided simply by Native/Indigenous sovereignty or cosmologies.

---

11. Genovese (2016) explains that *foco* theory or *foquismo*—"foco" being the Spanish word for "focus"—was a revolutionary theory coined by Régis Debray, a French intellectual that studied the tactical elements used in the Cuban Revolution with special emphasis on Che Guevara's (1960) book *La Guerra de Guerrillas* (Guerrilla Warfare) (p. 1). He continues, "*Foquismo* drew on the strategy of a protracted people's war—in which small bands of revolutionaries attempt to draw the enemy into the rural areas of the country while maintaining a positive image with the people. However, instead of relying on traditional Marxist theory of waiting on 'objective conditions' for the people's revolution (Marx and Engels 1960), foco theory re-interprets Lenin's theory of revolution and argues that a small vanguard of revolutionaries fighting in the rural areas could generate the people's support and jumpstart a revolution" (Genovese, 2016, pp. 1–2).

Subcomandante Insurgente Marcos read the First Declaration from the balcony of the Municipal building in San Cristóbal de las Casas. At the time, "three thousand members of the EZLN" were in occupation of "six large towns and hundreds of ranches in an armed uprising" (Hansen, 2002, p. 11). It took only twenty-four hours for the Mexican military to respond, "bombing indigenous communities" and killing at least 145 people (Hansen, 2002, p. 11). Fighting continued for twelve days. Mexican civil society and people in international solidarity came through with an outpouring of support against the bombing in Native/Indigenous communities, leading to a ceasefire declaration on January 12, 1994. A great majority of civil society was not in favor of an armed revolution against the government—led by an EZLN takeover on the path toward an eventual democratization as stated in the First Declaration—even if they did agree with many of the principles motivating this Marxist-Leninist-Guevarist strategy (Hansen, 2002, p. 11; Leyva Solano & Sonnleitner, 2000, p. 172). It would take another two years—until the signing of the San Andrés Accords[12] of February 1996—for an agreement to be reached between the federal government and the EZLN. As part of this agreement, the EZLN would be granted autonomous stewardship of agreed-upon lands in Chiapas.

To address the transition between the initial Marxist-Leninist-Guevarist guerrilla bent of the EZLN to more explicitly Native/Indigenous prerogatives and the NMZ, we must also name the strategic timing, nationally and internationally, of the First Declaration. The First Declaration of the EZLN occurred in tandem with the signing of the North American Free Trade Agreement (NAFTA)[13] on January 1, 1994. The EZLN explained the signing of NAFTA as signifying death to Native/Indigenous and farming communities (see EZLN, 1994). The EZLN took this opportunity to oppose NAFTA's modern/colonial global neoliberal capitalist agenda, anticipating the tremendous suffering it ultimately would bring on the Mexican people. The signing of NAFTA also came on the heels of a difficult political era for Mexican people, making

---

12. The full document of the San Andrés Accords can be read in English here: https://ucdp.uu.se/downloads/fullpeace/Mex%2019960216.pdf.

13. NAFTA was instituted by US president George H. W. Bush, Mexican president Carlos Salinas de Gortari, and Canadian prime minister Brian Mulroney. NAFTA is emblematic of the neoliberal age, as an agreement meant to allow for a freer trade and flow of goods and services between the three "North American" countries—the United States, Mexico, and Canada. What was notable about NAFTA was that the free flow of merchandise was not to be met with the free flow of people, meaning we did not see any simultaneous opening of borders or reforms to immigration, migration, and refugee policies, particularly for those flowing from South to North. In this political-economic agreement, Mexico was simultaneously claimed as "North American" because of sharing a southern border with the United States (thanks to the Spanish American war) and also as part of Abya Yala South / Améfrica Ladina, meaning its northern neighbor treats its people as "Third World" populations, accordingly.

buy-in to Zapatista ideology easier because of the timing. On July 6, 1988, fraudulent elections had brought President Carlos Salinas de Gortari to power. In 1992 Salinas reformed Article 27 of the Constitution (a gain of the 1910 revolution, signed into the 1917 constitution), "ending 75 years of land reform and allowing privatization of the ejidos"[14]—a pre-NAFTA acceleration into neoliberalism (Hansen, 2002, p. 11). This "corporate post-revolutionary" system installed by Salinas increased the tensions from civil society, leading the general population to question how the government was being run (Leyva Solano & Sonnleitner, 2000, p. 172).

The ejido (or government land parcel distribution) system itself had been corrupted time and again by waves of different electoral policies coming down from the federal government between 1917 and 1988. The ejido system played with peoples' livelihoods, distributing and redistributing land in the rural areas enough to "pacify" the campesinos (translated as "peasants") while ultimately appeasing the government's agendas for the land (Hernández Chávez, 2006, p. 252).[15] The largely Native/Indigenous campesinos, who had been independently organized by mestizo "ejidatarios" since the 1970s, were not willing to lose their only way of life; they arose in protest of Salinas's 1992 ratification to Article 27—a ratification that effectively ended land reform in Mexico (Leyva Solano & Sonnleitner, 2000, p. 172).

Feminist scholar of Zapatismo Mariana Mora (2018) also confirms— through her interview work with Zapatista community members regarding their recollection of the conditions of discontent among campesinos in Mexico in the period between the 1970s and 1990s—that the interpersonal conditions on the "fincas" or "ranches" of the ejidos, which had been owned primarily by mestizo families in Chiapas since the 1970s, degraded Native/Indigenous campesinos to the level of indentured servants. The relationships between mestizos and campesinos largely consisted of "suffering, trauma, oppression, and exploitation" (p. 26). Native/Indigenous people were "racialized" as less than, through their economic servitude on the fincas by their mestizo ejidatarios (what we could refer to as a new generation of conquistador-settlers in control of the ejido parcels). These conditions on

---

14. Ejidos were "a form of property under which certain lands may be used individually, collectively, or, in the case of pastureland, forest land, and water rights, in common" (Hernández Chávez, 2006, p. 238). People who had rights to the ejidos were called an "ejidatario," or land owners / settlers, and had "individual use rights or shares in collective use rights of a piece of land that forms part of the ejido. The *ejidatario* also has rights to property held in common by the *ejido*" (p. 238).

15. The Mexican federal government has been no different than other governmental bodies in treating lands like those found in Chiapas as terra nullius, contributing to massive deforestation and loss of human and more-than-human life. For more, see Ríos-Quiroz et. al. (2021).

the ranches contributed to twentieth-century restructuring of Native/Indigenous people as an underclass in Chiapas, then as part of the modern/colonial global neoliberal capitalist order in Mexico.

Mora (2017) emphasizes how this history affords us an opportunity to understand how processes of racialization were created through socioeconomic hierarchies—something that scholarly work in the Mexican academy often overlooks because of the longstanding whitening project of mestizaje that weds Mexican identity to nationhood (before race or ethnicity), labeling Native/Indigenous people as matters of "cultural difference" (pp. 30–31). Said differently, the treatment of Native/Indigenous campesinos by mestizos, played out in part on the ejidos, marks a unique history of racism,[16] specific to the Mexican state, that motivated and inspired large populations of civil society to get behind new forms of political participation. Mexico would enter a new era of self-reinvention as a "pluricultural" nation meant to newly honor Native/Indigenous people as subjects of respect and rights.[17]

Following the former series of discontentments, 1994 also marked moments of grave dispute among the Mexican people about the presidential candidate and the corporate and corrupt nature of the modern/colonial PRI (Institutional Revolutionary Party) system. On September 28, 1994, José Francisco Ruiz Massieu, the secretary general of the PRI, was assassinated in Mexico City. The brother of ex-president Carlos Salinas, with the latter's destabilizing reform of Article 27, was the suspect in the assassination. The investigations that took place around the murder marked a "political crisis in the revolutionary family" of Mexico's political scene (Leyva Solano and Sonnleitner, 2000, p. 173).

It was at this moment that the EZLN opened its symbolic doors to the "popular sectors and citizens . . . transforming its demands and its symbols" (Leyva Solano and Sonnleitner, 2000, p. 173). The EZLN's discourse changed from one with a clear Marxist-Leninist-Guevarist bent to one focused on "democracy, justice, and liberty." As Leyva Solano and Sonnleitner (2000) argue, "Zapatismo achieved attracting many Mexicans that were tired of being governed by an authoritarian and paternalist system that no longer fulfilled its principal obligation of procuring security and justice" (pp. 173–174). With the poetic and seductive articulations of the "official discourse" of Subcomandante Marcos, the EZLN became very attractive for Mexicans of all sectors of the

16. It is important to note that treating this issue as what it operates as sociopolitically (racism), as opposed to approaching Native/Indigenous people as an "ethnic" identity, is essential, because approaching Indigeneity through ethnicity has been an infamous omission by Mexican institutions of intellectual production (see Mora, 2017, p. 31).

17. For a longer discussion on this, see Leyva Solano (1999).

population interested in a new form of political participation (Leyva Solano and Sonnleitner, 2000).[18]

The leaders of the EZLN were savvy. They capitalized on the "fetishized symbols" of the Mexican nation, emphasizing, for example, how the "Zapatistas" named themselves after Emiliano Zapata, a famous Native/Indigenous political figure in the Mexican Revolution of 1910–1920 (Leyva Solano and Sonnleitner, 2000, p. 174).[19] Zapata championed agrarianism, even if he did not achieve a full agrarian reform. Calling the movement "Zapatismo" was a reclamation of this original promise. Therefore, one way to understand the organization of Native/Indigenous people in Chiapas into what also gets called "Zapatismo" is to see it as an umbrella term of conspecific relation; it is an ongoing coalitional strategy for gathering those who sought and seek a more dignified existence for Indigenous peoples. Some have belonged to the EZLN, others to the NMZ. The Native/Indigenous population of Mayan descendant in Chiapas, made up of Tsotsil, Tseltal, Chol, Mame, Zoque, and Tojolabal peoples, would also ultimately be organized in larger numbers (by their own and in coalition with the EZLN mestizo leadership) for Indigenous livelihoods.

The leaders of the EZLN capitalized on the folkloric fetishization of Native/Indigenous people and their dress by combining traditional garments with the markings associated with the EZLN's insurgent presence, like *paliacates* (handkerchiefs) and *pasamontañas* (ski masks). These markings serve as both a masking of individual identity and a turn to collective and visual seduction of outsiders, marking the clash of "old" and "new" worlds. In figure 1.2, we see three Zapatista women in a wooden room in Caracól Oventic, accompanied by three of their children. One woman wears a paliacate while the other two have pasamontañas on. They are all wearing Native/Indigenous dress of the Tsotsil and Tseltal peoples, which in their community includes Black lambswool skirts, a thick layer of protection in the crisp highlands of Chiapas.

---

18. The discussion of the Nuevo Movimiento Zapatista, or NMZ, that Leyva Solano (1999) and Leyva Solano and Sonnleitner (2000) develop is outside the purview of this chapter. However, there are some important elements to this distinction from "mainstream" (if you will) Zapatismo worth noting here. The NMZ, or "neoZapatismo," also originated in 1994 and consists of, they argue, five main divisions with specific prerogatives: agrarian, democratic-electoral, Indianist-autonomous, alternative-revolutionary, and internationalist-antineoliberal (Leyva Solano and Sonnleitner, 2000, p. 175). The civil society actors and militants that made up and continue to make up neoZapatismo are Zapatista sympathizers who were spurred on by "a charismatic leader, some academics, political leaders, and a broad popular base" (Leyva Solano, 1999, p. 66).

19. For a quick and important reference on Emiliano Zapata and Zapatismo for people who may not be familiar with this history, see this entry in the Oxford Reference: https://www.oxfordreference.com/view/10.1093/oi/authority.20110803133357216.

FIGURE 1.2. Zapatista women and their children in Caracól Oventic. Used with permission of the photographer, Moysés Zuñiga Santiago.

In figure 1.3, we see a group of about ten young Zapatista women and men, all in the clothes of their people and all wearing pasamontañas. Playing with iconography in their sartorial and scenic choices, they are positioned in front of the Mexican flag—a fascinating oxymoron as they deliver the Zapatista anthem.[20]

Taken together, the sum of strategies of EZLN and NMZ organizers, with an emphasis on the proliferation of the Zapatista image, brought together local, national, and international participation—branches of the NMZ—of people who would support Native/Indigenous sovereignty and the right to a dignified life as well as ideological and material struggles against modern/colonial global neoliberal capitalism. Native/Indigenous communities in the highlands of Chiapas continue to organize themselves internally and externally, holding their own systems of governance, schools, health care, and ways of working and existing with the land, as well as regulations about how they treat one another (like the prohibition of alcohol and religion) in honor and respect of millennial ways of living in harmony with one another, the land, and other beings. It was in these new life contexts that Native/Indigenous

---

20. The Zapatista anthem can be read in English and in Spanish here: https://www.struggle.ws/mexico/ezln/anthem.html.

FIGURE 1.3. *Himno Zapatista, 2007*. Used with permission
of the photographer, Moysés Zuñiga Santiago.

people of Chiapas began sharing their reclamation of their cosmologies as a
return to whole being.

My interest here in sharing some of the details of this history is to remember the people behind the masks operating in conspecific and coalitional relation for the sake of Native/Indigenous sovereignty and seeking for life during
modern/colonial global neoliberal capitalist takeover. In the reading in the
latter part of the chapter, we will be with what movements like Zapatismo
have politicized Native/Indigenous people into: their own cosmological compasses. Recalling the cosmological reclamation cited just above, we will listen
to culturally relevant articulations of a full existence, articulations that metrics
like "literacy" cannot account for. In the face of ongoing devastation from the
modern/colonial order, how might being confronted by racialized and gendered violence turn people toward other figurations of seeing and knowing?

Arte Acción in Chiapas and Necroliberal Refusal

Though revolutionary movements like Zapatismo have put Mexico on the
global scene of insurgent struggle, femicide/feminicide (and transfemicide/
transfeminicide) still rock the collective imaginary like a looming specter;

Chiapas is no exception.[21] This should remind us to be wary of mythologizing and monolithic narratives about place. As should be clear by now, most of the people affected by this violence in Chiapas are cisgender Native/Indigenous women. In 2019, the year I engaged in the performance exercise of "walking in the city" as a point of entry, one girl, young woman, or adult woman was killed every four hours in Mexico (Valencia, 2019, p. 182). Beyond the numerical significance of femicide, these are not your average homicides. Many of them are preceded by sexual violence and followed by a brutalization of the bodies long after the life in the person is gone—exaggerated forms of brutality that make manifest the existence of societal ills that create the conditions for such terror. The corporeal atomization that continues postmortem (borrowing a term originally coined in relation to the nature of the killing of Black trans women in the US) has been referred to as "overkill" by Eric Stanley (2011). This term is incredibly useful for our purposes, though here we are using it to refer to a different geopolitical context with a differently racialized population. It remains useful because the prevalence and brutality of the murders of Black trans women in the US exist on par with femicide in Mexico.

"Overkill," coined by Stanley (2011), describes "excessive violence" that "pushes a body beyond death" (p. 9). In the context of Chiapas and what prompted the inauguration of the actions against feminicide in 2012, overkill has included the very public displays of brutalized bodies after the physical murder. In instances like the case of Itzel, the viscera were "artfully" curated on the outside of the corpse and placed in public space with the intention of sparking fear, outrage, and disgust in the public memory.[22] The case of Itzel Janeth Méndez Pérez is a prime example of Native/Indigenous overkill that detonated a more urgent culture of refusal, exposing and publicly denouncing femicidal/feminicidal violence in the region.[23]

21. The context of femicide/feminicide in Chiapas is in the larger context of gender violence in Mexico—a country that has been in a "guerra no declarada" or an "undeclared war" in ways unprecedented before the signing of NAFTA, with ebbs and flows of extraordinary carnage. The "undeclared war" cost the lives of over a hundred thousand people during the presidency of Enrique Peña Nieto (2012–2018) alone. In this environment, it is seldom that femicide and transfemicide are met with any form of "justice" under the Mexican penal system. As we would expect from a justice system built on corruption, war, and racist exclusion, what redress is possible?

22. Images of overkill have been uncouthly published by local journalism platforms competing for attention, demonstrating that certain media outlets have not always had enough sense or tact beyond the sensationalism of the spectacle of extreme death in Mexico's necropolitical environment.

23. Feminists, lawyers, and activists of many kinds have been working to combat femicide and transfemicide in the region for decades. The important figures include the feminist lawyer Martha Figueroa Mier and the organization she founded in collaboration with CDMCH (the Center for Women's Rights of Chiapas), COLEM (the Women's Collective). Regular press conferences that include conversations and communiques to the United Nations have been

Sayak Valencia's (2019) astute transfeminist analysis of the tenor of this phenomenon in Mexico situates it as part of the necropolitical neoliberal machine that is at the center of how Western modernity/coloniality in the country organizes itself (p. 182). In other words, Valencia's work demonstrates how phenomena like femicide and feminicide are required by the OWW as fodder in its insatiable extractive war. Valencia (2019) explains that death becomes a "civilizing technology" where murder is a method of "indoctrination" into its order (p. 182). Valencia's (2019) transfeminist framework bridges the necropolitical with the neoliberal, coining the term "necroliberal" (henceforth replacing the term "neoliberal" in this book). "Necroliberal" is a deeply apropos term for the violence of neoliberalism that people like the Zapatistas have devoted their entire lives to refusing. We will engage in our reading practice within the purview of this necroliberal environment.

In that spirit, I invite us to understand this southern regional landscape through the lens of "grieving geographies" as we prepare for our visit with the first case study. Meztli Yoalli Rodríguez Aguilar (2021) defines "grieving geographies"—with "grieving" intentionally left in the gerund form—as "spaces of complex collective loss due to multiple interconnected forms of violence. Grieving geographies are where the deaths of humans and other-than-humans collide, compounding pain and sorrow" (pp. 2, 7). Though Rodríguez Aguilar's (2021) work emphasizes the environmental racism in Afro-Mexican communities on the coast of Oaxaca killing the lagoons, the context of "grieving geographies" is a useful framework for Chiapas's necroliberal eco-[24] and homicidal landscape.

Arte Acción, October 14, 2014

In the actions against femicide/feminicide and other forms of state-sanctioned violence, aesthetic choices are loosely charted in advance. Each living altar is collectively built as a large-scale container and public holding space to be with the beauty and humanity of those murdered, held alongside the horror of how they died and the holes left in their wakes. The actions are pedagogical for

---

essential to the frontline battle against these atrocious levels of violence. Though there have been some very real complications with the NGOization of feminism in the region, nonetheless there have been various stakeholders who have created crucial inroads for exposing the impunity around these murders. Organizations like K'inal Antsetik have also been crucial sites of feminist (largely lesbian feminist) and additionally Native/Indigenous resistance to various forms of gendered violence.

24. Zapatista territory still exists in autonomy. However, various kinds of extractive projects continue throughout the rest of the state, engaging in the same ecocidal necroliberalism that the Zapatistas warned about so many years ago.

the conversations they initiate and cathartic in their iterative nature, offering opportunities to be with the ebb-and-flow temporality of grief. In this intervention, held on October 14, 2014, we feel a heightened sense of the intersectional nature of necroliberal violence against Native/Indigenous people in the country. It has been just over two weeks since the September 26 disappearances in southwestern Mexico that have the entire country in a state of shock and indignation. Ayotzinapa, as the event is now referred to, was the forced disappearance of forty-three Native/Indigenous Mexican cisgender male students from an "escuela normal rural" (rural teacher-training school) called Escuela Normal Rural Raúl Isidro Burgos, or Ayotzinapa, in the town of Iguala in the state of Guerrero, Mexico (Walsh, 2023, pp. 14–15). The young men were abducted by bus by the local municipal police and "Mexico's narcostate" on their way to a protest. They intended to protest "Mayor José Luis Abarca's approval and signing of a law to raise the price of tuition for higher education in the state" (Keme, 2018, p. 57). Walsh (2023) relays the details that circulated on every news channel in the country at the time: "Three students were killed, eight were wounded, and forty-three were made to disappear" (p. 15). Recalling the energy that brought me into Chiapas for the first time in 2007—the ongoing threats to Zapatista autonomy and sovereignty despite signed government agreements—refusal is an ongoing act under conditions of conquest. The energy of Chiapas and the OWW of Mexico as a grieving geography is amplified by the shape of the current events rocking the nation. There is a general malaise and sense of fatigue.

This day, we coordinate with the family members to ask what they are desiring for the action. They make it clear that they are too preoccupied with the grief of their own lives, combined with the grief of the national alert, to make any creative suggestions. What they want is for us to take the lead and to be together in the Plaza. With this directive, ourselves also shaken by the current events, Difarnecio and I discuss ideas and images. We decide to address the various genders implicated in the violence against Native/Indigenous people being felt by the region and by the country, extending beyond while also remaining with femicide/feminicide. Through this decision, we attend to the large-scale mourning and targeted violence against Native/Indigenous people across all genders—to contest essentializing claims to gender exceptionalism when intersected with the racialization of Native/Indigenous people in the country of Mexico.

Like in the months of public interventions prior, Difarnecio and I initiate setting the scene for creative insurgency in the Plaza de la Resistencia—the same Plaza where the EZLN made its initial declarations. This day, we use large white paper and black paint, writing "no nos pueden matar a

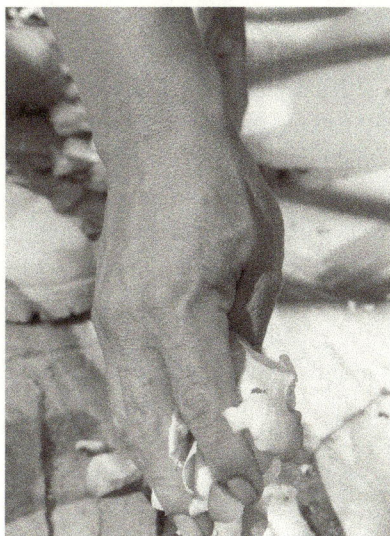

FIGURE 1.4. A hand holds flowers at a public *acción* in Chiapas on October 14, 2014. Used with permission of the photographer, Nelly Cubillos Álvarez.

FIGURE 1.5. A man and a boy sprinkle flower petals on the ground at a public *acción* in Chiapas on October 14, 2014. Used with permission of the photographer, Nelly Cubillos Álvarez.

todxs," or "they cannot kill us all," in massive letters, the "x" in "all" signifying genders beyond the binary and a gender-inclusive collectivity. I feel particularly ready for the task, having just begun my gender transition one month prior (on September 14, 2014). Difarnecio and I then line up the large-scale pages back-to-back so that they transversally cut the plaza in half. We dip our hands into a large bucket of a mix of cornmeal and water that we have brought with us to "paste" the pages to the ground using a method that will not leave lasting ecological damage, excited about the detritus that will be left behind. With bags of massive bundles of stemmed flowers and flower petals, sourced from a Native/Indigenous woman's surplus in one of the *mercados* in San Cristóbal, we invite the family members and the public to mark shared space with the stemmed flowers and flower petals, encircling and landing on the words (see figures 1.4 and 1.5). We also invite them to sprinkle the petals throughout. The flowers demarcate the outward limits of the altar and pepper it with colorful vitality. Intermixed between the stemmed flowers and words are small candles that threaten to flicker out from the harshness of the wind.

I lend my body as a holding space this day, meant to serve as a conduit for the implications of the imbricated violence at play. I deindividualize my body, instead marking it as a material space for a channel—a creative portal to help others externalize their grief. By bringing my physical, emotional, and spiritual bodies into relationships founded in practice, I understand myself to be in service of the collective as a spiritual practice. I place myself at the end of the start of the phrase, at the top of the word "no." I am wearing black clothes to symbolize mourning and a paliacate to shield my identity; the latter choice meant to tune in with the paliacate as a symbol of Native/Indigenous refusal in the region. To my right sits a red basin full of fresh cow's blood and a long black veil ready to be thrown over my head at the start of the action. I sit in silence, sensing when it is time to begin the walking action of the ritual I have chosen (see figure 1.6). I hear the rustle of the public all around me, moving throughout the plaza, some in anticipation and others chatting with those around them while trying to decipher the meaning behind what has been laid out before them.

The plaza, transformed into a space of public ritual, is an invitation to engage with those who have suffered the consequences of necroliberal violence, through embodied interaction in real time. By using my body as a holding space during times of such political unrest, I take the attention away from the mourning family members so that they are free to be held in their feelings without unneeded observation. These rituals allow for a sensing- and feeling-with that invites a critical reading of the powers and necroliberal environments being implicated in the construction of the live images. While living under the realities of a necroliberal OWW order set on individualizing the atrocious pain of violent loss, in this space, something else becomes possible.

Sensing it is time to walk, I stand up at the edge of the worded path before me and throw the black veil over my head—the latter a recognized symbol of mourning that women don in this region and in this country.[25] I place the red plastic basin of cow's blood on the ground to the left of me and step my feet down into it. My toes curl up slightly, my feet a little too long for the basin. I squish my toes around to ensure that I will leave clear footprints on the path. I begin to walk on the path, leaving footprints of blood with each step (see figure 1.7). I continue making steps forward until my footprints start to fade, nudging the basin alongside me as I travel. Once the prints become less visible, I step into the basin again to line the skin on the soles of my feet so that they will continue to leave marks. I only make it through one refill before I am spontaneously accompanied.

As I prepare to make my second set of steps, one of the aunties—notably older and a bit frail—of one of the murdered young women comes and stands next to me. Without exchanging a word or even making eye contact, she incorporates herself into the action, carrying the bucket of blood

---

25. For example, "lloronas," or "wailers," is a term used for women who are actually paid to grieve at funerary processions as a regular cultural practice in Mexico.

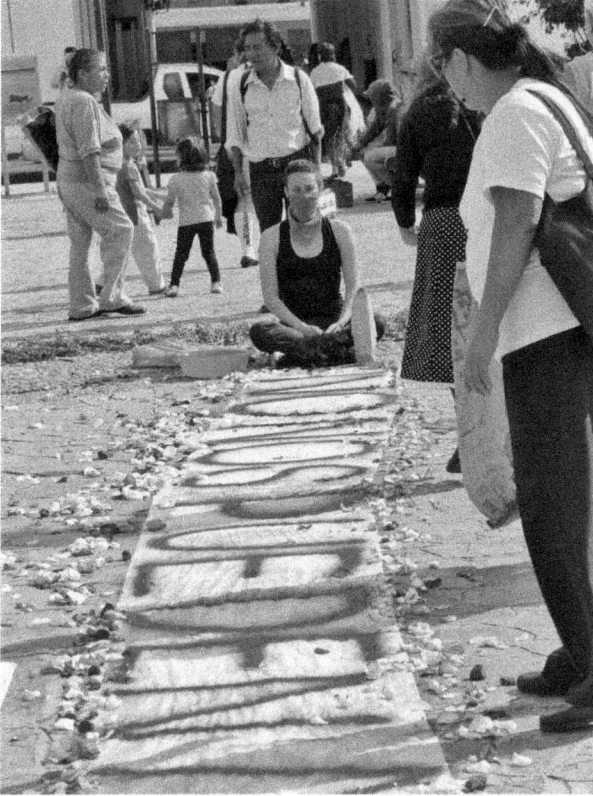

FIGURE 1.6. The author waits to begin a performance at
a public *acción* in Chiapas on October 14, 2014. Used with
permission of the photographer, Nelly Cubillos Álvarez.

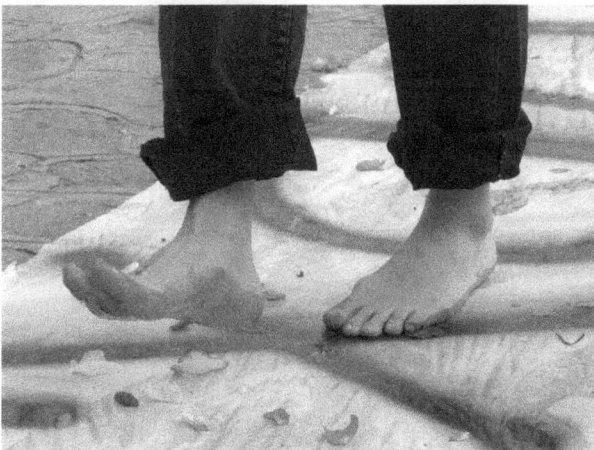

FIGURE 1.7. The author's bloody foot soles at a public
acción in Chiapas on October 14, 2014. Used with
permission of the photographer, Nelly Cubillos Álvarez.

FIGURE 1.8. The author steps into a red pail at a public *acción* in Chiapas on October 14, 2014. Used with permission of the photographer, Nelly Cubillos Álvarez.

alongside me, placing it down to my left when I pause to rewet the soles of my feet (see figure 1.8). We softly and gently fall into an organic collaborative ritual that moves at the pace of mourning. My breath catches and a wail crowds my chest as we sync into one another's rhythms.

We continue this way, taking our time, until we arrive at the end of the path. Feeling one another, we turn around and continue walking together,

FIGURE 1.9. The author walks covered in a black veil, accompanied by
an older woman, at a public *acción* in Chiapas on October 14, 2014. Used
with permission of the photographer, Nelly Cubillos Álvarez.

now moving in the opposite direction (see figure 1.9) As we walk together,
moving in slow and measured but perfectly synchronous rhythm, we tap into
something bigger than ourselves—something we can feel holding the space
between and around us. Though the ritual recalls blood, death, unresolved
murders, and the longevity of harm in this grieving geography, in the space
between us a tender sense of care is invited in.

In the plaza, we collectively unlearn grief as an individual process to be
held only by the aggrieved. Instead, we collectivize the pain of grief, within
the context of a grieving geography, as a pedagogical lesson about what it
means to hold grief's manifold implications and interlocutors. We put grief to
use to revalorize and reclaim the existence of other worlds and violent alienation from them. When we reach beyond the individual toward the struc-
tural and material realities that shape the lives of Native/Indigenous peoples
in Chiapas, we must simultaneously reach beyond the flattened framework of
Zapatismo-as-triumph or the visual constructions of Native/Indigenous lore

for the outside. Instead, we turn toward historical longevities present in this site.

Sitting with the externalization of grief in the practice walked through above, it remains instructive to hold the cosmological interventions inspired by the Native/Indigenous people and communities from within the Zapatista territories, to recall how Native/Indigenous people in the region lost access to themselves and their communities through the modern/colonial civilizing project. Part of the grief being held is this. Beyond what the outside world might remain fixated on or the prerogatives of life in modern/colonial global *necro*liberal capitalism, it is entire life worlds that people are fighting to regain. Dwelling in the images of this action—one that brings together forced disappearances of Native/Indigenous young men with femicide/feminicide—let us now use the "analytic of indigeneity" to listen to other cosmological sensibilities from Native/Indigenous worlds of the region that allow us to imagine grief as a portal into the pluriverse. In other words, let us listen—in imaginative pluriversal alongside—to what is on the other side of this grief.

Toward Life

"La tierra es de quién la trabaja" (The land is of those who work it) say the Zapatistas, in honor of Emiliano Zapata's legacy, named earlier in this chapter in our historical overview and mythologized in figure 1.2. Zapatista agrarian reform through its land-back revolution enabled a return to and new establishment of Native/Indigenous land politics—what is ultimately intended as an ecological politics of right relationship with all beings, including the self. This dynamic and integrated ecological relationship exists in many millennial Native/Indigenous cosmologies. However, as mentioned in the introduction, a notion of ecology that includes a contiguity with what the Anthropocene has called "the Natural world" continues to separate people from all else—it operates from a fractured locus. Integration and wholeness are not built into the modern/colonial global necroliberal capitalist world order and its manifestation in Mexico.

Moving with the grieving geography that is the center of San Cristóbal de las Casas, my walking alongside those most impacted by the pain of necroliberal femicide and state violence teaches me that there is something on the other side of this large collective grief. The depth of this grief—the reality of this grieving geography—shows that there is a wholeness that is longed for. Now, moving with Arvin's (2015) "analytics of indigeneity," let us think with some of the Native/Indigenous conceptions of a full self and life from the perspective of people who have existed in this region since time immemorial. While these frameworks cannot account for all Indigenous people in Chiapas, the conspecific and coalitional relationship that Native/Indigenous people have in Chiapas because of social movements invites a conspecific thinking-with Indigenous worlds beyond the violence and terror of coloniality's grip.

"Política kuxlejal" or "kuxlejal politics," for example—a theoretical and political praxis from Tseltal and Tojolabal peoples—has been used as a tool of Zapatismo to spiritually practice reciprocal relationship with the land as a holistic framework of ecological life. It is a cosmological framework that does not belong only to Zapatismo (Mora, 2018, p. 38). "Kuxlejal" means "life-existence"; one whose very definition grows and transforms when addressing the collective, as in "stalel jkuxlejaltik" (Mora, 2018, p. 38). "Stalel jkuxlejaltik" refers to "a way of being as a *pueblo* in the world striving for daily life with dignity, the goal, or 'lekil kuxlejal.'" The aspirational goal to live a life with dignity, *lekil kuxlejal,* is a "horizon of struggle" that is not only related to the "collective" as in being-with other people, but also "with the land, with the natural and supernatural worlds that clothe and feed all beings" as relations to be honored for all that they nurture and sustain in people (p. 38). "World," from this cosmology, already takes the pluriverse as given, seen partly in how Tseltal world-sense does not have a practice of possession, extraction, or thingification.[26]

To develop a deeper practice of listening to Tseltal cosmology, let us also be with theorization of the cosmology "a grandes rasgos" (in broad strokes), as articulated by Tseltal scholar Juan López Intzín. He opens up the world of the Tseltal people, also known as the "jp'ijil o'tanetik" or "the wise of the heart" (2013, pp. 181–182). Let us listen again: the Tseltal people are the people who are wise of the heart. Honoring the centrality of the heart, *o'tan,* in Tseltal cosmology, as the place where thought is born—where the thinking/doing intersect with feeling—López Intzín thinks/feels with a logic of "corazonamiento" or heart-reasoning of an "other rationality" (see López Intzín, p. 2013, p. 74, footnote 2; López Intzín, 2015, p. 184). Let us listen with our hearts to how Tseltal people come to be/become in their fullness.

The decolonizing spiritual work that the Tseltal people need to do / be doing to regain wholeness in the face of the modern/colonial global necro-liberal capitalist system, according to López Intzín (2015), happens in the labor of thinking/doing what it is to be/become Tseltal again,

---

26. "Thingification" is a concept that comes from Aimé Césaire. In his *Discourse on Colonialism,* he says, "My turn to state an equation: colonization = 'thingification'" (Césaire, 1972/2000, p. 42).

Once we had done the act of *xcha'sujtesel o'tan,* in other words, to make our heart return once again to the world-cosmos that we had been forgetting, then we could initiate the *yo'taninel sbentayel snopel sp'ijil jol-o'tanil,* heart-reason the walk/path reflecting on the wisdom of (the) mind-heart, that implied and implies going back to listen to and scrutinize the *Bats'il K'op,* the true word-language, our language of infancy, that guards many secrets and with which we can expect moments and times of revelation from within. (p. 182)

True to the nature of the Native/Indigenous languages spoken in Chiapas, language itself holds the cosmology. For the Tseltal, then, being-with the nature of the heart-thinking of their very language means to be/become Tseltal once again. The action of sending the o'tan back to the world-cosmos of their birth that López Intzín is referring to is part of what is required for Tseltal people, from their cosmology, to reencounter their "chu'lel," or soul-spirit-consciousness (p. 184).

All living things, human and more-than-human, have both o'tan and chu'lel for the Tseltal. López Intzín (2015) explains that one understanding needed to return the o'tan to the world-cosmos of their birth and gain the lessons that come from the wisdom of integrating one's chu'lel begins by accepting that all things have o'tan and chu'lel—a respect for human and more-than-human beings. The second aspect of the return of the o'tan that is needed is the acceptance of the collective aspect of chu'lel; or, to acknowledge that all things in existence have o'tan and chu'lel, one must also "recognize each element in their own grandeur" (pp. 184–185). Put another way, "You must see the human being, animals, and things in their 'just' dimension, in 'an act of recognition where *Ich'el-ta-muk'* is practiced" (López Intzín, 2015, p. 185). The practice of Ich'el-ta-muk' refers to a form of deep care for all beings, exemplified in the treatment of seeds that are going to be planted or harvested. If seeds have been thrown to the ground, each seed should be picked up again with care, recognizing that each seed has o'tan and chu'lel. By taking care to pick up the seeds, each seed is being recognized by another being as a being that is whole, with a heart and with soul-spirit-consciousness. It is the practice of this "principle" of *Ich'el-ta-muk'* that precedes a "transit toward *Lekil-kuxlejal*" (p. 185).

In Tseltal conceptions of being/becoming, people are given back to themselves as subjects when they unlearn the "domestication" of being and existence inherited from the modern/colonial civilizing project that denies the integration of the o'tan and chu'lel of racialized and gendered beings and of all other life, completely negating the existence of spiritual compasses to guide ecological interrelation-as-wholeness from Indigenous worlds (López Intzín, 2013, p. 76). Tseltales can return their o'tan to the root of their world/cosmos to reclaim their ontological life, in a community of other beings, recognizing and respecting all things in the justness of their grandeur, fullness, and completeness. It is here that one greets their chu'lel.

Returning to how we opened this analytical encounter with the Tseltal and Tojolabal cosmology through concepts like lekil kuxlejal, let us listen once more to López Intzín (2013). He explains that lekil kuxlejal refers to "this life where human beings live a full life, dignified and harmonious, an ideal state of humanity. Another world in which power is not the measurement but yes to the power to be or the power to feel-know-feel-think" (p. 78). A dignified life based in the principle of Ich'el-ta-muk' that practices recognizing the o'tan and chu'lel in all things, is the only path to wholeness for the Tseltal people; it is lekil kuxlejal.

Tseltal cosmology, understood through some of these broad strokes about being/becoming and thinking/doing, is a world not predicated on extraction from the earth's and one another's resources nor participating in the racialized gender hierarchy constructed by the colonial/modern gender system that, in turn, sustains the justification of said resource extraction. Recalling the practice of grief on September 14, 2014, let us imagine all that this grief practice is holding, in the longue durée of violence against Native/Indigenous peoples in the modern/colonial world order in this region.

Marking a sharp departure from these cosmological groundings, extractivism and racialized gender violence exist in symbiotic relationship—the former creating the conditions of the system that femicide/feminicide, trans-femicide/transfeminicide, and other state violences are the collateral damage of—requiring a dissociation from lifeworlds that honor the o'tan and chu'lel in all things. A dissociation that, for those experiencing the violence of power, is sometimes a strategy for survival. Here, the interconnection between how Native/Indigenous peoples have been racialized and gendered in symbiotic relation to extractivism in the modern/colonial order can also be understood as part of what has constituted the apparatus of the Anthropocene. A brief foray into the Anthropocene's logics is deeply instructive for our analysis of how the colonial/modern gender system operates for Native/Indigenous peoples. Let us momentarily scale out to the global design of the colonial/modern gender system and its relationship to the Anthropocene to then come back to its local implications to take in all that must be grieved.

Lugones (2010), guiding us around how to understand the location Native/Indigenous peoples were placed in within the colonial/modern gender system, says, "I propose to interpret the colonized, non-human males from the civilizing perspective as judged from the normative understanding of 'man,' the human being par excellence. Females were judged from the normative understanding of 'women,' the human inversion of men" (Lugones, 2010, p. 744). If we follow the decolonial feminist interpretation of the colonial view of Native/Indigenous peoples as outside the purview of the Human—via their hypersexualization and sexual passivity, as racialized, gendered, and sexed accounts of their being constructed to deny their humanness—we can see how, following the colonial logic of this interpretation to its end, "no women are colonized; no colonized females are women," and therefore, no men are colonized; no colonized males are men (Lugones, 2010, p. 745). The coloniality of gender at play allows us to, "understand the oppressive imposition as a complex interaction of economic, racializing, and gendering systems in which every person in the colonial encounter can be found as a live, historical, fully described being" (p. 747). The coloniality of gender is a lens to understand how the colonial condition "nailed down" those deemed "other" as nonpeople within the hegemonic order of things, categorized and marked for dispossession, death, and the obliteration of entire life worlds.

The Anthropocene, what we can partially understand as the complete anthropomorphic centering of the Human as the apex of all living beings, is coterminous with the colonial project and the site of emergence for necro-liberal global capitalism that was set into motion through a "universalist geologic commons" (Yusoff, 2018, p. 2). This means that the geological mapping of the earth as open for extraction (vis-à-vis doctrines like terra nullius) is co-constituted with power relations shaping dynamics like the coloniality of gender and racial caste systems—in other words, how the "bodies" of others were meant to be apprehended as "mattering" or not. Of the latter, Yusoff (2018) explains, "racialization belongs to a material categorization of the division of matter"—including the "mattering" of those deemed nonhuman (p. 2).

Now let us zoom out one step further to understand the global and hemispheric concerns the Anthropocene brought for Native/Indigenous peoples and other "others" of the hemisphere, important for bringing our local-global theorization home. The birth of the Anthropocene and its infamous genocide of fifty million Native/Indigenous peoples, ongoing and further dispossession of surviving Native/Indigenous peoples, justification of chattel slavery and all of its afterlives, and systematization of torture and violence in plantation cultures and ecologies demonstrates how the "annihilation of the colonial other" (recall Lugones in the introduction) was and is required to create (and to maintain) a globally hegemonic notion of space and place (Yusoff, 2018, p. 32). I appreciate Yusoff's (2018) connections between space, place, and time because, along with spatial inscriptions in geologic territory marked by dispossession, extraction, and accumulation comes warp-speed global environmental degradation, what Native/Indigenous populations like those in Chiapas have endeavored to halt. Notions of race (weaponized against Black/Afro-descendant and Native/Indigenous peoples in the Americas) and gender as an elemental grammar of the former, have been operationalized for the purposes of extraction, making race (and racialized gender as an inconvenient presence for necroliberalism) *foundational* to all structures of global space (Yusoff, 2018, pp. 2–10). From this vantage point, it is not difficult for conquistador-settlers to engage in a total discounting of Native/Indigenous cosmologies—like those of the Tseltales and their relationship to all beings—as an act of subjugation, dismissing other world cosmologies through discursively over-simplifying and weaponizing words and phrases like "'uses and customs,' 'traditions,' 'crafts,' 'beliefs,' 'witchcraft,' 'traditional medicine,' 'shamans,' 'exoticism,'" and so forth (López Intzín, 2015, p. 185). These gross misrepresentations and this utter disregard for entire other worlds is emblematic of the modern/colonial world order's hegemony over meaning and existence.

As a result of the justification of extraction via such thingification and nonmattering, entire populations of people have severed relationships to their land and ecologies, which is to say, to themselves. Stripping people of their sense of humanness allows conquistador-settlers to continue to displace and dispossess people of their land and the cosmologies of their worlds (Yusoff, 2018, p. 35).[27] Holding the co-constitution of nonmattering and extraction, let us now turn back to the practice of grief as a stepping stone out of the modern/colonial order's Anthropocene on the way to lekil kuxlejal.

Grieving Geographies

What if the ancestral and historical practice of grieving is the ignition that launches the journey of sending the heart back to the cosmos of its origination for the Tseltal people? Feet on the ground in the Plaza de la Resistencia, walking with those most affected by racialized gender violence in the region and by coterminous forms of extractivism, I feel the violences compound. The land is grieving. People, animals, plants, and even objects are grieving. Grief becomes a practice of collectively recalling a dislocation from entire cosmologies where

---

27. Colonialism's "geologic disruptions" have included the transplantation of foreign crops and diseases, mineralogic excavation that has permanently transformed the earth's ecology, and other forms of extraction like fossil fuels, oil mining, factory farming, and water damning that have all contributed to what we are now experiencing as global warming, erosion, degradation, chemical leaks, loss of biodiversity, etc. (Yusoff, 2018, p. 35).

all beings' (and even nonbeings') lives are apprehended in their "just" size—in the fullness of their being. "Todxs" now marks hundreds of years of grief—and all the emotions that can and do accompany and constitute grief as an affective register—from the ongoing onslaught of modern/colonial violence that marks this region.

In this "grieving geography," the land holds multitudes. This plaza is a site where many worlds intersect, interact, and even collide, symbolic of a region struggling to hold pluriversal meaning. To instill the capacity to brutally murder (to overkill) women, trans people, and other "others" in the public body is to witness the OWW machine functioning perfectly well without the oversight of its leaders. To be anthropocentric is also to be homicidal—a feature that most affects those deemed outside the project of the Human—even if those enacting the murderous behavior come from the same or similar population groups, in other words, hearts that have not yet been returned to their world-cosmos. The bloody footprints left from the violence that necroliberal regimes leave along their path chart the collision course of worlds—a government with claims to a one-world world in a geopolitical landscape of peoples from different worlds with other cosmological, ecological, and spiritual relationships with all that exists.

If we understand San Cristóbal de las Casas and the surrounding regions as grieving geographies, we might imagine the action of October 14, 2014, as a grief portal. If, according to lekil kuxlejal of the cosmologies of the Tseltal and Tojolabal peoples, to feel is also to know and to be, honoring the wisdom of the heart, in this grieving there is knowledge of other worlds that do not have to kill women, Native/Indigenous peoples, ancestral lands, and life as we know it as the very fodder of their existence. Grief as a portal—and the feelings contained with it—is the confirmation that there are other worlds that are not this. In a cosmology built on sensing with all the beings that exist and knowing interrelatedness and the dignity of their grandeur and magnitude, grief becomes a sensual exercise of acknowledging the ongoing destruction of other worlds that know interdependence, as a part of life, to be real—worlds that do not necessitate gratuitous violence as nutrition.

The ongoing murders of women (cis and trans) and other Native/Indigenous people in places like San Cristóbal de las Casas demonstrate that death is fodder for the necropolitical systems whose existences devastate our planet. With no solution to this violence in the OWW *from* the OWW, one way out is to grieve the unfathomable but ever-present violence and loss in the purview of the long durée of extraction and dispossession of entire worlds. To allow the feelings of grief to be big and witnessed, held by actions like those of Arte Acción in the Plaza, is to acknowledge the entanglements of violence that inaugurated and maintain modern/colonial modes of governance. To let the public feel the weight of the grief is to hold many worlds at once—to refuse to absent these worlds, regardless of the OWW's epistemological and ontological denials, amnesia, and coercive dissociation. *We must grieve all that the Anthropocene has destroyed* as one way to fully feel and be with the worlds that have been lost or suppressed. Grieving the loss of divine interconnectedness with cosmologies predicated on caring for all beings, acknowledging the o'tan and chu'lel in everything, along with the loss of public safety, is the pause needed to return to pluriversal openings. In other words, to move through and be with the grief that comes from experiencing the modern/colonial civilizing order's violence is to denaturalize individual experiences with violence as disconnected from the OWW's colonial/modern gender system and its global geological designs.

Here, grief is medicine. Grief is a teacher. Grief connects femicide and feminicide, tranfemicide and transfeminicide, and state violence to a historical trajectory of Native/Indigenous genocide and its afterlives. To grieve collectively is to feel all that has been lost in the service of global necroliberal capitalism—a grief far too big to be held by individual bodies. The decolonial feminist turn of this interruptive and public mode of necropolitical refusal that is established through the creative grief portal is a reminder that knowledge also arises from all that there is to feel. *Corazonando* (heart-thinking-reasoning) with Tseltal and Tojolabal peoples—for whom life-existence is one where the fullness of all beings exists in the recognition of their hearts and spirits—shows how grief is the recognition of the distance lodged between Native/Indigenous hearts and their world-cosmos.

The decolonial and transfeminist turns made within these grieving geographies are invitations to know and feel that "colonized, racially gendered, oppressed existences . . . are other than what the hegemony makes [us] to be" (Lugones, 2010, p. 746). Grief holds worlds where subjectivity is not something that is given from modern/colonial powers that cannot feel, fathom, or know these other worlds. Public grief, invited through actions against femicide and feminicide and state-sanctioned violence in the Plaza de la Resistencia, allows for reencountering the pluriverse of worlds, worlds where Native/Indigenous people are the stewards of their cosmological and ecological interconnectivity and subjectivities. Worlds where lekil kuxlejal—a full-dignified-just-life—is possible. Here, grief brings people home.

CHAPTER 2

The Wake Work of M/otherhood

I am standing in a confined room during my tour of Elsewhere Museum,[1] as part of a cohort of the Southern Constellations Fellows Residency in fall 2018. Elsewhere Museum is in downtown Greensboro, North Carolina, at 606

---

1. Though it is outside the scope of this work to take a deep dive into the history of Elsewhere Museum, some of the context proves interesting here. The museum is a converted secondhand and surplus store whose history follows that of the founder's grandmother Sylvia Gray. Sylvia Gray amassed an enormous collection of all sorts of items between 1939 and 1997—a fifty-seven-year period. Gray and her husband began the store as a furniture shop, buying secondhand furniture from the northern states and having it fixed and resold in North Carolina. After World War II, army surplus also became a part of their collection, along with discarded products left over from the upsurge in factory production. After Gray's death, the store remained boarded up for several years, the entire collection intact.

Then, in 2003, Gray's grandson George decided to move to Greensboro with some friends from college, with the idea of organizing and cataloguing the collection. Using all three floors, George and friends sifted through and sorted the collection. The collection was organized by classifying the items, placing like objects, materials, tools, clothing, etc. together in the same room or space. They relied on the aesthetic, functional, and metaphorical organization of the items in the old store to reveal possibilities to them. Some rooms began to show them what they wanted to become; others arose out of necessity. As Elsewhere began to develop, the crew opened the front door so that folks from the neighborhood could wander in as they pleased (Sherman et al., 2013, p. 37). The goal was to let the public life of downtown Greensboro shape and inform what Elsewhere was to become. Then, as it grew, they began to hold events, further animating the objects and ever transforming the space. With the help of a series of small grants and the events being held in the space, Elsewhere gained its name as a living museum (p. 38). The website for the museum is located here: https://www.elsewheremuseum.org/.

South Elm Street, just down the block from the International Civil Rights Museum—a museum that was developed around the Woolworth's counter where the famous sit-ins took place in 1960. I was intrigued by the compact size of this third-floor room (part of a former boarding house) approximately four feet by ten feet. I was also mesmerized by the purpose of the installation work of visual artist Antoine Williams that preceded me.[2] Williams created the installation *Because They Believe in Unicorns* as a response to ongoing Black death at the hands of law enforcement, white conquistador-settlers, and the prison-industrial complex. A unicorn, made from World War II army surplus tents, hangs in the back of the space as the centerpiece. Of the piece, Williams says, "I want to play with the perception of whether this figure is being hanged from the ceiling or being elevated out of so-called darkness" (Williams, Scheer, & Coleman, 2021, p. 253). Williams used Michelle Alexander's (2012) concept of "the new Jim Crow" to take a long view look at how the US government's 1980s "war on drugs"[3] leveraged the US melting pot's lie of a

---

2. The original piece by Antoine Williams that I developed my work into can be viewed on the Elsewhere Southern Constellations site here: https://antoinewilliamsart.com/section/467153-Because-they-Believe-in-Unicorns.html.

Here is what you are seeing in the images in this link: Williams continues Michelle Alexander's (2012) argument, refusing the colorblind discursive lie of race as a nonfactor in the war on drugs. He constructed a dilapidated army surplus tent "unicorn" to represent the Black man-as-mythical-unicorn mocking the political argument of race-as-irrelevant in the very intentional and exorbitant increase in prisons (popularly known as "cages") across the United States. In the top two-thirds of the room, Williams first collaged *Time* and *Life* magazine covers (all from the Elsewhere collection) featuring housewives romanticizing war. The images were subsequently sanded and painted over—leaving some of the images partially visible while others were fully obscured. This technique creates a palimpsest on the wall. The walls are overlaid with the color "haint blue," a popular color used on ceilings in the South because it was believed that bad spirits would see the color, think it was the sky, and exit the home. He also added splashes of red-brown brushstrokes across the walls, beckoning dimension out of the walls. The wall below these images is a solid brown color.

3. This is significant because the phrase "war on drugs" was first coined by President Richard Nixon, and it was declared in 1971. Its declaration (like many of the US's "wars") demonstrated how a "simple slogan's" performative power manufactured a literal war, not to mention that there was no self-consciousness on the government's part about the gravitas of this naming (Alexander, 2012, p. 74). Over the following decades, even as drug use declined significantly, Black men and other people of color continued to be disproportionately incarcerated, many framed as addicts-turned-criminals. I would like to draw particular attention to how Williams's work renders war visual/visible with his use of army surplus gear. This is significant because in 1997, the Pentagon "handed over more than 1.2 million pieces of military equipment to local police departments" (Alexander, 2012, p. 74). Then, between January 1997 and October 1999, an additional 3.4 million orders of Pentagon military equipment were transported to eleven thousand police agencies in all fifty states (p. 74). These decisions demonstrate that the "war on drugs" has historically been backed by militarism / police violence with the Pentagon handing over some of the most frequently used military weapons to domestic police forces.

"postracial" society as an attempt to occlude how said "war on drugs" was an internal war against Black people, by another name. This war has had many spokes and multiple faces, further criminalizing Black existence, denying the structures of anti-Black racism so foundational to US empire, while empowering the police force and conquistador-settler vigilantes. It was responsible for obscenely exacerbating mass incarceration, with Black men being disproportionately targeted. Through this history and this work, Williams is essentially asking whether the Black man is a mythical unicorn or an ever-lynched specter.

I build my piece into Williams's installation through slight modifications to the installation space itself and through live performance, largely based in movement.[4] In this piece, I conjure up the histories of Black women (transgender and cisgender) whose existence preceded mine and who we fight to keep here. I focus on Black women in the ancestral realm when I am moving, centering trans women who lost their lives due to transfemicide in the US South that year (some of their faces are added to the palimpsest on the installation wall). Both Williams and Alexander (2012) were intentional about their decisions to focus on the impact of mass incarceration on Black cisgender men. The specificity of their focus and the importance of their contributions cannot be overemphasized. That said, the purpose of my performance work and theorizations here is to pivot toward the ontological implications of mass incarceration for Black women (cisgender and transgender). I do so to feel into shifts in being/becoming and thinking/doing made possible through the work of Black queer feminist creative insurgency. Here, I argue that these practices are doing what Cristina Sharpe (2016) calls "wake work."[5] I make this pivot to ask how such insurgency does wake work by refusing new forms of Blackness-as-property vis-à-vis the necroliberal profitability of the prison-industrial complex. I ask how the creativity of this insurgency writes a new

Alexander names just what was contained in these orders, "253 aircraft (including six- and-seven-passenger airplanes, UH-60 Blackhawk and UH-1 Huey helicopters), 7,856 M-16 rifles, 181 grenade launchers, 8,131 bulletproof helmets, and 1,161 pairs of night vision goggles" (p. 74).

4. I invite you to witness the performance here: https://vimeo.com/309515075?embedded =true&source=vimeo_logo&owner=2318073.

5. Sharpe (2016) defines and redefines wake work as an episteme—in light of enslavement and its "wake" or many afterlives like police violence and mass incarceration—in her text *In the Wake: On Blackness and Being*. As she concisely puts it, "In short, I mean wake work to be a mode of inhabiting *and* rupturing this episteme with our known lived and un/imagined lives. With that analytic we might imagine otherwise from what we know now in the wake of slavery" (p. 18). I will continue to elaborate on the meaning of this term in the body of the text for the purposes of the analysis, but this starting point is important for folks who may be less familiar with her work or need a refresher.

history of Black women's gender through queer pondering of m/otherhood for a diasporic elsewhere[6] (Gumbs, 2016). First, I will explain how I got here and then where we are going.

I brought myself to this work through my residency and performance process at Elsewhere Museum in fall 2018. In my rehearsal experimentations and performance process, I kept coming back to the feeling of enclosure in this small space. I wondered what it would look like to consider the ongoing war against Black women's bodies (cis and trans) as part of the continuing conditions of conquest that are the systematized killing (literal and social) of those deemed not a part of the project of the Human. Blackness/transness and Blackness/queerness were not given the chance to form an antagonistic relationship through my decision to directly intervene in this installation by elaborating on the palimpsest already present. I recall all the cages that our people have lived and died in. I engage a movement repertoire invested in the symbolic nature of the installation and the enclosure of carcerality. I push against the space's walls that attempt to close in on Black existences, holding women's histories in my sartorial, movement, and musical choices, in my commitment to remaining in relation to the Black woman I once was and the Black women who came before me. Donning clothing items I had sourced from the clothing room of the museum, chosen because they reminded me of the period dress of the women in Julie Dash's *Daughters of the Dust,* I engage in a movement and somatic exercise exploring all the ways I can push against the walls of the space (see figure 2.1). In the performance itself, much of the movement repertoire revolved around this "pushing," while dancing and moving to Sweet Honey in the Rock's "I Don't Want No Trouble at the River." While moving, I recall the ways that Black women and queer people have led and keep leading people to freedom. In the space, I directed the light overhead so that it fell into the center of the room, casting shadows, recalling the lighting at the beginning of Alvin Ailey's *Revelations* as well as the historical memories of the beating rays of the sun. I dwell in the spaces conjured within me as I push on the walls, pondering Black un/freedom in the modern/colonial world order.

The performance moments of pushing against the walls of this conversational installation space in Elsewhere Museum bring me to the significance of what Jacqueline Hall (2005) has called the "long civil rights movement"—a fundamental historical intervention into the mythologizing and essentializing tendencies of the civil rights rhetoric that gets mobilized around a brief

---

6. Though an elaborate explication of Elsewhere Museum is not the emphasis of this chapter (see footnote 1 for more), I still find spiritual valence in the meaning of "elsewhere" as it relates to the pluriversal thinking-doing-being this study engages.

FIGURE 2.1. Still from performance of *Warriors: Beyond Unicorns and Erasures* (2018).
Used with permission of Elsewhere Museum. Image taken by Aurora San Miguel.

period in the 1960s—temporally and geopolitically sequestered to maintain a
convenient narrative about the South—cherry-picked away from its militant
edges at the expense of all that preceded this time and all that continues on.
Hall (2005) laments,

> By confining the civil rights struggle to the South, to bowdlerized heroes, to
> a single halcyon decade, and to limited, noneconomic objectives, the master
> narrative simultaneously elevates and diminishes the movement. It ensures
> the status of the classical phase as a triumphal moment in a larger American
> progress narrative, yet it undermines its *gravitas*. It prevents one of the most
> remarkable mass movements in American history from speaking effectively
> to the challenges of our times. (p. 1234)

Following the articulations of Hall (2005), I understand the civil rights struggle for Black Americans in the US to be one that never ended. The ongoing

reality of civil rights struggle is necessitated by the ever-present conditions of conquest and the modern/colonial order that structures the country. This reality was never so apparent as in the election of 2016—my reflections in the creation of this performance work sit squarely during the midterm election cycle of 2018.

Taking in the temporal and geopolitical expansiveness of this civil rights history, I ponder why I have dwelled so long on the tightness of the space I am in for this residency. I trust the intuitive artistic choice I have made and decide to remain here. In this dwelling, I go back to a moment that marks the colonial/modern gender system contained within this iteration of the OWW.

I recall my participation in the Black Mama's Day Bailouts as a part-time organizer with the multiracial queer organization Southerners On New Ground (or SONG) during the springtime earlier this same year (2018). I was struggling to make ends meet as a full-time lecturer with a 4/4 load (four courses to teach in both fall and spring semesters), looking for meaningful additional labor aligned with my ethical values of liberation. I applied for and joined the Durham chapter of SONG's bailout strategy in work partnership with another hired organizing fellow. The bailouts were an opportunity to pay the "ransom" of Black women being held in prison because they were too poor to pay for their pretrial release—a very profitable strategy for the prison industrial complex (PIC).[7] This organizing strategy, though partially useful for and intended to put pressure on local government (especially the city and county commissioners) to reform the corrupt system of cash money bail, was ultimately part of a longer-term abolitionist strategy that believes in a world without jails and prisons. This short-term strategy, as part of a longer-term goal of prison abolition, follows the ancestral lineage of newly freed Black people buying the freedom of still-enslaved Black people.

As organizers, we searched the available public databases to look up the public arrest records of incarcerated Black cisgender and transgender women who were mothers or caregivers, gauging who we would have the best chances of bailing out as well as who was being held on the most cooked-up pretrial stories. We also participated in court watching—providing a type of citizenship accountability and oversight board for the criminal justice system. We held multi-stakeholder community forums on policing and fundraised as

7. Whenever I refer to jails and prisons, I will refer to them as the "prison industrial complex"—a term that is now in popular use among "modern" abolitionists. The term tends to get credited to Angela Davis for its invention but has also been defined by the collective Critical Resistance. They define it the following way: "the Prison Industrial Complex (PIC) is a term we use to describe the overlapping interests of government and industry that use surveillance, policing, and imprisonment as solutions to economic, social and political problems." For more see: https://criticalresistance.org/mission-vision/not-so-common-language/.

much bail money as possible to pay the ransoms of Black women and care-givers in time for Mother's Day. Sometimes, we would simply show up at first court appearances and wait until the bail was named, offering to pay it on the spot. The point was to make jails and those who "man" them incredibly uncomfortable and to signal their complicity in the modern/colonial racist superstructure undergirding the criminal justice system.

In my decolonial pedagogical movements through the Southern US, I came to participate in such actions. Actions like the Black Mama's Day Bail-outs exist within the purview of the long civil rights movement in this region and this country. The purpose of this chapter is to be with the role of these actions in intervening in the business-as-usual character of this aspect of the afterlives of slavery—mass incarceration and the prison industrial complex in the US. As a preliminary question, I ask, What are the implications of the historical continuity of enslavement's coloniality that looks like targeting and locking up Black mothers and caregivers? The criminalization of poverty and its survival strategies is especially egregious ethically in a nation largely built by the labor of our predecessors' ungendered flesh—used as captive "breeders" for birthing new property into enslavement to keep the plantation economy going (see Spillers, 1987; Cooper Owens, 2017). Here I understand the preda-tory and misogynoiristic nature of the incarceration of Black mothers and caregivers (cisgender and transgender) within the historical and theoretical purview of the afterlives of slavery. Their bondage is a condition of continued conquest over the ontological terms of Black women's lives. The shackles of partus sequitur ventrem (that which is born follows the womb) is understood here as implicating all the descendants of Black people who were enslaved vis-à-vis the ongoing conditions of conquest.

I continue in the grammar of Spillers (1987), who, like Sharpe (2016), posi-tions the legacy of partus sequitur ventrem as one that structures a through line between the Middle Passage, the coffle, and the birth canal. It functions to "dis/figure Black maternity, to turn the womb into a factory producing black-ness as abjection much like the slave ship's hold and the prison, and turning the birth canal into another domestic Middle Passage" (Sharpe, 2016, p. 74). Important to note, because Black trans women are an indispensable part of this troubling dilemma, I am not limiting discussions of the "birth canal" to cisgender biomedical science's focus on anatomy. Instead, I imagine the birth canal as both literal and metaphorical to refigure the spiritual significance of the birth canal and m/otherhood relationship for Black people. In the geo-political context of southern regions like this one, I bring Black queer and feminist analyses like Alexis Pauline Gumbs (2016) concept of "m/otherhood," and my own queer reading of the cosmologies of Trans Atlantic diasporas, to bear on the "wake work" (defined below) of the Black Mama's Day Bailouts in forging pluriversal Black futures.

Like the organization of chapter 1, what follows in this chapter unfolds in two layers. First, I situate the long civil rights struggle of Greensboro and the surrounding region, briefly signaling key moments of its ongoing civil rights history, to position North Carolina as a significant site from which to think about creative insurgent projects like these. I focus on Greensboro's history even though the action occurs in Durham, because it is the performance site from which I am reflecting on these pluriversal openings and because its realities speak to important dynamics shaping the sociopolitical climate of North Carolina. Second, I share moments from the Black Mama's Day Bailouts and the pretrial release of the mothers as relevant moments of creative insurgency that invite pluriversal lenses on liberation. I then read this work through a Black queer feminist and spiritual diasporic lens to demonstrate how the thinking/doing of this wake work opens up pluriversal opportunities for Black people to be/become in a different legacy. I will demonstrate how this "wake work" is a collectively held and gender-nonspecific ontological rewriting of the ungendered flesh experienced by Black women and mothers (and, by virtue of legal doctrine, Black people) in systems of captivity like enslavement and one of its afterlives: mass incarceration.

"Wake work" is derivative of an expansive unraveling of the many definitions of a "wake," including a vigil of relatives next to the body of the deceased, through which to "enact grief and memory" (Sharpe, 2016, p. 21). Wakes also refer to

> "the track left on the water's surface by a ship; the disturbance caused by a body swimming, or one that is moved, in water; the air currents behind a body in flight; a region of disturbed flow; in the line of sight of (an observed object); and (something) in the line of recoil of (a gun);" finally, wake means being awake and, also, consciousness (definitions quoted in Sharpe, 2016, p. 21).

Tracking these many definitions for "wake," Sharpe (2016) attends to the multiple afterlives of slavery and how Black people might not "seek a resolution to blackness's' [sic] ongoing and irresolvable abjection" but rather "see Black being in the wake," landing on wake work as "a form of *consciousness*" (Sharpe, 2016, p. 14). My work here exists in the consciousness of Sharpe's (2016) conception of wake work that is not seeking after resolution to a modern/colonial global necroliberal world order that never included Black humanity in its design. Instead, I turn to creative insurgent practices like the Black Mama's

Day Bailouts to read their wake work of choosing life, despite the many after-lives of the terror of enslavement. The second part of the chapter will unravel how this wake work ontologically unfolds in the direction of life through an Afro-diasporic m/othering sensibility.

Long Civil Rights Histories, Elsewhere

Greensboro is historically marked as an important site of civil rights struggle, because it was one of the birthplaces of the national movement and organizing strategy of direct action called "sit-ins." Sit-ins were a strategy where, in highly organized and nonviolent action, Black people would come and "sit in," or occupy, all-white establishments or all-white areas of establishments as a method of refusing racist segregation laws in the Jim Crow South. The people engaging in these actions had to follow white protocols of decorum and respectability including things like grooming and dress as part of their tactic (Cohen, 2015). To be clear about the history: Greensboro was *not* the birthplace of the sit-ins as a strategy writ large, since the NAACP and the Congress of Racial Equality (CORE) had begun using this tactic after World War II. Rather, we should understand the events in Greensboro as emblematic moments that would spread like wildfire as a strategy for protesting segregation across the South, ultimately being taken up in other areas of the United States as well (Cohen, 2015).

The Greensboro sit-ins were devised by four women at North Carolina A&T—a historically Black college—but were ultimately carried out by four of their male counterparts because the fear of violence against women was too high.[8] Then, on February 1, 1960, four A&T men staged a sit-in at the Woolworth's lunch counter, to the great horror of the white establishment and its clientele. Their names were Ezell Blair Jr., David Richmond, Franklin McCain, and Joseph McNeil—all first-year students at NC A&T. They came into the Woolworth's, sat down, and ordered coffee. They were admonished for their decision to sit at a "Whites only" counter and denied service. They remained seated anyway, until closing time. On February 3, they came back with sixty others, and on February 5, three hundred more (Cohen, 2015). They refused to leave when they were denied service. They were met with vitriol in the form of physical and verbal harassment. As a result of the pressure of the sit-ins, the media attention, and the spreading of the strategy, Woolworth's was successfully desegregated in July of 1960. The International Civil Rights Museum

8. I learned this information from my tour at the International Civil Rights Museum in downtown Greensboro on October 9, 2018.

that I mentioned above, sitting just down the street from Elsewhere Museum, was built up around the original sit-in counter and remains in business today.[9]

Within two months following the initial sit-ins, other sit-ins were carried out in fifty-four cities in nine states. The sit-ins inspired sister direct actions including "wade-ins at pools and beaches, kneel-ins at churches, read-ins at libraries, and walk-ins at theaters and amusement parks" (Cohen, 2015). In the year that followed, more than one hundred cities had complied with some form of desegregation of public facilities (Chafe, 1981, p. 71). The Greensboro sit-ins shifted the terrain of the movement to one that included passive resistance and student-driven struggle (Chafe, 1981, p. 71). Part of the reach of this work resulted in the formation of SNCC (the Student Nonviolent Coordinating Committee) in April 1960 in Raleigh, North Carolina—a regional detail that signals part of the significance of North Carolina as a historic site of Black liberation struggles.[10] Without the intention of skipping over major eras of history, allow me to signal a few other defining moments and dynamics of the modern/colonial order's anti-Blackness in the region, demonstrating the need for the vision of the revisionist historical purview of "long civil rights" in this context. Let us look a bit ahead to understand how the history of Greensboro (and of North Carolina) remains one of push and pull.[11]

Greensboro and the rest of the US South are marked by ongoing police violence against Black people and their antiracist allies, as well as by plantation logics within the criminal justice system and prison industrial complex. On November 2, 1979, in a span of eighty-eight seconds, the Ku Klux Klan and US American Nazis opened fire in broad daylight into a crowd staging a "death to the Klan" protest, organized by the Communist Workers' Party.[12] This attack became known as the 1979 Greensboro Massacre, the memory of which was reopened "when, just over a year later on November 17, 1980, the

9. During the era of the Trump presidency, the museum was vandalized. Since then, visiting the museum has been limited to directed tours only. For more information, see: https://www.sitinmovement.org/.

10. An additional point of historical note: What is fascinating about Greensboro, situated in what has been called the South's most progressive state, is the history that led up to and that followed the sit-ins. Even after the sit-ins, Black residents did not see rapid change in access to various kinds of public services that they needed. Though Greensboro announced in 1954 that it would comply with the ruling of *Brown v. Board of Education* and desegregate schools, it ended up being the last city in the South to do so, not managing to until 1971 (Chafe, 1981, p. 6). Following the sit-ins, by 1963 Greensboro was the Southern city experiencing the second greatest number of protests and demonstrations, second only to Birmingham (p. 6).

11. Information gleaned from the most updated census information at the time: https://www.countyoffice.org/nc-guilford-county-jails-prisons/.

12. That day, five people were killed and several more injured. Those people were: Sandra Neely Smith (Black), James Waller (white), William (Bill) Sampson (white), César Cauce (Cuban American), and Michael Nathan (white) (Packer, 2021, p. 142).

Klansmen and Nazis were acquitted by an all-white jury" who had decided that the Klansmen had acted in "self-defense" (Packer, 2021, p. 142). The complicity between police officers and Klansmen was made horrifically clear in this incident; dynamics that many have only more recently become aware of in this country. It is important to recall the history of the Greensboro Massacre, because it emphasizes the significance of how long civil rights struggles have operated and how the upswing in right-wing white supremacist vigilantism that we saw in 2016 was far from exceptional. Multiracial coalitions of class-based organizing that desire to see an end to extreme racist organizations like the Klan have historically been met with characteristically extreme violence.

In another far-too-recent police tragedy, just one month prior to my residency at Elsewhere, on September 8, 2018, thirty-eight-year-old Marcus Deon Smith, a beloved unhomed Black man in Greensboro, was high on drugs and experiencing a mental health crisis. He was seen wandering in and out of traffic after the Greensboro Folk Festival (Taylor, 2019). He pleaded with police officers to help him by taking him to the local hospital. The officers put him in the back of a police car. When Smith did not see an ambulance coming, he began to panic and bang on the windows of the closed car. The officers and sergeants at the scene decided that they needed take Smith out of the car and use a RIPP Hobble on him—a form of hog-tie restraint that is combined with hand cuffs. He never resisted but pleaded for them to stop. Within half a minute, he was unresponsive. From his injuries and the distress, he quickly went into cardiac arrest and was declared dead at the hospital shortly thereafter. The police falsified their report, saying that Smith was suicidal and combative and that he had collapsed in custody, with no mention of the hog-tie or hand cuffs (Taylor, 2019). Eight police officers and sergeants participated in Smith's lynching, seven of whom received merit increases after the incident, including multiple bonuses and three promotions.

The Smith family protested the incident for three years and were met by nothing but mockery from the Greensboro Police Department (GPD). It was only after the murder of George Floyd, and the massive Greensboro protests that ensued, that attention was brought back to Smith's case. Smith's family and local organizers called the local communities' attention back to Smith, drawing parallels to Floyd, in an attempt to signal the long civil rights movement and the selective nature of media attention. It was only after these efforts that the Smith family won their lawsuit for wrongful death at the hands of the GPD, settling for $2.57 million.[13] These instances of police brutality—police

---

13. For more about the details of the settlement, see: https://www.rhinotimes.com/news/council-agrees-to-settle-marcus-deon-smith-lawsuit-for-2-75-million/.

as conquistador-settlers—are part of a larger, necroliberal, long civil rights environment that constitutes the prison-industrial complex's presence in the region and in the nation at large.

To make matters worse, the jail and prison systems in North Carolina have far too direct a continuity between the historic treatment of enslaved Black women and laboring bodies. It was only in the year 2021, after tremendous and ongoing organizing efforts led by the Black women and trans folks in SisterSong Women of Color Reproductive Justice Collective (with organizers Omisade Burney-Scott [she/her] and Ash Williams [he/him] at the helm of this work in North Carolina), that the shackling of pregnant and laboring incarcerated people in prisons, jails, and detention centers was discontinued. With Black women and gender nonconforming people already disproportionately represented within the prison industrial complex (part of a larger issue, the overall disproportionate representation of Black people in the PIC writ large), coupled with the fourfold greater likelihood of Black women and birthing people dying during childbirth,[14] shackling practices are nothing less than genocidal and eugenicist, by design.

When Tracey Edwards—imprisoned while pregnant in Raleigh, North Carolina, related to drug charges because of an opioid addiction—went into labor as an inmate, her wrists and legs were shackled "during transport, hours of induced labor and shortly after delivering her baby" (Browder, 2021). She notes that even postpartum, officers would not take her handcuffs off to allow her to comfort her crying baby, despite her pleas. Additionally, an IV line got entangled with her handcuffs, pulling it out and causing Edwards to bleed heavily (Browder, 2021). Given such treatment, it is appalling but not shocking that the new stipulations of the 2021 North Carolina law had to explicitly articulate the following: "Restraints should not be used when women are in labor, at the onset of contractions, during delivery, post-partum recuperation, during inductions, transportation for C-section and initial bonding with newborn" (SisterSong, 2021). Taken together as part of the context of the long civil rights struggle in Greensboro, neighboring regions, and in North Carolina, let us theorize, together, the wake work of the Black Mama's Day Bailout actions in offering something other than a lack of humanity.

---

14. The statistics about Black maternal mortality have become more widely known and generalized. For specifics about this and an excellent analysis of what she calls "birth geographies," I recommend Jennifer Nash's (2021) piece "Birth Geographies: Race, Reproductive Justice, and the Politics of the Hospital."

Wake Work of M/othering Ourselves:
Reclaiming Our Black Mothers

In Greensboro, like in Durham and cities throughout North Carolina, the jails (even at the advent of jails as a system) have been primarily filled by pretrial detainees. The primary purpose of jails, then, is as housing for people who have not yet been convicted of a crime but who typically do not have enough money to pay their bail.[15] Those working within the system continually cite the importance of jails, because they prevent FTAs (failures to appear), but never take into account the challenges that poverty poses to successfully making it to a court date: things like lack of PTO (paid time off) for blue-collar workers; lack of child care; lack of transportation; ongoing and untreated addictions that are often products of trauma, mental illness, or forms of abuse; housing instability; and situations of domestic violence, among other barriers endemic to racialized poverty.[16] Profiting off this systematically designed reality with its deeply ingrained racism, the cash bail system is meant to criminalize poor people—predominately Black, Native/Indigenous, and Latinx people, and their many deprivileging intersections—for simply existing and creatively utilizing all the survival and coping mechanisms at their disposal (all while navigating extraordinarily complex and ongoing trauma and systems of abuse).[17] People who spend time in jail because they are unable to pay their bail are more likely to be convicted of their alleged offense and transferred into the prison system, because poverty and racism make it nearly impossible to demonstrate "innocence" once targeted.

My primary role as an organizing fellow for the SONG 2018 campaign was to help organize the fundraising efforts for and the implementation of the Black Mama's Day Bailout in time for Mother's Day 2018. As such, my pluriversal theorizations here come from experience on the front lines of refusing

---

15. The Prison Policy Initiative has an excellent profile on North Carolina jails. It can be seen here: https://www.prisonpolicy.org/profiles/NC.html.

16. These realities are ones that we witnessed firsthand as organizers planning for the bailouts. Part of our job was to make sure that the people we bailed out made it to their court appearances—many of which were for infractions so minor that the cases were dismissed. Had they failed to appear because of a lack of resources, they would have found themselves in an endless cycle of being criminalized for being Black and poor.

17. For instance, simple possession of marijuana has been the charge behind a disproportionate percentage of Black people in prison, while white and wealthier people might have access to marijuana cards, be overlooked, or simply not targeted at all for either possession or use. Addictions to pain medication, alcohol, and other drugs to deal with the traumas of racism, gender violence, poverty, or chronic illness and pain due to similar factors and inadequate healthcare make for a snowstorm of possible reasons to be targeted as a "criminal." Many of the women that we met in the jail system were dealing with addictions or facing potential assault charges for standing up for themselves in domestic violence disputes.

the anti-Black silos of the modern/colonial order and its racialized gender formations. With SONG organizers throughout the Southern United States, there was a collective pot of money that served as a portion of the bail funds. Then, in community-led events like queer salsa lessons, open house parties, and other money-generating events, each location set out to raise a particular amount of money to "buy peoples' freedom." Our singular focus: Black women mothers and caregivers unable to pay their bail presently sitting in the Durham County jail, awaiting their trials. My participation in the Durham action is not meant to limit the geopolitics of these actions or turn our focus exclusively to Durham. Instead, I want to think about this action within the previously named regional North Carolinian context of the ongoing struggle for Black liberation. Instead of waiting for "rights" to become available to all, an elusive dream in a colonial/modern racialized gender order, we get people *free*.

Coordinating such efforts took a tremendous amount of collective organization and people power. The women imprisoned in the jail had to first be located and communicated with directly to get their consent to bail them out (since posting a Black mama's bail requires enthusiastic consent as part of SONG protocol). In the process of locating women to be bailed out, SONG hired a Black woman social worker to support the women during their release and also committed to a continuity of care for ninety days afterward as they adjusted to being back on the outside. The social worker's role included coordinating rides as a preventative measure against reincarceration for FTAs and organizing support for gaining access to addiction and mental health care services, job support, housing support, food vouchers, hygiene support, and child care so that the women could focus on holistically building stability and staying away from ensnarement in the PIC. As part of these creative insurgent and collective efforts, we stationed ourselves outside of the jailhouse during the days leading up to Mother's Day, with tables of food, flowers, cards, hygiene items, and gift cards as well as arms ready to embrace the women that would be freed, ready to greet the women one by one when they were released after we posted their bail (see figures 2.2 and 2.3).

Serena Sebring, Black queer organizer and mama who was the lead organizer of the Durham chapter of SONG at the time shared with *Ms.* magazine the impetus behind the decision to post bail for Black mamas and caregivers,[18] saying, "We wanted to call attention both to the importance and centrality of black women, black mothers and black caregivers to our communities, [as well as] to the particular impact mass incarceration is having on black women"

---

18. It is important to note, for the accuracy and respect of multiple organizing histories, that bailing people out of prison has been a national tactic taken up by different organizations throughout the US.

FIGURE 2.2. A table with gift bags and snacks at Black Mama's Day Bailouts 2018. Used with permission of the photographer, Kelly Creedon.

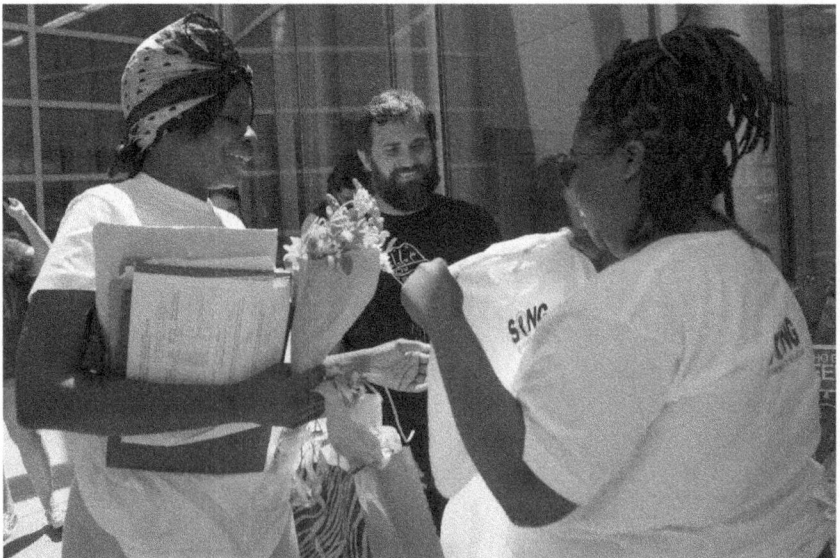

FIGURE 2.3. Organizers smile and laugh with a just-released Black mother at Black Mama's Day Bailouts 2018. Used with permission of the photographer, Kelly Creedon.

FIGURE 2.4. An organizer midchant at Black Mama's Day Bailouts 2018. Used with permission of the photographer, Kelly Creedon.

(Willets, 2020) (see figure 2.4). While SONG is not the only organization that has focused on pretrial bail as one prong of a larger strategy to abolish the prison-industrial complex in the US, the choice to center mothers and caregivers was a vision in particular of one of SONG's codirectors at the time, Mary Hooks. Mary Hooks, through her understanding of the long civil rights struggle, coined a mandate (also intended as a call-and-response chant) as a guiding principle for the bailouts and the long-term work to be done: "The mandate for Black people in this time is: To avenge the suffering of our ancestors, To earn the respect of future generations, To be willing to be transformed in the service of the work" (Carruthers, 2018, p. 135).

In this work, "avenging the suffering of our ancestors," responding to Hooks's call, means prioritizing Black mamas and caregivers as a form of "wake work." This is wake work, because it participates in historically refusing the continuation of abjection and nonontology for Black women, mothers, and caregivers and, by extension, Black people (see: partus sequitur ventrem) through the prison-industrial complex's treatment of Black women and caregivers. The longevity of the modern/colonial civilizing project's misogynoiristic scripting and scapegoating of Black women and mothers has included making them into chattel property, "breeders,"[19] "the 'mothers' of American gynecology,"[20] "Mammies," "medical super bodies,"[21] "matriarchs,"[22] hypersexualized "Jezebels" and "Sapphires," "welfare queens,"[23] and "unfit mothers,"[24] among other disparaging tropes throughout history, each existing

19. "Breeders" is the term that was used to refer to Black enslaved women who, after the banning of the importation of newly enslaved people after 1808, were used to develop gynecological science to cure medical issues like vesico-vaginal fistulae ultimately so that they could continue to successfully reproduce more people to service the plantation economy (Cooper Owens, 2017; Ross, 2017).

20. Cooper Owens (2017) explains how Black enslaved women's subjugation came to be framed in this light: "American slavery and early modern gynecology have intertwined roots that are distinctly southern. As much as white medical men are lauded for serving as the 'fathers' of American gynecology, black women, especially those who were enslaved, can arguably be called the 'mothers' of this branch of medicine because of the medical roles they played as patients, plantation nurses, and midwives" (p. 25).

21. "Medical super bodies" is a term developed by Deirdre Cooper Owens (2017) to describe "the myriad ways in which white society and medical men thought of, wrote about, and treated black women in bondage," how they spoke about their purported "fecundity, their alleged hypersexuality, and their physical strength, which was supposedly superior to that of white women" (p. 109).

22. The figure of the "matriarch" is one of the tropes that came from the anti-Black and misogynoiristic work of white sociologists in the 1960s desperate to frame Black women and mothers as "responsible for the disintegration of the Black family and the consequent failure of Black people to achieve success in America" (Roberts, 2016, p. 16). Further, the matriarch was said to harm their families in two primary ways: "They demoralized Black men, and they transmitted a pathological lifestyle to their children, perpetuating poverty and anti-social behavior from one generation to the next" (Roberts, 2016, p. 16).

23. The trope of the "welfare queen" is an infamous scapegoating of Black women and mothers whose impact continues to be felt. The mythology about the welfare queen describes "the lazy mother on public assistance who deliberately breeds children at the expense of taxpayers to fatten her monthly paycheck" (Roberts, 2016, p. 17). The image of the Black welfare mother has been linked back to a group of five Black unmarried sisters and single mothers who shared an apartment with their nineteen children (subsequently known as the "Chicago 19"). After the police raided the apartment in February 1994 and the story broke about the conditions the children were in and the amount of money the women were taking in collectively via welfare, this image became the trope that circulated about Black maternity (Roberts, 2016, pp. 18–19).

24. The trope of the "unfit mother" was part of the "war on drugs" and one of the reasons why we saw a rise in incarcerated women. Dorothy Roberts (2016) explains how reproduction was made into a crime for Black women by tracking things like traces of drugs in newborns' urine and arresting Black mothers postpartum for "endangering the lives of their unborn children" (see the case of Cornelia Whitner from 1992, cited in Roberts, p. 150). Law enforcement had no investment in rehabilitating mothers addicted to drugs or looking at the root of things like the crack epidemic. It was easier and more profitable to incarcerate women, and such treatment tracked with the treatment of Black women historically. The other side of the coin of treating Black women as "unfit mothers" was nonconsensual sterilization, such as lowering sentences if they agreed to receive the Norplant implantation (see Roberts, 2016, chapter 4; Goodwin, 2020). Sometimes even possessing drugs during pregnancy was enough to criminalize Black mothers (see Goodwin, 2020, chapter 7).

as part of the ongoing conditions of conquest. These disparaging tropes are steeped in the scientific, medical, and social racism helping to structure the United States' colonial/modern gender system's eugenicist formations.

Sitting with what appears to be an exaggerated historical fixation (on the part of conquistador-settlers) on disappearing the subjectivity and ontology of Black women—whether through dehumanizing them as commodities and terrorized flesh, defining them as hypersexualized deviants, or criminalizing their systematized impoverishment and methods of coping, or through minimizing the likelihood of reproducing, surviving childbirth, or being allowed to mother—it is not hyperbolic to comment on Black women's utter lack of reprieve as racialized subjects in this modern/colonial civilizing project and its racialized gender system. The many facets and phases of suturing Black women's lives to various forms of bondage and racist caricaturization shape fundamental pieces of the very blueprint of the Human. Of this "locus of confounded identities," Spillers (1987) notes the frailty of the modern/colonial order's requirement of an antithesis, which says, "My country needs me, and if I were not here, I would have to be invented" (p. 65). Capitalizing on this frailty, our wake work here delinks from the barbarity of this dialectic.

It is worth citing Iyko Day (2021) at length to borrow from her trenchant capitalist critique, developed from the theoretical contributions of what she calls "Afro-feminism." She maps the transition from the use value of Black flesh to the attempted eradication of choiceful Black reproduction in a way that helps structure the theoretical excerpt to follow. Day (2021) argues,

> If enslaved Black women were a continual source of relative surplus value under slavery, the aftermath of slavery dramatically reconfigured the inheritance of this value regime. While Black men "touched . . . by the mother" (Spillers 1987, 80) inherited a disinheritance under slavery, in its afterlife the disinheritance was recast as a devaluation of wage labor (as the enduring effect of temporal acceleration). However, for Black women, their association with acceleration was recast as temporal excess and a threat to the entire system of social relations mediated by capitalist value. No longer exclusively a source of white wealth as relative surplus value, the power of Black women's reproduction was redirected toward Black social reproduction. Thus the value tied to the temporal acceleration associated with Black women's reproductive labors under slavery was reconstituted as a *deviant excess* that threatened the social reproduction of white supremacy upheld by the value regime. (p. 75; emphasis added)

Building her articulations in this passage, Day (2021) culls her analysis from a history that saw Black women as only worthy of keeping alive, with "healthy"

reproductive organs, for the purposes of enriching the machinery of the plantation economy and reproducing the next generation of nonhuman labor—
predetermining the inheritance of the children born of enslaved women (see
also Cooper Owens, 2017; hooks, 2015; Roberts, 2017). Then, in the transition
from the plantation economy to the industrial capitalist system, the resentment of conquistador-settlers at Black "emancipation" is glaringly present
through the many modern/colonial figurations of Black women as anything
but autonomous subjects, eternally guilty by virtue of their existence, without
recourse to the rights of innocence afforded to "women" of the dominant race.
Again, echoing Lugones (2010), "the colonial answer to Sojourner Truth is
clearly, 'no'" (p. 745).[25]

Day's (2021) articulation of the "deviant excess" that Black women's personal reproductive labor has represented, and continues to represent, for
conquistador-settlers marks a striking shift in strategy, a compensatory move
responding to the fact that Black women and their offspring were no longer
useful for enriching white empire (Day, 2021, p. 75). To understand this further, we must tarry momentarily with conquistador-settler "resentment" of
Black emancipation, which has required an attack on reproductive rights as
part of the eugenicist project of white supremacy. Saidiya Hartman (1997)
articulates how "the texture of freedom is laden with the vestiges of slavery,"
so that we might "understand the nonevent of emancipation insinuated by the
perpetuation of the plantation system and the refiguration of abjection" (p.
116). Abjection has been refigured time and again through the aforementioned
litany of reconceptualized and reformed tropes designed to endlessly subjugate
Black women and limit their chances to renew and create life (whether in the
form of producing and raising children or any other life-generating work not

25. Here, Lugones (2010) is riffing on Sojourner Truth's supposed famous 1851 speech,
"Ain't I a Woman?," frequently acknowledged as a cornerstone of Black feminist thought. It is
very important to note, however, that this speech has been a source of contention because no
record of the speech exists. It was purportedly "recorded" by a white abolitionist by the name
of Frances Gage (who was also the President of the Women's Convention of 1851, where Truth
is supposed to have delivered the speech). What has called the speech into question are several
key details: it was recorded twelve years after it was purportedly delivered, it is written with a
Southern dialect and language meant to evidence "Black" speech (for example, some accounts
say "Ar'n't I a Woman?" while others say "Ain't . . . ?"), and it contains inaccurate information about Truth having thirteen children, where records show she had five (Sojourner Truth
Memorial Committee, 2022). It is important to note these discrepancies because its seems
that Gage was playing up ideas about Truth's Southernness, her accent, and the truth of her
life. Another version of the speech was written by Truth's friend Marcus Robinson, who heard
the speech and appears to provide a much more accurate account of Truth's accent and words
(see Sojourner Truth Memorial Committee, 2022). What remains significant about Truth's
testimony is the challenge she poses to the subject of "womanhood" in a white supremacist
society as an emancipated Black woman.

limited to physical or adoptive reproduction and rearing). The perpetuation of the plantation system can be seen in the existence and prevalence of the prison industrial complex. US Black women's ongoing subjugation has been facilitated by these new faces (recall Michelle Alexander's "new Jim Crow") of the plantation system. The conquistador-settlers' ongoing attempts to eradicate Black women, when no longer useful for the modern/colonial civilizing orders' establishment of itself as a capitalist empire (when Black women are no longer a *"being for* the captor"), is ultimately a war on Black people (Spillers, 1987, p. 68). The not-so-subtle intention of the disappearance of Black people, beginning from the root of our lives and lineages in this country—Black mothers and birthers—speaks to the threat conquistador-settlers see to "their" nation, one meant to preserve "a racial order on which the white republic was founded" (Hartman, 1997, p. 117).

Hartman's (1997) work is incredibly useful to think through here, because she establishes a historical and theoretical approach to the event of Emancipation as one that did not equal "freedom" for Black people. She argues, "the strategies of the individuation constitutive of the liberal individual and the rights-bearing subject" have had to continuously produce Blackness as "abject, threatening, servile, dangerous, dependent, irrational and infectious" to define and defend its existence (Hartman, 1997, p. 116). Tracing conquistador-settler shifts in strategy, Hartman (1997) examines how the profound transformations of the abolition of slavery and Reconstruction, with the growing entrenchment of a capitalist ideology of liberal individual humanism, meant a "burdened individuality" for Black people—a double bind that should not be evaded (p. 117). Said differently, Black people were late to the party of liberal humanist individualism because of their time as captive commodities for conquistador-settlers for the latter's establishment of their colonial empire. This dynamic has meant that within the purview of the OWW, Black people were never meant to be fully unburdened of our former status as property in a nation whose foundational logics required our existence as objects, chattel, and nonhuman beings. To make matters worse, through these transitions, the newly established nation-state's leaders and other conquistador-settlers were now "free" to continue subjugating Black people under the guise of capitalist production and population regulation through power garnered under liberal humanist "rights." This granted conquistador-settlers the power to manipulate institutions and the social order to fit their project of the Human and its ideological formations. This reality has been particularly harmful given that, *to this day,* there are those who have never desired to see Black people existing as freed beings, much less folded into the nation as respected and Human subjects of rights (see Hartman, 1997, pp. 118–120; Wynter, 1995).

Wake work, in the context of this history of resentment toward so-called Emancipation, lives within the tension point between flesh and body, property and personhood. After Hartman (1997), if we return to Spillers's (1987) always timely foundational articulations about Black women "made flesh" through the "pornotropic" conditions of their enslavement, it will help us to further set the scene for the aforementioned "symbolic substitutions in an efficacy of meanings that repeat the initiating moments" (pp. 66–67). Pornotroping, or the act of stripping enslaved Africans of their bodily integrity and subjective experience as a member of the human species, is what rendered captive people akin to animals—flesh. Flesh, for Spillers (1987) precedes the body. It is the nonmattering matter upon which the whip cracks and pierces and where all other forms of brutality—physical and sexual torture as well as grotesque forms of atomizing the flesh—were enacted. Flesh, a property of property, had no gender (pp. 67–68).

If we follow Spillers's (1987) logic to completion, enslaved women were not women, because they were not people. They also did not have a body, because they were degraded to flesh. As flesh, they were ungendered: stripped of culture, history, personhood, and the meaning-laden social relations that vanished during the crossing—meanings that "remained suspended in the oceanic" (p. 72). It is these fleshy nonbeings, then, who gave "birth" to new nonbeings, who inherited their value as property through the legal constraints of partus sequitur ventrem. Here, "'kinship' loses its meaning" because kinship and "property relations" are an incompatible proposition (pp. 74–75). "Birth" also loses its meaning as a "reproduction of mothering" because neither enslaved man nor woman had any parental rights (p. 78). Motherhood, in the syntax of power relations during enslavement, does not exist for the enslaved woman. All she (the flesh) reproduces is "the reproduction of relations of production" (Strobel cited in Spillers, 1987, p. 79).

Spillers's (1987) consequential theorizations of the conditions of fleshy property—which was the status of Black enslaved women in the formation of the colonial/modern race and gender system—are clearly not meant to be taken up and used to justify essentialized reifications of gender or sex as a rebuttal against what was denied to their ancestors during the conditions of enslavement (even if she does acknowledge the implications for representation that exist here on an "insurgent" plane) (Spillers, 1987, p. 80). Ungendered and dispossessed of motherhood, the ostensible Black "woman" poses a conundrum to traditional feminist theorizations, requiring that we add a pluriversal perspective to this lineage of thought—one that might be capable of tethering vestiges of what was suspended in the oceanic to the audacity of

Black survival, so that we might acknowledge the creative insurgent beings that have emerged in the wake, and all that their being/becoming has inspired.

I want us to now turn our attention to the action of the specificity of buying Black mothers' and caregivers' freedom from the jail cells holding them for ransom, as work that exists in a pluriverse of meaning that recalls the very long civil rights work of calling the "mother" home. Here, I want to imagine "motherhood" for Black American people in the wake. Motherhood signifies both birther and caregiver *and* something else. Said differently, we are going to remain with the "and" in an exercise of "yes/and," if "yes" is the action of the bailouts as a political strategy—a bus stop on the way to the abolition of the prison industrial complex (see Mariame Kaba's *We Do This Til' We Free Us*, 2021). Where "and" brings us to the spiritual dimension of this wake work—a breaking-open in the space-time continuum of the one-world world so that Black women (and by extension, Black people) might know themselves as something other than continuous with these legacies of un/freedom.

And

We watch Black women come out of the Durham County jail and receive their gifts, care packages, and bouquets of flowers. We are all beaming at the sight. Each woman sits down with their organizer or case worker, the one who will accompany them over the next ninety days, to create a provisional plan. The women are hugged and loved up on by the SONG organizers and by other organizers and community members who have been waiting in the hot sun to celebrate their release. Watching the bailouts become creative insurgent action, in real time, with material consequences in people's lives, it becomes clear to me that there is something bigger going on here.

BYP100, or the Black Youth Project 100, accompanies our action that day. They are here to remind us of life and to keep the energy elevated. Toward the later afternoon, they engage us in call-and-response (see figure 2.5) with some of the freedom songs, liberation chants, and political action messages (some original, some reappropriated) that have since been integrated into their album *The Black Joy Experience*.[26] Echoing through our bones at the end of these long and emotional days are freedom chants the likes of,

---

26. *The Black Joy Experience* is available as an album here: https://www.youtube.com/watch?v=L1C6LcbRT6s&list=OLAK5uy_lezl9a_sSVUNmuQO4WUSEkGIHRkHoil3E.

FIGURE 2.5. A group of organizers stands in a circle at Black Mama's Day Bailouts 2018. Used with permission of the photographer, Kelly Creedon.

Call: I. Response: I. Call: I believe. Response: I believe. Call: I believe that. Response: I believe that. Call: I believe that we. Response: I believe that we. Call: I believe that we will. Response: I believe that we will. Call (now shouting): I believe that we will win. (Response and call join in together and continue, shouting), I believe that we will win! I believe that we will win! I believe that we will win!

I recall witnessing the energy and joy of BYP100 and select members of SONG like Serena Sebring (seen participating in the chants in figure 2.5) and feeling my way through the exhaustion and tears gathering in my chest. The feelings evoked in me are not mine alone: I feel generational spirits and ancestors taking up residence in my chest, my emotions blended with theirs. In the pluriverse of possibilities, these actions remind us that we have already "won"; the price has already been paid.

At the end of the bailout days, those of us who have brought the community together to organize these women's release linger in the shade, desperate for some reprieve from these unusually hot late spring days. The muggy hot day produces a recollection of the exhaustion this beautiful work creates. We process with one another, riding the high energy of BYP100's chants, and make plans for what else needs to get done that day and the one to follow. Occupying the entire front entrance to the jail with our massive signs and banners that read "Money Kept You In. Black Love Got You Out" and "Libera-tion in Our Lifetime. #Endmoneybail," we maximize our civil rights to public space. Watching Black women exit the jail, we witness how little time it takes to break someone's spirit through incarceration. We watch their affects shift to glee at the warm reception awaiting them. Bearing witness by participating in this work creates molecular shifts. Mary Hooks's voice echoes on repeat in my head—"to be willing to be transformed in the service of the work." In these moments, we choose to remain with the jubilation of knowing a few more people have a chance of escaping the prison-industrial complex and its goal of recidivism (because even pretrial, Black people are "convicted" in the eyes of *this* state). I reiterate, something so much bigger than us has happened here.

When we choose to mobilize community resources to get Black mothers and caregivers free, we do not make any evaluations of worthiness, nor do we run them through assessments of character meant to determine the quality of their personhood. To be alive, breathing, and Black is to be deserving of freedom. Still, engaging in this process does not presuppose a romanticized or utopian relationship to motherhood or caregiving. We are not ignoring the reality that some Black mothers and caregivers socialized into this colonial/modern racialized gender system also cause harm and can be problematic. Simultaneously, we refuse the tropes, caricatures, stereotypes, and respect-ability politics that keep our people unfree. We do not let anyone individually serve as a stand-in for all Black humanity. Collectively holding an abolition-ist ethic within the purview of the longevity of anti-Blackness we desire to eradicate, we make decisions to practice freedom together. We practice what it feels like to honor one another's humanity by holding the stickiness of us, as a collective, unraveling the Black mother or caregiver as a stand-in for the nonontology of Black people.

By engaging in the process of hacking the predatory and racist money bail jail system by posting bail for Black mothers and caregivers in time for a national holiday in celebration of motherhood, we spiritually reckon with the role of mothering and caregiving as a labor whose foundational logic in this country was not intended for Black people. In so doing, we are tapping into something deeper and longer than any of the individual participants of this action. We are doing wake work, which is also to say, the spiritual work of healing our relationship to the figure of the Black woman and the Black mother and to the labor of Black mothering and caregiving in the afterlives of enslavement.

In the pluriversal vision of this wake work, we need a queer definition for the role of the mother and the labor of mothering. Let us build upon the Black queer feminist seeing of Alexis Pauline Gumbs (2016) when she queries,

"What would it mean for us to take the word 'mother' less as a gendered identity and more as a possible action, *a technology of transformation* that those people who do the most mothering labor are teaching us right now?" (pp. 22–23; emphasis added). Gumbs (2016) continues,

> This means that "mothering" is a queer thing. Not just when people who do not identify as heterosexual give birth to or adopt children and parent them, but all day long and everywhere when we acknowledge the creative power of transforming ourselves and the ways we relate to one another. Because we were never meant to survive and here we are creating a world full of love. (p. 23)

Gumbs's work, inspired by the literary production of a lineage of queer Black mothers and caregivers from the 1970s and 1990s, uses the queer imaginative space of yes/and to offer us pedagogical possibilities for Black "motherhood," as a technology of transformation—the actions and energy of caring for and loving one another as Black people. "Mother" or "caregiver," in this Black queer feminist reading practice, comes to represent a horizon of relational dynamics where Black people mother one another and ourselves into wholeness as a birthright of our very existences, in the wake.

Gumbs (2016) invites us to honor both those who have nurtured the children who were and are "not supposed to exist" as well as the mothering "to end war, to end capitalism, to end homophobia and to end patriarchy" as very queer things (p. 20). She acknowledges the tremendous and impossible labor of mothering against all odds as the force that has shown us how to love ourselves and one another into fullness in this wake. This mothering energy is queer, because it makes strange the ways that hegemonic and modern/colonial formations of gender and sexuality—through enslaved peoples' utter lack of bodily autonomy and right to chosen kinship formations—were and are used to exclude Black people from the very category of the Human vis-à-vis the very grammars of the colonial/modern racialized gender system. "The queer thing is that we were born," Gumbs (2016) reminds us, standing squarely within Audre Lorde's (1978) lineage, the latter another Black queer woman whose poetry affirmed for us: "We were never meant to survive" (p. 19; Lorde cited in Gumbs, 2016, p. 24). If one of the "queer" things here is that we were born at all and then had the audacity to survive, then mothering is any spiritual force that supports the defiance of Black joy in existence, survival, and flourishing, in the present and into the future.

Though it is important that we recognize the significance of more traditional notions of mothering and caregiving, and the way that cisgender Black women exercise their own forms of refusal by claiming their place within these spaces, our consideration of mothering and caregiving here is not limited by these gender constraints. This is the queer proposition here. If—speaking to the symbolic order of the modern/colonial global necroliberal capitalist order in the United States—the very notion of gender-based mothering and caregiving loses coherence in the hold of the ship that crossed the Atlantic and on the property of the plantation that built the world's most devastating empire, what is the creatively insurgent pedagogy that comes from a pluriversal reconfiguration of the energy of mothering or caregiving?

To attend to this question, I invite us to hold the remainder of this chapter's wake work of queering mothering and caregiving in a pluriversally diasporic and spiritual container. This container detaches the being/becoming of mother/caregiver from gender—what Black people have not been afforded in the OWW due to the past and ongoing conditions of conquest. In the forced movement of Africans across the Atlantic, the spiritual forces and energies that accompanied them were required to engage in different strategies when up against the totalizing force of colonization. Though the spiritual forces that are central to today's Afro-diasporic cosmologies and spiritual practices and religions—like Lukumí, Palo Mayombe, and Arará of Cuba; Kôngo Angola and Candomblé of Brazil; Petro Lemba and Vodun of Haiti; Vodou of New Orleans and the US South; and Spiritual Baptists of Trinidad, St. Vincent, and Grenada, et cetera[27]—"did not require the Crossing," they made the Crossing with our ancestors and predecessors, shape-shifting in form as many times as necessary to refuse the eradication of our worlds through Black genocide in all forms (Alexander, 2005, pp. 292–293). Let us linger with the practice-based wisdom of M. Jacqui Alexander for an extended moment to help us grasp the implications of this shape-shifting, molding what would become Afro-diasporic spiritual energies and practices, through the Crossing.

Alexander (2005), as if in prayer, shares,

> Mojuba: an expansive memory refusing to be housed in any single place, bound by the limits of time, enclosed within the outlines of a map, encased in the physicality of a body, or imprisoned as an exhibition in a museum. A refusal that takes its inheritance from the Crossing, which earlier prophets had been forced to undertake from the overcrowded passageways in a place called Gorée, the door of no return, still packed centuries later with the scent of jostled grief so thick that no passage of human time could absorb it. It hangs there, this grief, until today, an indelible imprint of the Crossing,

---

27. Here I am expanding upon M. Jacqui Alexander's examples (2005, p. 291).

fastened by a pool of tears below, constantly replenished by the tremors of human living.

   Once they crossed, they graced all things with the wisdom of Ashé. Wind. Sky. Earth. Fire. Thunder. . . . For once they intuited that the human will was long intent on capture, they all conspired to rest their Truth everywhere. . . . Being everywhere was the only way, they reasoned, to evade capture and to ensure the permanence of change—one of the Truths of the Ocean. (Alexander, 2005, pp. 288–289)

Mojuba—I salute or pay homage to, I honor—the beginning of all prayers, demonstrating a reverence for the energies that keep us here. Sacred energies could not be enslaved the way that people were (though there were certainly many attempts to do so, calling such forms of practice "devil worship," "black magic," and the like). Alexander (2005) is addressing the way *asé* or *ashé* navigated the diaspora. Asé is life force. (Recall how in Tseltal cosmology, all beings and things have chu'lel, a spirit-soul-consciousness.) Asé is a similar conception of the energy of life that also demonstrates the existence of spirit-soul-consciousness in all things. What is primal about asé is that it is a neutral conception of energy of life force unattached to moral judgments about how "good" or "bad," "evil," or "pure" it is. It just is—element force. For this reason, "asé," when uttered, is a way to seal the fate of an energy—to say "asé" is to say, "it is so"—a knowing that some call "faith" and others call ecological interrelatedness of what just is. Embedded, then, in African and Afro-diasporic understandings of the asé of elements like the wind, sky, earth, fire, and thunder that Alexander (2005) names above is a trust in the inherent intelligence and wisdom of our planet's ecological liveliness and its vast manifestations—a trust that, when left unmanipulated by human extraction, nature will do what it needs to do. Destruction and calm, death and life, chaos and serenity are all required elements for maintaining the homeostasis of our biodiverse planetary system. As beings that understand our inseparability from the ecological life of our planet—the existence of planetary elements within our bodies as proof of our coextension with them—our worship and work with these energies is central to our spiritual practices and how we go about making life.

   Before continuing any further, and in the spirit of refusing to mythologize any of these systems, it is important to note that the African continent has been no stranger to internal or intracontinental colonization and imperialism, including battling for the supremacy of spiritual systems. The supremacy of the Yoruba pantheon, for instance, had already made its way around massive portions of the behemoth African continent prior to and during part of the Transatlantic Slave Trade, "as a result of wars of conquest, in the name of religion, and for the sake of capturing people and owning territory" (Alexander, 2005, p. 291; see also Law, 1992). For this reason, "African-based cosmological systems are complex manifestations of the geographies of crossing and dislocation. They are at the same time manifestations of locatedness, rootedness, and belonging that map individual and collective relationships to the Divine" (Alexander, 2005, pp. 290–291). The cosmological systems that now make up the varied spiritual practices, religions, and technologies of the African diaspora, then, "engage the different inventions of the social" as creativity, ingenuity, and pure viscera have worked to keep Black and Afro-descendant people alive in the Western Hemisphere (Alexander, 2005, p. 292).

To complete the unpacking of Alexander's (2005) work crucial to our pluriversal revision of mothering and caregiving, we must also be with how the energies that made the Crossing with our ancestors and predecessors through the Transatlantic Slave Trade knew that the Human (conquistador-settler Humans) was "intent on capture" (p. 289). For this reason, the Truth of these energies—the materiality of their asé—permeated all things, beings, and bodies, making itself uncapturable and inviting peoples of the diaspora to make their way back to them, differently. For these reasons, taken together, we have all the varying Afro-diasporic traditions that we do. Geography, local conditions of conquest post-Crossing, and intracontinental migrations and dispossessions of these energies and pantheons that preceded and exceeded the Crossing have resulted in a richness of Afro-diasporic traditions and cosmological systems in this Western Hemisphere (now also existing elsewhere). It requires residing in the wake as a consciousness of the consequences of dispersal to hold the sheer pluriversality of what we now call the Afro-diasporic.

Recalling now, for a third time, what Gumbs (2016) asks above, "What would it mean for us to take the word 'mother' less as a gendered identity and more as a possible action, *a technology of transformation,*" invites an attention to the asé of the Black diaspora (pp. 22–23). Here, if the diaspora's asé is "a technology of transformation" that made the Crossing, then when we say African diaspora to the "Americas" we are also referring to a site of endless creativity and insurgence—African diaspora as mother; a mother who holds and gifts spiritual practices as permutations of countless worlds coming together under the umbrella of who and what we call "Black people." This mother is not bound to any one land or any monolithic constructions but is instead a spirit-soul-consciousness who carries asé across any distance necessary to imbue its forces in all the beings and things required to keep us alive. We are cared for by their (this mother's) energies through this ongoing labor in their various bids for our survival in a manufactured version of a singular world that still feels justified in its defense of the Crossing.

Let us take our thinking one step further to ground our pluriversal theorizations here. Here, we bring our thinking full circle. Gumbs (2016) articulates, "The radical potential of the word 'mother' comes after the 'm.' It is the space that 'other' takes in our mouths when we say it. We are something else. We know it from how fearfully institutions wield social norms to try to shut us down" (p. 21). If the radical potential of the word "mother" comes after the "m," what sutures different Black people together is our existence as "others," in the modern/colonial global necroliberal capitalist order that paints itself as "a" world. The ongoing reality of our existence in these modern/colonial systems defies the eugenicist logics established to eradicate us for the barbaric aggrandizement of conquistador-settlers, logics predicated on the colonial white supremacist fear of whiteness and white people losing supremacy.[28] Black life, under the one-world world construction of Black ungendering and nonbeing established through the Old World grammars, is a queer proposition. Othered through these grammars yet still surviving well into this "New World," Black people *are* something else.

With queer Black people and allies situated squarely at the helm of the work of bailing these women out, the spiritual otherwise that stops giving credence to the historical grammars that birthed the carceral descendants of the colonial/modern gender system's foundation is a portal held among our bodies. By this I mean that the bubbles of safety and protection we create by liberating one another from the confines of the carceral/plantation system demonstrate our knowledge of and existence in the pluriverse. We are transformed in the service of this work, dwelling in the knowledge of the capacity for transformation that we have held for centuries; we must harness our power for accessing other worlds. We do this because, at some point in our lineages, we (descendants of enslaved people) were also descendants of orphans of colonial empire. It is unsurprising, then, that queer people exist at the helm of this work. We are unthreatened by any cisgender or heterosexual Black women and caregivers being liberated in this process because of the expansively queer legacy of motherhood and caregiving that binds us and that will set us all free.

Here, mothering is practice birthed from the knowledge of ungendered nurturance that sustains entire worlds in the diaspora. When queered or divorced from OWW logics, nurturance is removed from its patriarchal cisgender and essentialist headlock, becoming a pathway to places other than here and the multiplicity of what we know as "here." Mothering and caregiving

---

28. See, for instance, David Bauder on the present-day "Great Replacement Theory" here: https://www.pbs.org/newshour/politics/what-is-great-replacement-theory-and-how-does-it-fuel-racist-violence.

actions such as the bailouts, while they do not change the conditions the OWW was predicated on, do the wake work of un/becoming nonbeings as we are reborn through one another's creative insurgence that keeps our millennial knowledge of asé alive—the knowledge that we have always been complete members of the species and other than anything the OWW would come up with. When Black mothers and caregivers are held with abolitionist grace, we are breaking centuries of grammars established for our undoing. As we rebirth ourselves into one another's arms, we learn something new about home.

With the wake work of this, I leave us with this pluriversal pedagogical lesson on mothering and caregiving that cuts through any normative or sequestering jail cells that Black motherhood and caregiving is otherwise put into. Following the layers present in the creatively insurgent exercise of bailing out Black mamas in time for Mother's Day, may the Black queer feminist pluriversal magic of returning nurturance to its role as ungendered guide find us on paths to creating better places. When we move in this way, we can see, anew, the centrality of mothering and caregiving as an energy also belonging to other cosmological guideposts that teach us that there is more than this, that there has always been and will always be more than this. These are tools we will need for the road ahead.

CHAPTER 3

Into the Trans Break

In this chapter, I turn to reading the work of my friend and colleague—Lia García—for the pluriversal openings that her trans performance and pedagogical work offer us. I use the metaphor presented in her performance piece *Cocinar la memoria,* or "cooking memory," which was developed during shared time in the last two days of the residency at Elsewhere Museum in 2018 discussed in chapter 2. I will thoroughly visit this metaphor as an invitation to coalitionally reimagine—for Black/Afro-descendant and Native/Indigenous peoples—how we might think/do ontology (being/becoming) as something other than a philosophical exercise whose truths are predicated on a singular OWW idea of the "modern" (read: modern/colonial global necroliberal capitalist world).

Bringing together the conversations about the thinking/doing of the being/becoming from the previous two chapters, here I am curious about how the trans pedagogical work of García's creative insurgent performance practice, studied through the performance piece here, can be mobilized as a poetic pluriversal opportunity for holding Black/Afro-descendant and Native/Indigenous ontologies in the US and Abya Yala South / Américka Ladina alongside one another. What does a trans woman of color's stewardship in this territory allow us to see, feel, and do? The stakes of our task here are to approximate a pluriversal lens of analysis for hard-won ontological conceptions in the OWW as neither ontological equivalents nor in ontological hierarchy. Instead, we will mark them as geopolitically, historically, and cosmologically relational, with their nuanced and real differences. The goal is not to solve or answer the question "What are the definitive ontological positions for Black/Afro-descendant and Native/Indigenous peoples in this place called 'The Americas?'" but to demonstrate that from a pluriversal perspective, it is impossible to make definitive theorizations about Black/Afro-descendant and Native/Indigenous ontologies that are universally applicable to Black and Indigenous peoples.

In this chapter, I trace and read the inner workings of García's performance for the metaphor for the pluriverse that it forwards as a needed break from the business-as-usual essentializations about being/becoming in the OWW. Elaborating upon the metaphor she draws for us—"brokenness"—I unpack what I see as some of the pluriversal encounters it allows us to have about the Wynterian concept of man/Human within the context of the modern/colonial civilizing project, the OWW. Ultimately, I uplift breaking and brokenness as desirable doings in the present world order. This metaphor furthers theoretical engagements with pluriversally sanctioned revolutions in being/becoming, or how we talk about the study of ontology. This chapter emphasizes the transfeminist significance of what I am calling the *trans break*, or where transness's slippery transgressions and misrecognitions in the OWW are a site where we might become clearer about both Black/Afro-descendant and Native/Indigenous relationships to the Human by epistemological (thinking/doing) departure from it.

This chapter unfolds in three parts. First, I begin by introducing my relationship to García through transfeminist transnational activism and performance. I then walk through her performance in November 2018 to establish the centrality of the organizing metaphor. Third, exhausting the possibilities of the central metaphor, I explicate García's trans pedagogical practice's framework for transness as an opening to the pluriverse and disruption of singular and definitive ontologies—at the level of being/becoming and meaning-making—meant to encompass an essence of Black and Native/Indigenous experience in hierarchical relation.

Some of the questions guiding the theoretical and spiritual contemplations prompted by García's performance here include: What if we predicate plural ontologies on a question of the species to hold Black/Afro-descendant and Native/Indigenous notions of being in appropriate pluriversal complexity, rather than in hierarchical and comparative relation always based on a conspecific center? What value is there in dwelling in the breaks in the OWW's system of representing being/becoming, so that we might long after an ontological break from its confines, allowing us to inaugurate our subjectivities from Sacred otherwise locations? To the latter question, what value does trans pedagogical work of performance practice hold in spiritually accessing pluriversal conceptions of being? Finally, how does a trans woman of color's performance stewardship into the pluriverse allow us to imagine and engage more capacious integrations of being, knowledge, and practice for Black/Afro-descendant and Native/Indigenous personhood?

Trans Kinship and *Cocinar la memoria*

Lia García (also known by her performance names Lia La Novia Sirena, or Lia the Mermaid Bride, and La Mujer Espejo, or the Mirror Woman) is a mixed-Afro-descendant transfeminist and antiracist transwoman and performance artist from Mexico City. Her Black lineage descends from the coast of Colombia. Lia was born and raised and is based in Mexico City but spends a lot of time on the road because of how her transformational work as an artivist, performer, and scholar has her constantly being invited to cross transnational geopolitical borders to share her critical pedagogical performance praxis around the world. As a transwoman in constant transnational friendship, kinship, collaboration, and labor, she refers to herself as a "trans woman of color" in English. Thusly, I will use her language when referencing the racialized gender location that she reappropriates and the site from which she experiences the world transnationally and from which she creates and conjures.

García's performance at Elsewhere Museum, *Cocinar la memoria,* inadvertently sutured the US South and the Mexican South together by virtue of the affective sanctuary García and I have created with one another as kin who call one another our trans sister and trans brother, respectively. Though García and I had had numerous shorter moments together in the years prior, in the summer of 2017, we got to spend deep time together, in community, through a collectively organized convergence in San Cristóbal de las Casas planned for cisgender and nonbinary lesbians and trans people who find strength in living a feminist life. My home in Chiapas at the time served as the landing place for all but one of the five transwomen who had come from other parts of Mexico to be at the convergence. The purpose was to build coalitions between lesbians and trans people through a shared love of feminist principles, without resulting to violent and exclusionary positions and language. The underlying goal was to unearth internalized transantagonism without harming people in the process. I was one of the organizers because of my years of work against femicide and transfemicide in the region, as a (then) transnationally based

Black feminist, and because of having publicly transitioned in feminist performance activism and queer community in that context and in transnational artist residency homes.

That summer, a group of lesbians (cisgender and nonbinary assigned-female-at-birth people) and transmasculine folks brought together a local, national, and transnational contingent of scholars, organizers, artists, and radicals interested in building ethical relationships between lesbians and trans people through the lens of nonexclusionary transfeminist thought and praxis. The convergence was meant as part of a larger conversation about the very challenging colonial/modern necroliberal racialized gender system in Chiapas and in Mexico at large, where the high levels of pointed violence directed at cisgender and transgender women (though much higher against cisgender women only because of population; statistically, it is now common knowledge that the violence against transgender women is extremely disproportionate) create a particular flavor of acritical and transantagonist relationships between cisgender and transgender feminist organizers and academics in Mexico (local and foreign).

We called the event Las Jornadas Lesbo-Transfeministas, or the Lesbian and Trans Feminist Convergence. Initially, we had planned to hold a "casa adentro" (or "inner house") gathering of folks organizing at the nexus of the tension between lesbians and trans people in Chiapas. As the word got out, the needs and desires made the scope of the event explode. People were insistent on being a part of what local feminists were calling a "historical moment," especially because of its location in San Cristóbal de las Casas, Chiapas. We ended up holding four full days of feminist workshops, teach-ins, talks and conversations, dance nights to feminist music from feminist musicians, rappers, hip-hoppers, and reggaetonerxs from around Abya Yala South / Amé-frica Ladina, live concerts from people from different parts of the Americas, poetry events, performance, interventions, pop-ups with DIY feminist merchandise, and more, with at least one hundred people from across the hemisphere and Europe. It took place at K'inal Antsetik, which translates to "land of the women" in Tseltal—an organization that, since 1995, has supported the autonomy of Native/Indigenous women to sustain themselves, particularly those who have left their communities due to patriarchal abuse. K'inal Antsetik was founded by a coalition of lesbian mestiza feminists and Native/Indigenous women of the highlands of Chiapas.

Though there were many moments of beauty and solidarity, as the result of the very human, messy, and toxic behavior that you would expect when you put a bunch of unhealed, multiply marginalized people in one place, this was the first and last Jornadas that would ever occur, some relationships ending with the conclusion of the convergence. Part of the problem was simple: we had needed to have an emotionally and spiritually responsible trans people of color analytic governing the space. The one-twentieth of us holding Blackness did not cut it. That said, and even with the painful and sometimes irreversible ruptures that occurred—in part because of getting too big too fast, out of what felt like a desperation for dialogue and shared space—the Jornadas was an indisputably memorable encounter of transnational feminist alliances.

In this learning process, I was the most impacted by the pedagogical and performance offerings of my transfeminine and transwoman kin from Abya Yala South / Améfrica Ladina, particularly García's.[1] Additionally, this experience of learning about our alignments in transfeminist practice, performance, pedagogy, and antiracist work deepened an already beautiful friendship based on accompanying one another's journeys, regardless of the geographical distance at any given point. The charged nature of the Jornadas brought Lia and me closer. For this reason and as an investment in our kinship, Lia is in Greensboro, North Carolina. The performance is simply taking advantage of the opportunity to be in artmaking in the same space again. It is for this reason that I bring these two geopolitics together in this chapter. I present this way of coming together and featuring one another's performance work, because these entanglements are how we invite one another into accessing pluriversal worlds and how we create worlds between and among one another. García's performance/pedagogy serves as a guiding force for our times. For these reasons, I think with what it has taught me, here.

With the previous lessons in mind, García has become more specific about the audiences of her work. García has tasked me with very specifically inviting women, queer, and trans and gender expansive Black people and other people of color to join her around the Elsewhere Museum kitchen table for a new performance she is calling *Cocinar la memoria*. I have coordinated her performance with Elsewhere Museum as the performance that will close the Southern Constellations Fellows Residency.

García begins her performance/pedagogy by walking into the room, where Black people and other people of color from the local community are sitting around a large performance table and others (a mixed audience) are standing around the outside. She explains that the red dress she is donning and the makeup she is wearing are just for us, her audience members. She says she

---

1. See Coleman (2019), where I elaborate the challenges that trans people face when confronting trans exclusionary radical feminist lesbians in the context of Mexico when feminism is a tool for our survival as well. I discuss why learning from transwomen and performance practice within the context of Las Jornadas Lesbo-Transfeministas was a profoundly transformative moment for myself and others involved—to such an extent that debates about our personhood or right to access a space fell away.

FIGURE 3.1. Lia García and the author share a moment of kinship at Southern Constellations Residency: García, 2018. Used with permission of Elsewhere Museum. Image by Aurora San Miguel.

wanted to look beautiful for us. García decided to engage the spoken element of her performance in English tonight, rather than opt for simultaneous translation, emphasizing the importance of allowing the words she is speaking to land upon our skin from her trans voice without going through translation—throwing notions of imperfect grammar and octaves not typically assigned to femininity into crisis. She knows how to disarm people like few I have ever seen.

García begins by building anticipation, walking around the table while narrating the process through which she selected the contents of a cardboard box on the table in front of us. She pauses at moments to make eye contact with various audience members as she tells the story. Like many skilled performers, she uses engagement with audience members to anchor her affective presence. She pauses for a moment at what she has designated as the front of the table and where I happen to be sitting. García and I share a moment of kinship-meets-performance/pedagogy complicity. She looks down at me, and I look back up at her (see figure 3.1).

We lock eyes and I surrender to the role of witness in my beloved chosen sister's work. My face still glistens with sweat from the performance rounds I have just completed upstairs of *Warriors: Beyond Unicorns and Erasures,* the performance work that framed our entry into chapter 2. García's smile and her words light me from the inside out. When García looks down at me, her hands resting gently on the edges of the box, whose contents and García's framing of them are about to shift our sense of space-time, I soften my gaze and meet her eyes with respect, wonder, and anticipation. I feel poised to learn from her performance/pedagogy, my emotions "a flor de piel."[2] The performance has begun.

As I witness her while also witnessing others witness her for the first time, I wish I could hear glimmers of what is going on inside the heads of the people present, to *presence* the percolations in their minds as the performance builds momentum. García's performance encounters disrupt normative ways of relating to transwomen's bodies and to the cisheteronormative colonial/modern gender system of the modern/colonial civilizing project. García is not afraid to get close to people, talk to them, and ask them questions, challenging the walls they put or have up.

Her performance work, actions she calls "affective encounters," stage incredibly intimate exchanges between her trans body and the bodies of those that constitute her publics, inviting energetic giving and receiving of consent, and confrontations with discomfort. The mother of the phrase "radical tenderness," she moves with seductive affection that foregrounds emotional connection, unsettling the too-familiar violence of the hypersexualization and fetishization transwomen often experience by reversing the gaze. In her performances, you never question who is in control of the situation.

After García and I exchange a moment of performance encounter, she continues to circle the table, laying her hands gently on peoples' shoulders, arms, and heads while she narrates how she came upon what awaits us in the box. García's strategic use of touch is a form of engagement Cynthia Citlallin Delgado Huitrón (2019) calls a "haptic tactic." García's hands work to move energy between us, connected to each other's bodies by her "haptic tactic" as she takes her time, circling the room. Delgado Huitrón (2019) explains that the haptic "demands a disordering of the senses," by virtue of the emphasis on the centrality of tender nonsexual touch (p. 166). In this performance/pedagogy instance, one of the ways that the disordering of the senses happens is through an alienation from the space of the "public" and "properly behaved" audience member, to that of a vulnerable witness stewarded by the conjures of García's ongoing and circulating touch. In her performances, each audience member becomes a museum of histories, memories, and feelings,

2. A metaphoric phrase that refers to having one's emotions at the edge of their skin.

FIGURE 3.2. Lia García stands at the head of a large table during her performance at Southern Constellations Residency: García, 2018. Used with permission of Elsewhere Museum. Image by Aurora San Miguel.

invited to hold our complexities and vulnerabilities in that space, together (and usually completely unspoken).

As García moves from person to person, her light touch softening us more and more, she asks about the last time we were touched and what memories arise with it. She asks us things like "Have you ever touched or been touched by a transwoman before?" "In what context, if you have?" "If you have not, how does it feel to be touched by a transwoman of color?" "What feelings does it evoke in you in this very moment?" García adeptly disburses any tensions that energetically arise, her tender haptic tactics serving as invitational engagements, while she holds the collective agency in the room. As her palms rest on our shoulders and cradle our cheeks, I witness the audience members smile with softness and delight; others acknowledge their stiffness at the haptic tactic, working to release their resistance, leaning into her, and out of their discomfort.

García pauses again around her box, her rounds of tender touch or "haptic tactics" coming to a pause for now (see figure 3.2). García explains that when trying to figure out what objects in the museum she wanted to work with, she had to meditate longer than expected on the museum protocol. In Elsewhere Museum residencies, all objects and artifacts in the building are a part of the collection. They are all open to be used and modified if nothing is added to or removed from the collection.

FIGURE 3.3. Lia García places broken crockery pieces on a large table during her performance at Southern Constellations Residency: García, 2018. Used with permission of Elsewhere Museum. Image by Aurora San Miguel.

García explains that she struggled to settle on what objects she wanted to use to ground her performance action. She had some ideas that were not conducive to the museum space at the time (like working with water in the kitchen on an old floor that would get damaged by water). Then, *they* jumped out at her. García explains that on the third floor, in a corner of the room where the workshop is located, she found a box of discarded crockery (plates, bowls, and cups)—all broken and living as fragments of what they once were. She explains that she immediately felt a connection to these items because of how they seemed to be tossed aside and not integrated as a part of the collection—something that felt ironic in a living and preserved museum space where every single other item, from a paperclip to bolts of fabric, has been carefully organized, used, or repurposed for some creative end. She asks us, rhetorically (and by default, also asking the museum curators that are in attendance), what it is that made these broken dishes unworthy of being a part of the museum and its protocol? Did these dishes somehow transcend the protocols of Elsewhere? At this point, without requiring any movement on our part, García reinvites us and reintroduces us to what is now being referred to as a dinner table and begins to introduce our "special guests" (see figure 3.3).

As García places the broken crockery items onto the table, one at a time, she recounts her life as a racialized transwoman living in Mexico City and as a transwoman of color who regularly crosses international borders to share her art and her life.[3] By tenderly and vulnerably sharing from her life, without ever surrendering her agency, she invites us to find ourselves by identifying with pieces of what she shares, forging pedagogies of radical tenderness and kinship suspended in time. She expresses her deep affection for these special guests both because of their existence, as they are, and the conditions she found them in. They remind her of what has happened to her sense of wholeness after having experienced and being regularly afraid of myriad forms of violence that are not uncommon when moving through the world as a racialized transwoman. She explains that her lived experiences have sometimes left her feeling like a portion of a once-whole self. Some of these experiences have left her feeling discarded, fearing she does not deserve to be invited back to the table by virtue of her new form: now only a semblance of an unbroken version of herself.

With the accumulation of life experiences, García vulnerably shares how the trauma she has experienced has led to feelings of brokenness—that these broken pieces of herself are ones she may never get back, a product of moving as a transwoman in a world that says that Black people, that Brown people, that trans people cannot be part of the Human (by design). Here, her pedagogical work continues—García explains that from this place, the risks taken to love and be loved as a trans person can bring about their own kinds of brokenness. The underlying theoretical tenor of this tender pedagogical work signals the limitation of asking others to validate or recognize our existence from within the modern/colonial civilizing project, the OWW. Doing so can result in violently horrific invalidation in a one-world world that has no real investment in normalizing or protecting gender expressions outside of its colonial/modern binary gender system.

García, as she continues to unravel the metaphor of brokenness, making sure everyone has a piece of crockery before them, asks questions meant for our silent contemplation, about what kinds of brokenness we find in our body memories (see figure 3.4). She continues to signal back to her beloved "trastes," each time with increasing tenderness, imagining their life trajectory, ultimately leading to their treatment as disposable objects because of their purported brokenness.[4] García urges us not to forget that every dish once served food or liquid. She has us creatively conjure sensuous memories of

---

3. I use "racialized transwoman" when referring to Mexico City and "transwoman of color" when she refers to her border crossings, because these are how she distinguished racial differences in her own performance, as grammars that shift with the geopolitical contexts she moves in.

4. "Trastes" translates to "dishes."

FIGURE 3.4. Yellow flowers rest inside a broken yellow ceramic vase during a performance at Southern Constellations Residency: García, 2018. Used with permission of Elsewhere Museum. Image by Aurora San Miguel.

meals and gatherings that these dishes could have experienced and enjoyed—these objects are now also treated as sentient beings. We are to imagine what kind of food or drink they might have held, reimbuing them with sentience. She asks us to also conjure up the emotions the dishes might have held because of the warmth of their contents or the scent flowing out of them. She has us reflect on the capitalist society that would have us throw things out at the earliest sign of wear or when the next upgrade becomes available. "We are afraid that we cannot be loved like this," she says, "a piece of a dish."

García explains that we do not need to find the other piece of the bowl or plate and try to "fix" it to invite it once again to the table. "In a table of broken dishes, we have a banquet," García explains.[5] García brings home why she feels a powerful connection to these dishes, her "trastes"—because they serve as material representations of the sentiments of her embodied transwoman of color experience. Pain and brokenness are part of it—speaking vulnerably to

---

5. In each of these moments of citational practice of what García said in performance, I am paraphrasing from memory.

the pieces of her that will never be put back together the same way again. Yet, she continues, when we come back to the table as subjects of memory and history, collectively, we have everything we need. The smiles that break through her tears reassure us as we each work through the devastatingly simple yet profound metaphor she has laid out on the table for us.

At this point in the performance/pedagogy experience, tears have flooded the dam that is the world that we are holding together tonight, as our eyes sweat saltwater. We each feel where we have broken. Silent streams pour down many of the solemn faces of those around the table as people contemplate the moments when they felt disposed of or not enough because of their purported "broken pieces." Through my own eye puddles, I glance around the room to bear witness once again to the witnesses, curious about the stories and memories being recalled by each of the people present. I watch people's eyes light up as they begin to process the experience she has taken us through: we bear witness to one another's humanity without sharing a word.

García's trans pedagogical performance *Cocinar la memoria* invites Black people and other people of color across the gender constellation to learn from the knowledge of the experience of a transwoman of color who has crossed borders to be with us. We learn that within the knowledge of embodied trans experiences there is much that we can ascertain about our species and our ways of making meaning.

In a final moment of reflection, García has us write a letter to our pieces of crockery on colorful pieces of paper. She asks us to write a letter to them that reestablishes their relationship to the kitchen—a futurist invitation to be whole in purpose, without the promise of recovering any missing parts. In some way, we seem to be inviting ourselves and these pieces to let go of previous conceptions of what it is to be singularly "whole"; in this new conception, we are whole by bringing our broken pieces to the collective. Through reflections and tears, this convening of people grieves the pressures and the impossible impositions the OWW places upon our psyches, bodies, and senses of identity. I reflect on how we are asked to strive after that which was never designed for us—systems that have no concept of who our people are. There is no whole to which we can aspire to arrive as women, queer, trans, and nonbinary Black people and other people of color if our source of validation is the modern/colonial global necroliberal capitalist order. There's a collectivity to this grief that sends a sense of release around the room as we realize that no one can be whole in this system. At the table tonight, breaking is full of agency. We tuck our letters into places they can fit into, to be stored as part of the archive of these reanimated objects. At the end, García re-collects each piece, with our papers loosely jutting out of the broken parts (fitting them in where we can make them sit). The performance closes with whoops, hollers, more tears, and then a sea of people covering each other in warm embraces.

It is performances like this one that have shown me the way, that have taught me the possibilities trans pedagogy creates in many peoples' lives.

In *Cocinar la memoria,* brokenness becomes the spectacular potential for a necessary undoing. Around the table, in what feels like a guided meditation bordering on performative hypnosis, we gather our broken pieces as we love on the dishes that are no longer whole. We imbue our broken pieces with worthiness and life, turning our attention to other ways to be with this brokenness.

Sitting with García's performance over a period of years brings me to a clear theoretical revelation: brokenness is the condition of possibility for existence in the modern/colonial civilizing project, the OWW. Said differently, there is no possibility for wholeness within the confines of the OWW project for subjectivities that were never contemplated as part of its design. Brokenness, as a metaphor staged with broken crockery pieces in *Cocinar la memoria,* is an invitation not only to feel our broken pieces, like the crockery we have caressed just moments before, but *to aspire to* break. To break, following the lineage of this metaphor, is to recognize another kind of wholeness that acknowledgment of the deeply fractured and violent OWW could never provide, a wholeness as an erotically full[6] existence that cannot be contained, enclosed, fully named, or known within the OWW Human project as we know it. To break is to know that there is something else, rather than an invitation to turn against or feel sorry for oneself. It is leaning into our brokenness that provides a way out of the denials of the OWW (at least psychically and spiritually), welcoming other ways of relating to our existence.

García's trans pedagogical "breaking" is what we might imagine as a "trans break" that can carry us through this sense of incompleteness, to find home in the interstitial places of this "world"—the places where all the other worlds emerge—that many do not know how to see, much less police. To the latter point, we could argue that when people and practices are policed, there is a lack of pluriversal reckoning with all that is happening. The trans break is a space just out of sight. It troubles the visual regimes of necroliberal governance and its minions by existing outside of hegemonic displays of being/becoming, thinking/doing. It is what we create by being together, beyond what any external interpretation of what we create could name.

---

6. Here, I am speaking of the kind of erotics that Audre Lorde gave us in 1978. To hear the essay read by Lorde, visit https://www.youtube.com/watch?v=aWmq9gw4Rqo.

While existing in these interstices, the "trans break" allows us to see that the OWW's hegemonic hold over the project of the Human and other forms of sentient life does not foreclose upon all possibilities for wholeness of being beyond its limits. I want us to remain in the space of the broken pieces of crockery as the initiation of an existential transit that can move us from an atomized existence to that of being/becoming and thinking/doing in an uncapturable wholeness. This brings us to our metaphysical and spiritual need for the framework of the pluriverse and its ontological and epistemological otherwises.

Before continuing, a word on how García's embodied trans pedagogy shapes the frameworks for the knowledge production that happens collectively in her "affective encounters." What is at stake in forwarding a metaphor of "brokenness" is being met with the wrong uptake. In exhausting the length of this metaphor for our material-philosophical theorizations here, I am refusing to reinscribe transness-as-abjection by focusing on one or all parts of the following: the spectacle of necropolitical trans brutality, individualized trans devastation, and the denial of trans agency by viewing transness as a *crisis* and *deviation from* "normal" humanity. Rather, we are breaking with the conditions that create violent experiences and universalizing knowledge about "the real" and "humanity."

García's performance manages to bring us to a shared sense of agency by watching her stand, move, and speak fully within hers. Encounters like *Cocinar la memoria* are a reprieve from the hyperscrutiny of trans subjectivities and embodiments. García's work is a capacious trans offering that allows people who are not trans to learn *with* us, allows trans people to learn all the ways we will forever be learning from one another, and locates us in shared pluriversal gender spaces that do not reinscribe transness as an object to be debated, observed, fetishized, or scrutinized. Lastly, by naming García's trans pedagogy—also the language she uses to refer to her own work and what shaped her choice to pursue a PhD in pedagogies at the National Autonomous University of Mexico (UNAM)—I am not referring to trans people as a teaching tool but rather as people creating new worlds through how we carve our existences and find our wholeness, teaching other people how to do the same. Trans pedagogy invites people out of proving themselves or killing and harming others to hold up their totalizing claims to a singular world. Transness, when allowed to mobilize for the collective good, births us into rest.

I understand García's performance/pedagogy to be a form of tranifesting or tranifestation. Marshall (Kai) Green and Treva Ellison (2014) coined the term "tranifesting," saying,

Tranifesting, or transformative manifestation, describes the theories, methods, and modes of self-representation that attempt to call into being flexible collectivities or groupings whose articulation transforms normative understandings of race, gender, sex, and sexuality. (p. 300)

Self-representation here refers to continuing to magnify pluriversal thinking/doing on a planet full of people convinced the OWW is all there is. When operating this way and encountering others doing the same, the collective agency found, when gathered, restructures entire worlds. For Green and Ellison (2014) "tranifest" is a verb that challenges the limitations of state politics that attempt to prevent people from assembling flexible collectivities through which to generate new identity formations (p. 222). Creative, insurgent, flexible collectivities invite witnesses to existentially board a plane to the pluriverse. Additionally, Green and Ellison (2014) articulate that tranifesting serves "an epistemic" function connecting Black feminism and trans studies in its capacity for "mediating particular individual experiences and operationalizing identity—not as ends in themselves but as places from which to generate transformative politics"—precisely what García has done in narrating her connection to these broken pieces of crockery (p. 223). Tranifesting is not simply manifesting oneself in the world as one wishes to be, but it is the possibility for coalitional relationality that this manifestation, embodiment, and existential pluriversality engenders. It is the appearance of subjectivities that rupture the notion of a singular realm of the real by finding possibilities of expression through what they are seeing in communities of practice. It is here where the light comes through in the cracks of the OWW. The refiguring of self-in-relation to more, made possible through the collective witnessing that tranifesting allows, marks the value of coming together to steward one another into the pluriverse of worlds, held where a heterogenous group of people is gathered.

Before turning to what this breaks open for Black/Afro-descendant and Native/Indigenous people ontologically, I have one additional reading on the role of tranifesting in García's trans pedagogy and its "breaking." The greatest epistemic, or knowledge-creating, function of tranifesting is found in what Black trans people and other trans people of color learn from one another when gathered in the same place: none of us will experience, define, or understand our trans embodiment, identity, and place in our worlds in the same way. It is by continuing to be in community with one another and others that we give ourselves permission to endlessly ask about the limits of the OWW's construction of the real and its impact on our possibilities for authenticity.

These pedagogical spaces—never based on exclusionary or essentializing relationality—have taught me that transness's proliferation as a possibility for the self at this historical juncture signifies what was always an inevitable eruption from singular totalities about gender, sex, and sexuality—totalizing claims that were never capable of accounting for species diversity without simultaneously reifying totalizing one-world world ideologies along with them. Ancient, presentist, and futurist cosmologies of gender beingness temporally commingle in the embodied brilliance of trans tranifestation and existence through our ancestral spiritual access to many other ways of being/becoming and thinking/doing our existence (as gendered beings and otherwise). It is this point of rupture, the trans break, that I forward as the site from which to hold our pluriversal pasts, presents, and futures.

The Call Is Coming from Inside the House: The Ontological Pluriverse

What does it mean to limit beings to the status of nonontological without recourse to an otherwise at a time when the Human project is telling on itself for the ouroboros that it is? The theoretical precision of philosophical projects like Afro-pessimism aims to provide us with a totalizing explication for the unconscionable levels of violence against Black people around the planet. Projects like this do important work in helping us to articulate the inhumanity of the Human project and the brutality of the conquistador-settler.[7] With the current crises of meaning that we find ourselves in, however, it could be dangerous to make these claims our end point. I find no life there. Let us listen to Sylvia Wynter's (1995) historical-theoretical formulation of the OWW and how it established a hierarchy between Black/Afro-descendant and Native/Indigenous ontologies. We will then read this through the pluriversal openings of the trans break to bring us elsewhere.

Wynter (1995) establishes an important hemispheric conversation between Blackness and Indigeneity that is useful for us here because she begins at

---

7. I can appreciate the Afro-pessimist sentiment that the world would have to collapse and begin again under a new world order for anti-Blackness to be eradicated. Since this is not the case, there is no possibility where Blackness and ontology live inside one another in the OWW. In an environment where Black death is extraordinarily mediatized and met with almost complete impunity, how else could we explain these acts of extreme violence except as the expression of beings who lack Being? We know full well that nice professorial offices and PhDs at the ends of names will never stop the police from killing and threatening Black people. In the OWW system predicated on enslavement and genocide, Black people *cannot just be*. Where my romance with the nihilism of the Afro-pessimist project begins to lose strength is in the presence of the current world demolition self-inflicted by the minions of the OWW. The project is undoing itself, and the power of those excluded from the Human project is in a new era of force.

the level of meaning-making and knowledge production. She employs Merlin Donald's (1991) concept of "symbolic representational systems"—or how humans represent our lives to ourselves through the cognitive technology that we have come to call "the mind." Through our "symbolic representational systems," we justify and police our and others' behaviors, beliefs, perceptions, and cultural systems (Wynter, 1995, p. 8). Wynter employs this term to make sense of how the Portuguese justified the expropriation of the Neolithic Berbers they encountered on the Canary Islands. The Portuguese deemed these people "idolators" for their non-Christian practices. The pope supported this categorization, allowing the Portuguese to have papal defense and therefore feel rightly justified to expropriate the Berbers. Columbus used the same logics within his "symbolic representational system," allowing him to continue to conquer Native/Indigenous land and peoples, shipping Native/Indigenous people to Spain as slaves as a symbolic reward for and expression of gratitude to the monarchy for funding and religiously sanctioning the voyage, underwriting its success. The precedent of labeling Native/Indigenous people as subhuman "idolators" began with this juridic-theological legitimation based on that historical moment's symbolic representational system (p. 8).

Using this same juridic-theological legitimation, the slave trade was established by the Portuguese after 1441. It was enslaved Africans that substituted for the labor force of the Native/Indigenous people of what the OWW calls "the Americas." The African "disposable, coercible and unpaid labor force" further ushered in tremendous economic development of the Americas and revolutionized the social structure (Morgenthau cited in Wynter, 1995, p. 11). The substitution of Africans for Native/Indigenous people freed many of them from their enslavement from the intra-Caribbean and Caribbean mainland Native/Indigenous slave trade, where they had been formally sold as "cabezas de indios/as," garnering the Spaniards great fortune (p. 11).

Wynter argues that the "excluded difference" (read: Indigenous people-as-idolators) of the Native/Indigenous people granted them the status of a legitimately enslavable group. Thereafter, in the transfer of social relations through the importation of enslaved Africans, Native/Indigenous people were socially bonded to their Spanish settlers as "hereditarily free subjects of the Spanish state" (Wynter, 1995, p. 11). Wynter further argues that since enslaved African people entered as a third population group, they embodied a new, symbolic system of representing race, in which they were seen as possessing an inherent difference that permitted the Spaniards to justify their sovereignty over the Americas on postreligious, legal terms. Africans, as the new subhuman category that legitimized the legal treatment of Africans as European property, were the symbolic stand-in for race in general. This meant,

continuing with Wynter (1995), that Europeans could create moral and philosophical legitimations for the status of Africans and "rudely" accept Native/
Indigenous people into their midst (p. 12); Native/Indigenous people were
still considered a nuisance but were no longer enslaved. I am in historical
alignment with Wynter's breakdown of how the conquistador-settlers justified their treatment of African and Native/Indigenous people as subhuman,
a dynamic that played out—albeit with different players and across distinct
periods of time—in almost every country of the Western Hemisphere.

In Wynter's historical articulation of what she calls the White-Native-
Black social schema emerging from the colonial situation, African/Black
people are placed below Native/Indigenous people socially, ontologically,
politically, and epistemically on the hierarchy of being. The ontological hierarchy, in her schema, descends from left to right. While I can see how Wynter arrived at this conclusion and subsequent codification of a racial scheme
based on how she historicizes her accounting of the initial relationships that
the Spaniards had with Native/Indigenous peoples, I also see how there is
perhaps a one-world world dynamic at play for the purposes of her philosophical work. We will need to suspend this triad as an immutable ontological hierarchy, or fact, for the sake of approximating pluriversal ontologies that
do not predicate one's being on one's categorization and treatment in the
OWW. It seems to me that locating enslaved Africans and Black people with
respect to an unmovable and categorically subjugated ontological position
serves an important theoretical function for emphasizing the deep anti-Black
nature of the world. In this way, the point is well taken. However, considering
contemporary relationships between Afro-descendent, Native/Indigenous,
and Euro-descendent people and mixes thereof throughout Abya Yala South
/ Améfrica Ladina and the dramatically different histories, peoples, cosmologies, languages, and cultures that these conspecific categories include,
I would argue that, for our purposes of thinking/doing from a pluriversal
conception of the planet, it is impossible, if not simply inaccurate, to provide a definitive ontological ranking between Native/Indigenous and Black/
Afro-descendant people. To do so would mean to take conspecific categories
created and maintained by the modern/colonial global necroliberal capitalist world order / OWW as capable of fully representing realities of being/
becoming and existence for Black/Afro-descendant and Native/Indigenous
peoples in all worlds.

The differences between Black/Afro-descendant and Native/Indigenous
people must never be conflated or equated, particularly because specificities of
skin colors and physiognomic characteristics have been part of what has been
used to systematically dehumanize Black/Afro-descendant people in different

ways than Native/Indigenous people, the severity of the consequences of which vary greatly by geopolitical reality. When we are talking about specific historical realities, these relationships can also be more intertwined than some historical-philosophical accountings make them out to be. Though Wynter focuses specifically on the "Americas," she is also taking aim at how symbolic representation systems with supremacist, colonialist, imperialist doctrines create epistemological supremacies that shape global ideas about race. As such, we must also hold space for the Black/Afro-descendant people of our planet who are Native/Indigenous to their lands; for the Afro-Indigenous peoples (especially throughout the Americas) who are often forced to straddle the lines of tension between Blackness and Indigeneity, often founded under conditions of conquest; and for those of Black/Afro-descendent and Native/Indigenous diasporas who understand that multiple generations of diasporic descendance distances one from being "indigenous" to place. Then, the fluidity of Black/Afro-descendant and Native/Indigenous ontology in relation to the project of the Human shifts and moves with geopolitical location; internal and external diasporas; dispossessions and displacements; racial and ethnic commingling; decisions of local, national, and transnational institutions; and other forces that continuously mark Black/Afro-descendant and Native/Indigenous subjectivities under varied conditions of duress with an OWW system. Then, I take mass genocide, Native/Indigenous enslavement, and ongoing attempts at complete Indigenous eradication as seriously as African enslavement and its ceaseless afterlives in the wake and other forms of institutionalized subhumanism. The dynamic interplay between Indigeneity, Blackness, and "the scaffolding of the human" (King, 2017, p. 176) invites us to read Wynter's original formulation as a useful theoretical "strategic essentialism" (Spivak cited in Grosz, 1985) for the OWW and not a basis from which to build pluriversal ontological understandings. Part of our job is to properly locate ontology within the purview of the pluriverse and the specificity of distinct Black/Afro-descendant, Native/Indigenous, and Afro-Indigenous peoples and cultures, rather than to use racial rankings, epistemological supremacies, or the flattened realities of conspecific relation as the only site from which to understand the endless pluriversal beings/becomings of a people. As such, the Human and its exclusions do not need to be the barometer that we use to measure our ontological lives.

Rather than enter the binary battle between abandoning the Human versus not abandoning the Human, I believe what we are to do now is to treat the Human—a categorical partition that has been co-opted by the modern/colonial civilizing project—as an *interface*, as in what *Merriam-Webster* defines as "the place at which independent and often unrelated systems meet and act on or communicate with each other."[8] We must approach the OWW's Human with an element of detachment, since, at best, it is supposed to be a categorical possibility of conspecific relation for our species. Since the OWW's modern/colonial Human is an interface most of us are forced to interact with, our job, in my mind, is to do so without forgetting that the stranglehold on its meaning is not something we have to adapt or take in, regardless of the power being wielded to evaporate other worlds.

What I am arguing, then, is that we *trans* the ontological appropriation of the "real" in the modern/colonial Human project by proceeding with its Human as an interface, holding nonattachment to its ignorant and supremacist symbolic representational systems. If the Human is an interface, it can mean something in the OWW and something entirely else in other worlds, even using other language entirely. We are to treat the OWW's Human and violence justified in its name as the least rational possibility for a pluriversal "real." The nonontology that might be true about some positions within the OWW does not attend to how the wholeness of our ontology is *held elsewhere*, in the pluriverse. What we ultimately must abandon, then, is ontological theorization predicated on Western metaphysics.

Only now is it appropriate to explain why I introduce a slash between being and becoming throughout this book—placing being and becoming always in coextensive relation. Being, in a pluriverse, is a constant unfolding—an endless becoming in worlds predicated on ecosystem relation, who then are also alongside and sometimes intersecting one another. Because we are beings always in the process of transformation by virtue of living in bodies that are entire ecosystems themselves—a widely applicable trans pedagogical lesson that invites us to embrace transition/change as the only constant for our species—absolutist claims and fixed natures have no place in our constant unfolding. Being, as science of thinking/doing, or pedagogically interacting with the meaning and nature our existence, is not static like in this dystopia of the modern/colonial global necroliberal capitalist world system. Many of us exist in many worlds at once.

At some point, what we need is to feel the brokenness produced by attempting to source our entire senses of being/becoming on the modern/colonial world order's Human. It is my understanding that the trans break launches us into these feelings, which, when used productively, garner us access to the pluriverse and to a sense of whole being/becoming not predicated

---

8. Tiffany Lethabo King (2017) understands that to abandon the Human is a privileged theoretical position that does not honor the materiality through which most of us must continue to move. I agree with her completely. It gives too much power to theorists, a notably anthropocentric position.

on symbolic representational systems who mark some members of our species as nonontological. Leaning into the transformative possibility of the break, we gain access to other cosmological ways of apprehending and experiencing ourselves and our worlds. I invite us to welcome this devastation of ontological humanism as the only thing that could even approximate a "real" that we could hold together. Still, all of this said, how do we live whole ontological lives while being forced to interface with the abstract, supremacist, faux-universal modern/colonial Human? How do we remain grounded in our experiences of embodied life?

After first plunging into the trans break to sever our relationship with the OWW and its Human as "all there is," we must come to practice. By coming to practice, I do not necessarily mean being a spiritual practitioner of something. What I do mean is that we must practice knowing the pluriverse. Arturo Escobar (2020) puts it this way:

> It must be stressed that the pluriverse is not just a trendy concept; it is a whole practice. Living in accordance with the idea that there are multiple worlds, partially connected but radically different, entails an entire [sic] different ethics of life, of being~doing~knowing. It means attenuating the capacity of modern certainties about the real and the possible (and their most important correlates, such as the individual, economics, and science) to mold our personal and collective lives. Ultimately, pluriversal politics aim to create conditions favorable to the flourishing of the pluriverse, other ways of world making. (p. 27)

We must live, embodying our knowing of the existence of the pluriverse regardless of what the OWW is doing.

I add one final layer to our thinking here. What we are practicing—as was outlined in regard to an "analytic of indigeneity" foregrounded in the introduction—is not just harnessing the power of our pluriversal cosmologies for purposes of trying to manage to outlive the planetary-level destruction being caused by the modern/colonial global necroliberal capitalist order. Our larger task is to *refuse*—to refuse to spend our embodied lives fixated on getting the OWW to assimilate us into its fold. At this point, to be in practice is to do what is in our power to keep the pluriverse alive to ensure that our cosmologies will outlive us—to leave a spiritual record of members of our species who never gave up on the pluriverse.

Like the two chapters that precede this one show us, a decolonial pedagogical relationship with life is one way to transition into treating the modern/colonial Human as interface. From this kind of thinking/doing, we have a greater chance of finding our ways to the elements and energies of our other worlds, honoring the cosmologies that they come from, and learning from the peoples past, present, and future who have maintained and evolved or adapted these knowledge systems to keep them alive, despite all the endless and ongoing attempts at eradication. These cosmologies precede, exceed, and will outlive the grammars of ecological nonrelatedness and Anthropocentric design that the modern/colonial global necroliberal capitalist world order is predicated on, even if our bodies do not. In Black/Afro-diasporic and Native/Indigenous cosmological understandings of our beingness, we understand that this "energy simply does not obey the human idiom" (Alexander, 2005, p. 309). Therefore, the Human, and its grammars that would limit ontological life to those outlined within the OWW's domain, do not know the power of the eco-cosmological roots of other spiritual and cosmological systems and their sacred knowledge that we have access to in the pluriverse.

Returning full circle to our opening metaphor of brokenness, we must disconnect brokenness, once again, from its connotations as a negative self-constitution and nonexistent being. Alexander (2005) offers,

> The breaking of waves does not compromise the integrity of the Ocean, so too anything broken in our lives cannot compromise the cosmic flow to wholeness. The body cannot but surrender to make way for this tidal flow. And this, too requires practice (Alexander, 2005, p. 322).

I see the body's surrender to the cosmic flow to wholeness that Alexander (2005) reminds us of as a practice space that becomes available through the trans break. As the trans break moves us through the grief of realizing that what we strive after in the OWW will never give us recognition or dignified wholeness of our ontological lives, we feel and learn that the cosmic flow (our ecological-ontological beingness in other cosmological worlds) cannot be broken, regardless of the ways in which the OWW might fracture and fragment us. This energy (partly seen in the ever-more-voracious takeover of the planet by the "natural world") is far stronger than the OWW can comprehend, systematize, or stop. To be in intimate relationship with those energies is, indeed, something else.

The cosmologies that subtend the practices I am thinking through here are ultimately healing systems (Alexander, 2005, p. 299). They are healing systems because their function is the work of "Divine self-intervention." In Divine self-intervention, we align ourselves with our ecological beingness as species-beings by recognizing ourselves as held by pluriversal cosmologies, "accompanied" and "non-individuated" by virtue of the beings (deities, forces of nature, ancestors, etc.) that walk with us (p. 300). We live within and among ecological cosmologies that reshape our relationships to ourselves as part of the species, despite what the OWW is doing at any given time. The collective nature of our accompaniment while walking this spiritual path is Sacred companionship. There is an "intimacy between personhood and Sacred accompaniment"—an engagement with unseen realms that put us in touch with the pluriverse. This means we do not belong to the domain of the OWW, even if part of our embodied species experience occurs within its domain. We must interface with its Human as part of how we carry out the spiritual labor of any given lifetime.

Through cosmologies of the pluriverse, like those of Afro-diasporic and Native/Indigenous peoples, we (re)turn to the powers that have always been and will always be stronger than anything the project of the Human can come up with. Case in point: the forces that have been colonially called "nature" are taking over, and no god can stop them. We will never be as we were before. There is no "back." The trans break is an invitation to surrender to this being/knowing. Reminded that eventually the OWW project will be forced to succumb to the will of "nature," we turn to these forces and regard them as the wisdom holders that they are, to learn how to remember our Sacred subjectivity. Herein lies a form of "hope" that insists not all the problems are looking for "solving."

Allow me to turn to Alexander (2005) once again to understand the nature of Sacred energies of pluriversal origin:

> Sacred energies would want us to relinquish the very categories constitutive of the material world, not in the requisite of a retreat but *as a way to become more attuned to their ephemeral vagaries and the real limits of temporality so as to return to them with a disciplined freedom capable of renovating the collective terms of our engagement.* (p. 329; emphasis added)

To return to the material planet (colonized by the OWW) with a disciplined freedom is to engage in the Human project-as-interface and not as all that we are or can aspire to be. When we acknowledge that the external ecological sources of nature that give us life and energy are also the forces that live within us, we can further make sense of the OWW's incredibly limited explication of our existence. I am not convinced the OWW knows much about this form of the Sacred.

A rhetorical question: What if we are not being asked to find a solution or to find theoretical "answers" that can explain the violence and the chaos that surrounds us? The Human cannot even fathom the planetary, much less consolidate around collective solutions for planetary problems like ecological devastation. The choice is to die: to die to our ways of loving, of living, of embodying ourselves, of making family, and of relating to our and other species and the planet, and to learn other ways of being that come from crafting Sacred subjectivity. Sacred subjectivity expands our consciousness outward by going deeply inward—we get to die to any nonexistence that the OWW would predicate our lives on, by engaging a breaking that cannot be and need not be glued back together. In doing so, we turn toward a wholeness, an ecological beingness, aligned with how the forces of nature manifest inside of us and how we can then use them to propel us forward.

The trans break tenderly invites us to learn how to move through the OWW differently—to be in it but not of its confinement, interfacing with its Human—while engaging practices that will keep guiding us to and in our Sacred subjectivity. We can acknowledge who the Human contains versus who it does not and still know that we must interact with it as an interface that corrals our political lives as a species. To approach the Human as interface is to abandon the spiritual hubris of the Human's totalizing ideas about itself and to find sanctuary in the unfathomably rich ontologies of the pluriverse. Spiritually, we can take refuge in our nonbelonging to the Human's ontology, because we can see a larger picture—the one of the species in the pluriverse.

Our interfacing with the Human is the site through which we grow by learning to navigate its many violences and limitations, including our [partial] exclusion from it. "It," this project of the Human, is real insofar as there are material consequences for our locations in its hierarchies as they are maintained by the OWW's Human minions and other members of our species. However, in sacred subjectivity, the violence of the Human has no bearing on our position in and with the Sacred. The fullness of our ontological lives and accepting the shortsightedness of the Human (while relating to it as interface) means understanding that we belong to a species. The very setup of the Human, as Warren (2018) makes impeccably clear for us, requires its outside to exist. Then, in a way, the shortsightedness of the OWW's ontological understanding of our species is our opportunity to bring forth what is stronger: a species in relation to entangled ecological realities, after Wynter (1995). Our belonging to this species is sanctioned by the spiritual beings that hold us, even if others of our species (and those with worldly power to determine the confines of the OWW) do not recognize the fullness of our being. If the very powers that threaten to destroy the Human and his modern/colonial civilizing project are the powers that move through us and around us, then by coming into ecological-spiritual relation to them, what we have access to, quite literally, is otherworldly power. Once we acknowledge and practice embodying this, we have permission to release our minds from the shackles of the OWW.

I defend Black and Brown trans breaking that asks us to be in pluriversal spiritual relation to all beings. When we part ways with the OWW's silos, we can come into the fullness of our own being. I am talking about a pluriversal fullness of ontology available to Black/Afro-descendant and Native/Indigenous people through transing or rupturing with the binary of ontology or nonontology—predicated on the perceptions of the OWW—through moving into other worlds. The trans break is what demolishes this binary and allows our bodies to experience other worlds. This means that our capacity to render a full ontology is not exclusively or primarily contingent upon the limited metaphysical reality of the Human project in the OWW. Rather, our ontological lives are held within our pluriversal cosmologies.

CHAPTER 4

Shoal Ecopoetics and *Otroas*

Starting in the year 2015, I began to regularly hear the Zapatistas shifting their language from "compañeros and compañeras" to "compañeros, compañeras, and compañeroas" during public seminars and lectures, especially in spaces like CIDECI-UniTierra (Center for Comprehensive Indigenous Training—OnePlanet). During the summer of 2015, I was in attendance of a good majority of the Zapatista seminar "Pensamiento crítico frente a la hidra capitalista," or "Critical thought in the face of the capitalist hydra."[1] Two things were very memorable to me about the seminar: (1) the EZLN made a conscious effort to center the leadership of cisgender women and to revise some of the ways that cisheteropatriarchy from within the movement has made men (and mestizo men like Marcos) the (covered) "face" of the movement, while erasing and occluding the participation of women who have been important historical figures in the movement (Comandanta Ramona, for example). And (2) when addressing the public collectively, the three versions of the word "companions" are now being used consistently and back-to-back—"compañeros, compañeras, compañeroas"—expanding on their usual "compañeros and compañeras." I remained curious about each of these things but trusted that the opportunity would come to explore more about the Zapatista's way of sharing

---

1. The full archive of this event can be found and watched or listened to here: https://seminarioscideci.org/category/seminario-pensamiento-critico-frente-a-la-hidra-capitalista/.

transformations and additions to their critical thinking about being/becoming and thinking/doing for a pluriversal world, while continuing to honor all that they are in their Indigeneity.

That said, I am also clear on the fact that the EZLN, because of its international reputation, must be particularly careful about what it presents as its "official discourse," so as to avoid inviting unneeded critiques of the movement or revealing any internalized colonialism that has not yet been worked out intramurally. Since they started opening the doors of their communities in 2013 for their international Escuelita Zapatista, or Little Zapatista School,[2] they have come up against increased criticism about things like gender dynamics, their position on queer people in their communities, and whether patriarchy was a factor of colonization or a complete Western misread of their cultures (see Oyěwùmí, 1997). They are an example of what happens when you mythologize a people: you dehumanize them by expecting a perfect coherence that no humans on earth can have. I accept the EZLN and the Zapatistas as imperfect people who have committed their lives to maintaining Native/Indigenous sovereignty and decolonization through the Anthropocene's late modern/colonial global necroliberal capitalism while still living in extreme poverty. Holding all these complexities simultaneously, in this chapter I spend time uplifting the pluriversal wisdom from the creativity of their relationship to gender and ecological fluidity through reading one last creative insurgent case study.

In April 2021, seven members of the EZLN headed off on a maritime voyage—designed as a performative "reverse colonization"—from Mexico to Spain. Squadron 421 had seven members: four women (Lupita, Carolina, Ximena, and Yuli), two men (Bernal and Felipe), and one *otroa* (Marijose). Their boat, *La Montaña*, or *The Mountain,* set sail on a voyage they called "the voyage for life," starting from Isla Mujeres, Quintana Roo, Mexico, and navigating through the Atlantic Ocean by way of Cuba and onward to the port of Vigo, Galicia, Spain. The boat left from a site that was historically sacred to the Maya, Casa Ixchel, on the southern tip of Isla Mujeres (see figure 4.1) (Oropeza, 2021a). Casa Ixchel is where they would begin their fifty-two-day voyage, followed by a five-continent tour, with the intention of sharing what they have learned in "their world," as Tsotsil, Tseltal, Chol, Tojolabal, and Mame peoples; all this, before it was "too late" (Oropeza, 2021a).[3]

---

2. For more on the history of the Escuelita Zapatista, I recommend visiting: https://ausm. community/escuelita/.

3. Here, "too late" refers to the rapidly increasing effects of global warming permanently changing the weather patterns and topography of the planet. "Too late" also suggests that in the future, such voyages will be too risky to undertake.

FIGURE 4.1. Casa Ixchel, Isla Mujeres, Mexico. Used with
permission of the photographer, Daliri Oropeza.

In this chapter, I read the EZLN's "reverse colonization" maritime journey of Squadron 421 on *La Montaña* for the decolonial pedagogical work the
voyage performs. Sifting through its various symbols, motivations, and intentional performance choices (including the "official discourse" documented on
the EZLN's website), I ecopoetically read the EZLN's decision to sail across
the Atlantic Ocean as one that *shoals* (more on this below) Native/Indigenous
life with a queer / Black Atlantic life. By "performance choices," I mean something between the real and the staged, where the action of staging a symbolic
"reverse colonization" to spread pedagogical knowledge about their world is
meant to create waves of response to the modern/colonial civilizing order's
hegemonic logics.

This chapter takes seriously Rinaldo Walcott's (2020) contention that we
must "think about transatlantic slavery and Indigenous colonization as a cultural revolution that is still unfolding in ways that remain deeply traumatic but
that now are also complicatedly implicating and entangling" (p. 347). I engage
with transatlantic slavery and Indigenous colonization as still-unfolding cultural revolutions in a complex local/global modern/colonial civilizing network
that implicates and entangles by inviting us into an ecopoetic and imaginative space. I use the work of queer, Black feminist, and decolonial/Indigenous
feminist thinkers to poetically read the Atlantic that carried *La Montaña* and
its squadron safely to the other side as spiritual accompaniment of Indigeneity

by Blackness across charged modern/colonial waters. I am motivated to consider this creative insurgent example as one in conversation with the others in the previous chapters because of the EZLN's intentional choices to have the otroa squadron-member, Marijose, be the first person to set foot on Spanish soil (we will unpack the meaning of "otroa" below). I will analyze the significance of Marijose's presence in the squadron, the official discourse around it, and how and why the nexus of her subjectivity as a Native/Indigenous otroa makes her performative proclamations about a new land relationship to the former colonial power a decolonial pedagogical gesture of Native/Indigenous "modernity."

To engage the readings of the decolonial pedagogical work of this creatively insurgent action, the chapter proceeds in two layers. First, I will story in the ecological urgency of this voyage in the face of environmental racism and megaprojects in southern Mexico. In this section, I will first set a pluriversal shoal container that practices a Native/Indigenous and Black/Afro-descendant ontology-alongside. Then, thinking with the poetry of the buildup to the journey, I develop an ecopoetic imaginative space through the shoal relationship I claim the EZLN are forging with the Black Atlantic through this voyage. By "ecopoetic" here, I mean the theoretical work of this chapter, a type of writing that bridges poetry and ecology-as-theory (for more, see Hume and Osborne, 2018). As a transitional space between the preparation for and lead-up to the maritime voyage of the delegation and its decision about directives for Marijose, I contextualize how the shoal analytic brings us to a union with the *queer* Black Atlantic, becoming a *cuir* Black-Native / Indigenous Atlantic. Second, I will read part of the EZLN's "discurso oficial" (official discourse) about the directive given to Marijose upon disembarking the ship on Spanish soil, for its decolonial feminist and ecopoetic gestures (Levya Solano, 1999, p. 58; Leyva Solano & Sonnleitner, 2000, p. 166). In the folds of this second layer and to set up the relationship to the directives given in the "discurso oficial," we will think with Native/Indigenous feminists in Abya Yala South / Amérfrica Ladina, querying Indigeneity's relationship to modernity. We will do so to help anchor how the Zapatistas have navigated their relationship to critical gender and feminist thought within the modern/colonial OWW through a degree of what we could call Sacred opacity. Ultimately, this chapter is invested in the symbolic universe generated by Squadron 421's voyage and its contributions to pluriversal being/becoming and thinking/doing.

Modern extractive projects held in the purview of the coloniality of the modern/colonial world order—in this case motivating Native/Indigenous people to take to the sea to report back to those living in the geopolitical origin of their first conquistador-settlers—sutures Black/Afro-descendant and Native/

Indigenous modern/colonial experiences through a common experience of being treated as ecologically irrelevant. The origin of this interstitial relation comes together where land and sea meet. This ecological entanglement moves us away from the power play of equivalencies also distanced from in the previous chapter, suspending the belief that we can apprehend the modern/civilizing projects' hemispheric-scale attempt to eradicate Indigeneity enough to render the reality of Black enslavement and dispossession as an always-already graver ontological reality.[4] Moving with a shoal analytic, then, expanding upon the work of the last chapter, we are not required to rank ontologies. Instead, we will read for the ecological poetry of this interrelation.

Shoal Ecopoetics along the Queer Black Atlantic

Imagining Squadron 421 out at sea, I picture the bioluminescence below *La Montaña* carrying the ship and its crew forward, assuring their safe passage (see figure 4.2). In Afro-futurist visioning, Alexis Pauline Gumbs (2018), writing with and after M. Jacqui Alexander (2005), muses on the bioluminescence of the ocean and how some of it must be produced by "the bones of the millions of transatlantic dead" (p. 11). Gumbs (2018) reminds us that bioluminescence is catalyzed by calcium and by magnesium, recalling that each of these elements also exists in the contents of bone—"the bones of the captives who would not live as captives" (p. 11). Her scientific Afro-futurist poetry continues, explaining that the marine decomposition of the bodies of those who were tossed over the rails of enslavers' ships or who jumped to their freedom and death means that over time their bones have been ground "as fine as sand," and have "infiltrated the systems of even the lowest filter feeders. so [*sic*] any light that you find in the ocean right now cannot be separated from the stolen light of those we long for every morning" (Gumbs, 2018, p. 11). In the poetry of the spiritual, historical, and scientific conjuring that Gumbs (2018) creates for us, we come to imagine that part of the light that can be

---

4. As a Black scholar who has spent significant time in Chiapas, I have felt compelled to spend deep time with Indigeneity. In my life experience in the United States, I have felt how disconnected from Indigeneity and Native/Indigenous peoples many Black people are. We must be wary of the epistemological moves we make because of this. Our understanding of Indigeneity must become not only more hemispheric but more planetary. It is witnessing Native/Indigenous life in Chiapas that has brought me to the desire to stand at the shoal. It is also important to note that in this ontological exercise, I am continuing with the destruction of Heideggerian ontology, importantly reckoned with in the work of Nelson Maldonado-Torres (2007) and Calvin Warren (2018). It is the interpellation into this form of ontology in the OWW that gets refused through these other onto-epistemic formations.

FIGURE 4.2. *La Montaña* out at sea. Used with permission of the photographer, Daliri Oropeza.

found in the Atlantic Ocean contains catalytic elements resulting from the disintegration of those who would never know what it was like to be a captive in the New World (in this case, we can imagine those that joined the spirits of the water en route to Mexican shores). The watery grave of the transatlantic spirits exists in the lower half of the ocean, where the deity Orisha practitioners call "Olokun"[5] lives—the deity I hear Alexis Pauline Gumbs making homage to in her work here. What happens if we imagine the ancestral spirits of those whose lives ended at sea as collaborating with Squadron 421 as they cross the Atlantic, ensuring their safe passageway, in Black/Afro-diasporic and Native/Indigenous spiritual, historical, and coalitional relation?

It is possible for me to imagine this ecopoetic ancestral coalition of Black/Afro-descendant and Native/Indigenous people and deities fighting in co-constituted space of the spiritual and material realms—on land and at sea—to propel this journey safely forward, thanks to the framework of the shoal. King's (2019) concept of "shoal" refuses to render Blackness and Indigeneity as separable, incompatible, and incommensurable geographical and ecological

---

5. Olokun is a water deity of the Orisha pantheon and is considered one of the most mysterious by the human species because it is the owner of the deep ocean. Olokun gets depicted as a gender androgynous/ambiguous deity who holds some of the most terrifying and mysterious aspects of life and death on earth—especially given our morbid fascination with reaching and exploring the mysteries of the ocean's floor.

concerns. King (2019) foregrounds the shoal as a geological and ecological metaphor, because it challenges the idea that Native/Indigenous people are stably sutured to land whereas Afro-descendant and Black people are errantly tied to the sea (pp. 2–4). When Black people meet Native/Indigenous people, they are "not just water (fluid, malleable, and fungible) but also a body landed" (p. 9). To this I would add that, given the broad areas of Mexico that border the ocean, like this Atlantic Coast—in a nation-state whose territory was stewarded by Native/Indigenous people for millennia—Native/Indigenous people are not just land but also bodies of water.

As a geological formation, a shoal refers to an area in the ocean where it is shallower but not quite at the shore (p. 2). When "shoal" is used as a verb, it represents a danger for navigation (p. 4). It is also a formation that can "erode over time, drift, and eventually accumulate in another location," creating an "unpredictability" that "exceeds full knowability/mappability" (p. 3). King's (2019) shoal, like the book that inaugurated its use,[6] exists in a "liminal space between the sea and the land," also fundamentally shifting the people who engage with it—"where one becomes an ecotone, a space of transition between distinct ecological systems and states" (p. 4; p. 9). The shoal helps unsettle the overdetermined rooted/rootless dichotomy made between Black/Afro-descendant and Native/Indigenous people, emphasizing what is unearthed at the points where the sea's movements make for fluid land—geologically, ecologically, corporeally, and spiritually (p. 4).

King's (2019) shoal takes some of its epistemological contours from Kamu Braithwaite's (1999) "tidalectics." In tidalectics, Black Caribbean understandings of temporality, in confluence with sea rhythms, part ways with the linear temporalities that are a product of modern/colonial thinking. She further explains, "tidalectics confound the binary and dialectical thinking that would separate ocean from land and render Black people and Native/Indigenous people as an antagonism" (p. 7). Following King (2019) and the tidalectical contours of the shoal, we have an analytic that allows us to engage Squadron 421's maritime journey as one that moves with the temporality of the waves at sea, "where Black studies attempts to engage Native studies on ethical terms that unfold in new locations" (p. 10). Let us now turn to what preceded the journey.

Subcomandante Insurgente Galeano (2021), in his "discurso oficial," describes his attempt to dissuade those considering putting forth their candidacy as delegates and volunteers for the would-be squadron, with the tenor of typical sardonic EZLN humor saying, "I told them horrible things about the

---

6. I am referring to *The Black Shoals: Offshore Formations in Black and Native Studies.*

high seas: the interminable vomiting; the vast monotony of the horizon; the corn-poor diet, with no popcorn or (the horror!) Valentina salsa; the fact of being shut in with other people for several weeks" but to no avail. He mentions also describing "in extreme detail" the "terrible storms and unknown threats" but how it was the women that stood up and insisted that the journey's locomotive mode would be by boat (SupGaleano, 2021). The people who would give their lives in the defense of their land sovereignty, with almost no prior exposure to the vast ocean, were not going to be dissuaded from carrying out their mission of sharing the wisdom that has come from their world as the descendants of those that survived the empire that intended to colonize all their ancestral lands. Ultimately, such humor-laden scare tactics by people like SupGaleano were meant to help those who would join the squadron do so with psychological sobriety and realism to prepare their bodies, minds, and spirits for the journey ahead.

During the COVID-19 pandemic that forever transformed our worlds, Squadron 421 and their supporters were spurred on by the reality of the ever-encroaching extractivist megaprojects in Mexico. These projects contributed not only to the motivation behind their mission but also to the significance of carrying out the delegation. Insurgenta Jaquelín delivered the message of the CCRI-CG (the Clandestine Indigenous Revolutionary Committee–General Command) as part of the communications that framed the journey, sharing, "We were forced to make the decision to leave despite the virus that has us locked-down. The capitalist system doesn't stop and advances with its plunder, its dispossession, and its destruction of living beings, as with the projects of the Mayan Train and the Interoceanic Corridor, among others" (Oropeza, 2021a). Here, Insurgenta Jaquelín signals two environmentally racist and devastating megaprojects in southern Mexico that demonstrate the Mexican state's and conquistador-settlers' ongoing attempts at Native/Indigenous genocide and Afro-descendant dispossession and erasure. A bit about these projects for context.

The Mayan Train or Tren Maya, was a project proposed in 2018; its construction was officially underway in early 2022. Its construction is meant as a boon for the Mexican tourist industry. The Mayan Train "is an intercity railway line stretching 950 miles around the Yucatan Peninsula, in a rough loop around the states of Chiapas, Tabasco, Campeche, Yucatan, and Quintana Roo, connecting beach resorts with ancient Mayan sites" (Kishwari, 2023). Besides the bulldozing of massive swaths of forest throughout the region, what is perhaps most environmentally devastating about its construction is that it is happening on top of a "fragile cave system" of *cenotes,* or "water-filled sinkholes formed by the collapse of limestone," making up the largest underground aquifer in the world and providing water to approximately five million

Mexicans (Kishwari, 2023). More and more cenotes continue to be unveiled throughout the construction of the train; its very construction threatening the existence of the cenotes as a trusted and reliable water source and, therefore, threatening the life of the region.

The second project Insurgenta Jaquelín names, the Interoceanic Multimodal Corridor, or Isthmus of Tehuantepec Megaproject, by another name, is yet another railroad and multimodal project in process. But in this case, rather than serving the tourist industry by moving human species cargo, its goal is to rival the Panama Canal, moving goods cargo between oceans. Its reach impacts "thirty-three municipalities of Veracruz, forty-six of Oaxaca, fourteen of Chiapas, and five of Tabasco," meaning it is primarily Native/Indigenous and Afro-descendant people who are feeling the brunt of the impact (López y Rivas, 2022).

The Interoceanic Corridor is an extractive megaproject that is in its third iteration over the course of the past 164 years—beginning with the 1859 McLane-Ocampo Treaty,[7] later reactivated by the government of Ernesto Zedillo in 1997, and now in its current iteration. What has been so devastating about the current iteration of the project is its many-pronged extraordinarily extractivist aims; beyond the smokescreen of the railroad are the multiple harmful modalities for producing and moving commodities. These include

the modernization of the ports of Coatzacoalcos and Salina Cruz, a parallel network of highways, 10 agro-industrial and industrial parks or corridors for the chemical, petrochemical, oil and gas industries, petrochemicals, petroleum, refineries, wind farms, hydroelectric dams, automotive and machinery assembly plants, manufacturing of other products, gas and oil pipelines,

7. The McLane-Ocampo Treaty of 1859 was

an agreement between the US and Mexico regarding transit rights. Negotiations were conducted during the War of the Reform (1858–1860) by Robert M. McLane (1815–1898), United States ambassador to the Liberal government of Benito Juárez in Veracruz, and Melchor Ocampo, Minister of Foreign Affairs. The treaty gave US citizens transit rights across the Isthmus of Tehuantepec and across northern Mexico from the Gulf of California to the vicinity of the lower Rio Grande and allowed the US government to send in military personnel to protect the route and US citizens in transit. US citizens would not be charged for transit at a rate different from that charged to Mexicans. In exchange for these transit rights, the United States was to pay Mexico $4 million, half upon ratification and the other half to be applied to the claims of citizens of the United States against the government of Mexico. The treaty was rejected by the US Senate in 1860 and a subject of much controversy in Mexico, where some feared the loss of significant territory to the United States. Had it been ratified; it would have given the United States a large measure of control over areas of Mexico that were crucial to the passage of persons and goods to and from California. (Barry, 2019) timber plantations, and high voltage power lines, as well as hotel infrastructure, services and communications for luxury tourism. (López y Rivas, 2022)

What is worse, the project is beneficial to US economic and military interests, as well as securing more of Mexican economic hegemony in Abya Yala South / Améfrica Ladina, helping it compete with other economically imperial nations and continents like China, Europe, and Japan (López y Rivas, 2022).

This megadevelopment project of mass-scale ecological devastation and sanctioned environmental racism and terrorism has been met with protest efforts by various members of civil society in the affected states, led by Native/Indigenous and Black/Afro-descendant peoples. In 2019, the El Istmo Es Nuestro[8] (the isthmus is ours) campaign was formed, with its stated goal being to prevent the triple devastation "against nature, against indigenous and black peoples, and national sovereignty" (López y Rivas, 2022). Within the context of these megaprojects that have been devastating major swaths of environmental relations and land needed by the Mexican people and the planet (the isthmus is home to 10 percent of the planet's biodiversity), the urgency of the delegation could not be overstated (López y Rivas, 2022). In these examples, it is not a stretch to hold the ecological devastation (which is also to say, species devastation) with shoal simultaneity.

There is one other important consideration for us here that grounds the ecopoetic readings that follow. This occurs at the level of culture. It is my sense that how we listen to Native/Indigenous practices of being/becoming and thinking/doing from their worlds must challenge the way that the modern/colonial civilizing project, the OWW, deploys "culture." This is important, because when "culture" is positioned as contiguous with a "belief" system about things like the modern/colonial construction of "nature," it makes "culture" an inconvenient particularity antithetical to all things "modern" so that it is considered more "primitive" than that which has been "universalized" for the benefit of the modern/colonial civilizing project. De la Cadena and Blaser (2018) explain that there are "limits to deploying culture to represent such heterogeneity" in our species, since "categories that made the difference apparent in the first place may amount to explaining the difference through 'the same,' or difference in terms that are homologous to the self to which difference disappears" (p. 7). In other words, "culture" is a term that has come to be deployed against the people and cosmologies the modern/colonial OWW considers to be in competition with the necroliberal economic interests protected by its colonizing "universal truths"; still, "culture" is mobilized and

---

8. The full "El Istmo Es Nuestro" declaration by the CNI (National Indigenous Congress) can be read here: https://www.caminoalandar.org/post/declaratoria-el-istmo-es-nuestro.

explained from within the terms of the OWW. This requires that its Human represent *the* universals around which the OWW universe can be organized while trying to force others into the coloniality of its meaning-making, using "culture" to explain what it considers to be a nonsignificant "difference" or heterogeneity. "Culture," mobilized in this way, is still about marking a difference up against a norm or center to justify the total lack of regard for and deprioritization of other worlds and knowledges considered invalid information for the OWW. What happens in this rendition of "culture" is that the modern/colonial global necroliberal extractive capitalist mode of relating to the rest of living beings on our planet is maintained.

Deploying "culture" allows other people's interdependent connections to all other living beings to be framed as mere "beliefs" that "cultures" hold (see Escobar, 2021). For example, if treating a body of water as a subject of agency, rights, and dignity is made out to be a cultural belief and not a cosmological truth and one that helps sustain our ecologies, there is no convincing the OWW to treat that water as deserving of protection and care. Refusing the conquistador-settler framework, I follow Escobar's (2021) call for "an ontological perspective that avoids translating them [cosmological-ecological understandings] into 'beliefs'" (Escobar, 2021, p. xiii). In other words, when we speak of cosmological prerogatives that guide the Zapatistas' ecological relationships and knowledge, we are speaking about real knowledge from other worlds, regardless of their framing as cultural "beliefs" within the modern/colonial world order. Within this pluriversal perspective, "environmental conflicts," like the ones named above, that the Zapatistas have been drawing attention to for twenty-eight years, are simultaneously "*ontological* conflicts" because how we treat our ecologies has everything to do with which worlds we are coming from (Escobar, 2021, p. xiii; emphasis added).[9] To further drive this point home, as Blaser (2012) argues, "multiple ontologies are not cultures" (p. 51). Said differently, as we continue to expand our relationships to other notions of ontology, we must suspend the Western urge to treat people as representations of cultural diversity and therefore diminish ontological conflicts to "caring about nature." Instead, we are tarrying in entirely different worlds who have a wholly different set of ecological relationships and ways of understanding existence. It is from this perspective that we can more accurately hold the Zapatista leadership of the EZLN and the CCRI-CG, as representative of intentionally chosen conspecific relationships of Native/Indigenous

---

9. The thinkers writing about the pluriverse who I am thinking alongside have coined the idea of political ontology. However, I do not use their term, because the ontological-theoretical foundation of the OWW *is a political ontology.* I do not think that placing "political" in front of "ontology" offers anything different. Instead, as should be clear by now, I am interested in pluralizing forms that ontology takes and where its origins arise.

peoples and worlds in Mexico whose creative insurgent mission is to move in shared right relation to planetary resources, as members of our species who are inviting others to do the same.

Now, with this understood, let us engage poiesis to further comprehend the imbricated nature of Black/Afro-descendant and Native/Indigenous ecological ontologies. Alexis Pauline Gumbs (2018) asks us if we "remember?" Do we "remember that the whole planet was ocean" "everywhere" [sic] we have been, "that desert valley was the bottom of the deep where something sentient used to swim. and every grain of sand and mineral and currently growing tree is breathing in the ghost of ocean, the infinite face of deep" (p. 112). Squadron 421 holds land and ocean as one—remembering that this place we call "planet" was once all ocean. The presence of their bodies moving across the Atlantic asks us to remember that approximately 60 percent of our species' body composition lives as saltwater, paralleling and closely approximating the 71 percent of this planet that remains ocean. If we continue moving with Gumbs (2018) in ecopoetic and Afro-futurist imagination, we might envision any relationship to ancestral land on this planet as one that lives with the ghosts of oceans past as well as the interruptions of the present and the potentially grave ecological devastation of our watery futures.

The shoal journey of the Native/Indigenous stewards of the highlands of Chiapas is not simply a matter of Indigeneity's dance with water and the relationship to Blackness to be found therein. It is also a reminder that though they are Native/Indigenous peoples of Mayan descent from a place of land and sweet waters (Chiapas), they are departing for the colony from a site where other Mayan descendants have lived alongside and with the ocean for millennia (Casa Ixchel), recalling the Native/Indigenous Atlantic and Caribbean lands along the coast of Mexico. The people in Squadron 421 shoal any distinctions between land and water as they relate through conspecific Indigeneity, simultaneously inviting a reading and being-with Blackness and challenging the extractivist projects impacting Black/Afro-descendant and Native/Indigenous people in their homeland.

From the Queer Black Atlantic to the *Cuir* Black-Native/Indigenous Atlantic

As should be clear by now, "Black" in this chapter does not just mean African American from the US but rather a diasporic constellation made possible, in part, by the many stops of the ships along the Atlantic and the Caribbean Oceans. The maritime journey of Squadron 421 materializes *La Montaña*, the squadron, and the water, following Omise'eke Natasha Tinsley's

(2008) insistence that maritime theorizations ground themselves in materiality (p. 197). Concerned with the literal impact that these forced migrations had on bodies, Tinsley (2008) stresses how figuring people who experienced the Crossing as merely "oceanic imaginings" ends up stopping "short of its most radical potential" (p. 197). Tinsley's work is also useful here, because she reimagines Paul Gilroy's (1993) Atlantic, which she summarizes as "a trope through which he imagines the emergence of black modernities" (p. 195). She reimagines Gilroy's (1993) Atlantic by queering it. By this, she moves beyond a limited scope of "queer" as in (her words) "'gay' or same-sex loving identity" to also conceive of queer "in the sense of marking disruption to the violence of normative order" by "loving your own kind when your kind was supposed to cease to exist" (p. 199).

Tinsley (2008) poignantly describes queer relationality forged at sea—a type of survival affect for gender-segregated enslaved African peoples shackled together in the hold—as one developed through experiencing the extremes of bodily reactions to the seascape, everyday eliminations, and sickness, in shared vulnerability. "Queer" here is the *"feeling for"* an-other experiencing the uncensored and uncontrollable bodily functions in the hold, forging intimacies through the nonconsensual sharing of bodily fluids and the torture of the sickness, pain, stench, and dehumanization (Tinsley, 2008, p. 199; emphasis in original). Building on Tinsley's (2008) queer Black Atlantic, I once again shoal normative theorizations of the oceanic to invite a conversation between Blackness and Indigeneity through Squadron 421, in ancestral and relational entanglements with disrupted geographies.

First, what if we transition from "queer"—a definitively North American–produced term—to "cuir," or Abya Yala South / Améfrica Ladina's reappropriation of the term meant to more accurately reflect geopolitical gender and sexuality politics located in and emerging from histories in Abya Yala South / Améfrica Ladina and meant to refuse Anglocentric epistemological imperialism (see Falconí, Castellanos, & Viteri, 2018). By bringing the otroa Marijose on board of Squadron 421, giving her a prominent role in their "reverse" colonization, the EZLN performs a shoaling of the queer Black Atlantic. They do this by bringing Native/Indigenous modernity into the fold, by loving on and appreciating other-gendered beings and ways of being, beyond the OWW's cisgender heterosexual norm, as some of the stewards of other worlds.

"Otroa," while not a novel concept to Native/Indigenous gender but certainly one to semantics, normalizes differences in gender ontologies[10] and expressions, as well as sexual subjectivities, without contorting them to fit the

---

10. I use "ontology" here instead of "identity," because the all-too-common idea that gender-diverse people "identify as" perpetually invisibilizes the possibility of a gender ontology. To me, it is a pluriversal *fact* that other genders "are," and as such, I refuse to use the phrase

modern/colonial civilizing world's "inclusionary" logics or ways of naming. Instead, the presence of the otroa is featured as a primary agent of an/other/ their world, an "other-other" whose role is to share about the lessons from the Zapatista pedagogical breach of the universe and their role in maintaining the wisdom of their world in the pluriverse.

Before turning to the role of Marijose in Squadron 421, a note about Indigeneity's relationship to Western "modernity" in Abya Yala South / Américha Ladina. Aymara feminist scholar Silvia Rivera Cusicanqui (2012) says, "The indigenous world does not conceive of history as linear; the past-future is contained in the present. The regression or progression, the repetition or overcoming of the past is at play in each conjuncture and is dependent more on our acts than on our words" (p. 96). Cusicanqui's (2012) thinking is crucial for moving with Zapatista cosmologies—in this case, meaning the worldview where nature and gender are held—because the Zapatistas also move with a temporality parallel to that which Cusicanqui articulates from an Aymara perspective. I cite Cusicanqui (2012) here not to collapse Indigeneity into a coherent and singular whole but rather to acknowledge the spiritual-theoretical network of Native/Indigenous scholars in Abya Yala South / Américha Ladina who are challenging the discursively premodern place that Native/ Indigenous people get bound to from the colonization of the Americas. Simultaneously, I am acknowledging some conspecifically shared aspects of Native/ Indigenous cosmologies as they relate to temporality and intervene in world and knowledge-death. The Zapatistas are just one conspecific group of Native/ Indigenous people who have always contemplated and participated in their own form of modernity (rather than their place inside of the modern/colonial civilizing project)—living their Native/Indigenous autonomous future *now*.

"Modernity," in Native/Indigenous worlds, means the concomitant construction of past-present-future that can be read, for instance, in Zapatista communications (more on this below). I understand Native/Indigenous futurism in Zapatista cosmology to be a futurism that understands that *the future already was,* because if we imagine a future predicated in the OWW, we only see the imminent end of our capacity to sustain our lives here on earth because of what the exploitation of planetary resources is doing to its habitability. If "future" means only an endless upgrade of technological prowess, ecologically sound planetary relations cannot coexist with modern/ colonial extractive civilization. The onto-epistemic rewriting of the Zapatista's relationship to "future" and ecology vis-à-vis their autonomy and the

---

"identify as," which participates in continuing to recenter a singular conception of a binary gender universe where cisgender men and cisgender women are the norm and center.

maintenance of their world is the Native/Indigenous "modernity" that they continually construct.

The decolonial pedagogical work for the Zapatistas is in retrieving their worlds, moving in the service of pluriversal epistemologies and ontologies that suture past-present-future in ways that linear notions of necroliberal capitalist time in modernity (the modern/colonial civilizing order) cannot comprehend on its terms. They move away from this destruction. Here, the Native/Indigenous person is not relegated to the figure of a primitive being who refused to come into modernity but instead are beings who have their own "modern" and whose present is the future and whose future is the past. Their lifeways hold some of the keys to ecological survival that might just inspire other worlds—this is what they are traveling to share, and they have chosen an otroa to initiate their landing to share it.

Marijose: *Otroas* and Other Modernities

The concept of otroas has begun to emerge with more intensity recently, from within the Zapatista movement as another category of struggle. And it implies a new conceptualization that Zapatismo makes out of a "sex-gender" reality that is very present in the struggles of the LGBTTTI+ movements. However, this category of "otroas" ("others") ([gender neutral, plural] children, companions, etc.) implies the recognition of a reality that emerges from thinking on political struggle that is frequently based on categories of Mesoamerican philosophy. So we can think of it as contemporary emergence of what was ancestrally lived as gender fluidity. It is the identity of a being in fluidity. (Marcos, 2021a, p. 408, footnote 6)

Marijose is the one otroa present in Squadron 421 aboard *La Montaña*. She is thirty-nine years old and Tojolabal. Marijose also speaks Spanish fluently and knows how to read and write. In her community, she has worked as a "*milicianoa*, a health *promotoroa*, and an education *promotoroa*, and an education trainer"[11] (SupGaleano, 2021, italics in original). Marijose, relating her story in her own words in Zurich, Switzerland, during the visits that followed the maritime trip we will briefly analyze here, explains that she knew that she was not of a binary gender when she was about five years old. After many years of

11. "Miliciano" or "militia," seen here in the gender-fluid form, "milicianoa," positions Marijose as a member of the EZLN or the militia forces of the Zapatistas. "Promotoroa" is the gender-fluid form for "promotor," a designation commonly used for the organizers of the work. So, in this instance, Marijose has worked as a health organizer and education organizer.

experiencing bullying in school, her home, and her community, she turned to the Zapatistas as a space without religious doctrine or modern/colonial ideologies where she could find acceptance and respite by involving herself as part of the movement (Marijose cited in Sirenio, 2021). She explains that becoming a member of the Zapatista movement is what allowed her the space to be free, live without discrimination, and live within a world where it is not a problem for her to be who she is.

Marijose has been given an undeniably prominent role in Squadron 421. In Galeano's words, "Marijose spent six months preparing to be a delegate and volunteer for the voyage to Europe and has been designated to be the first Zapatista to get off the boat, which will initiate the invasion . . . okay, the visit to Europe" (SupGaleano, 2021). Assessing Marijose's background and how they are spoken about, we can deduce that Marijose's history and brilliance has made her an important person in the community and someone who is treated as worthy of holding leadership roles.[12]

Now, let us listen, in its entirety, to the directive given to Marijose upon landing on Spanish soil, or what Subcomandante Insurgente Galeano humorously calls an act of "consensual sado-masochism":

Thus, our first footstep on European soil (assuming of course they even let us disembark) will not be that of a man, nor that of a woman, but that of an *otroa*. In what the late SupMarcos would have called a "slap in the face of the hetero-patriarchal left," it has been decided that the first person to disembark will be **Marijose**. Upon stepping for the first time on European soil and recovering from seasickness, **Marijose** will shout:

"*Surrender hetero-patriarchal pale-faces who persecute those who are different!*"

Nah, just kidding, but that would be cool wouldn't it?

Rather, upon landing, the Zapatista *compa* **Marijose** will solemnly say:

"*In the name of the Zapatista women, children, men, elderly, and of course, others, I declare that from now on this place, currently referred to as 'Europe' by those who live here, be called:* **SLUMIL K'AJXEMK'OP, which means 'Rebellious Land' or 'Land which does not give in nor give up.' And that is how it will be known by its own people and by others for as long as there is at least someone here who does not surrender, sell out, or give up.**"

(SupGaleano, 2021; emphasis in original)

---

12. The rest of the squadron members can be read about on the Enlace Zapatista page dedicated to the voyage: https://enlaceZapatista.ezln.org.mx/2021/04/20/421st-squadron/.

Through their "act of consensual sadomasochism," or playful use of the master's tools to performatively dismantle the master's house (Lorde, 1984), the EZLN have a very different message with their "invasion." Citing the infamous image from schoolbooks of Christopher Columbus planting the Spanish royal flag on the lands of what came to be known as the New World, Marijose becomes the stand-in for a symbolic Native/Indigenous takeover of Europe. However, this time, the first thing they name is the autonomy of the *land,* not the ownership of the people, in a historical, however symbolic, reversal. If there is at least one person who will continue to steward and protect the ontology of Slumil K'ajxemk'op, the *land* shall live in full recognition of its status as a sentient being. And so, Spain gets poetically renamed "*Land which does not give in nor give up,*" suspending its place among the modern/colonial civilizing world's superpowers by pluriversally reducing it in size, imagining what it would be like to return the people to the land; for, in this world, land cannot "belong" to people, it can only be "of" them, in reciprocal relationship.

As we listen to the comedic spark of Subcomandante Galeano (2021) describe how the performance events will unravel and what will be said, it is poetic to have Marijose as the first person to set foot on Spanish soil and to make these pronouncements. Joking about what they "would" say but will not actually say, SupGaleano retorts, "*Marijose* will shout: '*Surrender heteropatriarchal pale-faces who persecute those who are different!*'" In the ecological cosmologies of Mayan-descendant people that the Zapatistas' autonomous land struggle is built from, it is a given for them to connect the race of the colonial powers' "pale-faces" and heterosexist patriarchy to the colonization of the earth. Ecological relationships require that all people participate in the process of being-with other beings, which means intimately caring for the earth, abandoning modern/colonial orders.

There is a prophetic nature to the ecopoetic content of Zapatistas' "official discourse," exemplified in their decision about Marijose's pronouncements upon "invading" Spanish soil. It is important to connect this to their previously mentioned relationship to modernity, given that their gender relations have long come under scrutiny, particularly when witnessed by outsiders who have been invited into communities in the spirit of Zapatista openness, pedagogy, and witnessing. It is outside the purview of this book to rehearse the entirety of those arguments here. However, it is important to note that part of the problem lies in the lens through which gender is being read in community—particularly given that purported "traditional" gender roles are replicating patriarchy—without even interrogating the Western lens from which these accusations are made (see Marcos, 2021a; Oyěwùmí, 1997; Zapatista Women, 2018, 2019). As mentioned in the beginning of this chapter, one of the results of these critiques has been to foreground the role of Zapatista women in birthing the uprising and the autonomous stronghold (see La Comisión, 2015, pp. 109–136). The long-term positive residual of this historicizing revisioning work was the creation of the International Encounter of Women in Struggle in 2018. The second year, they canceled the event due to threats to their territory that they had to attend to, though it does not seem like a stretch to also imagine that the pressure to respond to Western gender ideals about liberation would also be a reason for their exhaustion (see Zapatista Women, 2019).

There is a particular passage from a communiqué related to these critiques that converses with the epigraph definition of "otroas" that Sylvia Marcos provides us with (2021b). It requires our close listening (and therefore its full citation) to approximate a closer understanding to the significance of Marijose's presence. I take the time to emphasize it here because it speaks to a more recent (2019) Zapatista articulation of their position on gender and feminism that very clearly locates how they "feel" about the modern/colonial civilizing project's expectations of them (even from those on the margins of its center) and how they embrace the otroas in their midst. It is also significant that it is coming from a collective of Zapatista women:

> Maybe we don't know which feminism is the best one, maybe we don't say "*cuerpa*" [a feminization of "cuerpo," or body] or however it is you change words around, maybe we don't know what "gender equity" is or any of those other things with too many letters to count. In any case that concept of "gender equity" isn't even well-formulated because it only refers to women and men, and even we, supposedly ignorant and backward, know that there are those who are neither men nor women and who we call "others" [otroas] but who call themselves whatever they feel like. It hasn't been easy for them to earn the right to be what they are without having to hide because they are mocked, persecuted, abused, and murdered. Why should they be obligated to be men or women, to choose one side or the other? If they don't want to choose then they shouldn't be disrespected in that choice. How are we going to complain that we aren't respected as women if we don't respect these people? Maybe we think this way because we are just talking about what we have seen in other worlds and we don't know a lot about these things. What we do know is that we fought for our freedom and now we have to fight to defend it so that the painful history that our grandmothers suffered is not relived by our daughters and granddaughters. We have to struggle so that we don't repeat history and return to a world where we only cook food and bear children, only to see them grow up into humiliation, disrespect, and death. We didn't rise up in arms to return to the same thing. (Zapatista Women, 2019)

The Zapatistas perform themselves out of the logics of what the OWW would call "diversity" and the measuring stick that has been projected onto them by onlookers. They challenge outsider condemnations and assumptions about their relationships to feminism and gender through their sarcastic and savvy criticism. In this passage, they call out the way that necroliberal politics of ever-linear "progress" infiltrate some of even the most "radical" of political movements and discourses. For example, spaces who emphasize the use of the word "cuerpa," or the feminization of the Spanish work "cuerpo," become a marker of holding properly radical feminist political currency vis-à-vis modern/colonial semantic conversions. In such spaces, "cuerpa"-users would denote more militant feminists. Pausing here for one moment longer: this play on words is an interesting example, because given the Latin origin of the Spanish language, "el cuerpo" as a "masculine" word has nothing to do with dichotomous gender formations attributable to the modern/colonial civilizing project (like playful reappropriation from history to herstory in US feminist politics). "Cuerpa," then, though seemingly innocent and playful, can easily slip into becoming an overdetermined semantic attribution that materially manifests as feminist virtue-signaling-turned-policing, inadvertently replicating racist colonial dynamics.

The Zapatista women make clear that they are not familiar with terminology like "gender equity" or the LGBTQIA "alphabet soup," as some would have it. I do not see this as dismissive of the social justice struggles and movements in other worlds that also have done important work in countering the modern/colonial hegemonic business-as-usual but rather as an invitation to pluriversal humility and a recognition of how the ethnocentricity of this language ends up reproducing colonial dynamics. The Zapatista discourse emphasizes that they quite literally live in a world that is divested from the modern/colonial civilizing project, the OWW, and its ways, even if there are certainly influences, given that they have not maintained the insularity of say, noncontacted peoples (see figure 4.3). Therefore, they are also divested from other worlds' solipsistic and myopic epistemologies that claim to be the most "advanced" while destroying planetary habitability for many species.

A tone of weariness marks the passage. Modernity's arrogance rears its ugly head as it looks judgmentally upon the Zapatista women. They cancel that year's encounter, opting to turn inward. In the second portion of this passage, they mock how the OWW sees them—as *supposedly ignorant, and backward*—and yet "even they" acknowledge expansive gender formations beyond the man/woman binary (otroas). They question how otroas are treated in other worlds and express that *even they,* the "backwards ones," know that the proper way to treat otroas is how they want to be treated. The simplicity

FIGURE 4.3. Squadron 421 women and *otroa* aboard *La Montaña*.
Used with permission of the photographer, Daliri Oropeza.

of this communication and its move beyond the identity wars, oppression Olympics, and politicking/policing plays of other worlds allows us to see how simple it is for them that otroas are a part of their world. What feminism, womanhood, and otroa life means in the Zapatista Native/Indigenous communities of Chiapas is what it means within their ecological cosmologies and their entire ecological relations and is not predicated on the modern/colonial world's misperception of its own "more" advanced civilization. Otroas are a part of their ancestral beliefs in complementarity and pose no threat to their world. No Western grammars could ever fully attend to these gender ontologies and relationalities. It is an expansive, fluid gender relationship in the ecological ontology of the Zapatistas that stages their "invasion" of Spain.

Returning to the pronouncement in preparation of Marijose, the subtext behind her first hypothetical pronouncement, "*Surrender hetero-patriarchal pale-faces who persecute those who are different!*" brings together the persecution of those who are different with the renaming of the land. Marijose's fluid embodiment, as a Native/Indigenous modern Tojolabal otroa, sutures the violence done to "others" to the ongoing extractive relationship the modern/colonial civilizing project has with land, water, and other ecological relations (conceived of as "resources"). Marijose's presence is the last image that the colonial/modern civilizing order, the OWW, would expect of a voyage undertaken by Native/Indigenous autonomous peoples who do not share their

FIGURE 4.4. Squadron 421 *otroa* Marijose aboard *La Montaña*. Used
with permission of the photographer, Daliri Oropeza.

vision of modernity (see figure 4.4). The Zapatistas capitalize on presumptions
of their "backwardness" and perform something else—something not easily
understood in the terms of other worlds—signaling their existence in the pluriverse for those who know how to hear it.

The Tojolabal otroa becomes a human species embodiment of ecological beingness—honoring Native/Indigenous fluidity of relationships to land
and to sea and with deep regard for their shared ecological imbrication with
Black/Afro-descendant people—there to teach colonial forces a lesson about
the entangled nature of land and water, Blackness and Indigeneity, and the
fluidity of gender in other worlds. The Tojolabal otroa signals a multiplicity of
fluid relationships to bodies, land, and water and a categorical partitioning of
humans that cannot be named or fully conceived of by the grammars of the
OWW. Said differently, in worlds with ecologically appropriate relationships
to sustaining the planet, *of course* otroas would be integral and normalized
parts of society. The presence of otroas in society signal a not-yet-foreclosed
possibility for entering renewed and right relationship with the land and
beings that make up our planet. The Zapatistas do not require any theoretical discourse to overly theorize this connection—their being/becoming is the
thinking/doing.

Out on the cuir Black–Native/Indigenous Atlantic, Marijose's duties can
be read as their own genre of decolonial pedagogical work—something that

approximates transfeminisms, Native/Indigenous feminisms, and ecofeminisms in other worlds but that should be taken on their own terms. The pedagogical lessons, in this instance, require holding subjectivities as possibly *other* ontological positions from pluriversal worlds that are not beholden to the semantic engagements and symbolic representational systems from worlds on the fringes of the OWW (even if carrying relational entanglements because of interfacing with the OWW's Human and choosing to engage it in such lessons). The fluidity of Marijose's otroa gender ontology is a pluriversally fluid subjectivity, making them the perfect person to stage a message for the shore—where land and sea meet. It is through these intentional actions that the decolonial pedagogical lessons of Squadron 421 emerge.

Final Notes on Pluriversal Ontologies, Thought Together

I remember the power of seven Mayan-descendant land defenders setting sail to "reverse colonize" Spain, whose colonial descendants, conquistador-settlers perpetuating the modern/colonial global necroliberal capitalist world project, work "against nature, against indigenous and black peoples, and national sovereignty" (López y Rivas, 2022). I recall the African elders who jumped ship to avoid knowing a life in captivity and envision them as protective ancestors in solidarity with Native/Indigenous people fighting to keep their worlds alive. Where the land meets the sea, an otroa emerges to announce the return of the land, sanctioned by the protection of the sea and all the beings fighting to guard these sentient life-forms. It is through performing an interruption into the modern/colonial business-as-usual that we find Black/Afro-descendant and Native/Indigenous ontological revolutions in the pluriverse. We are ready to hear the messages from the pluriverse when we are no longer astounded by leadership of otroas at the helm.

Tuning In to the Wood Wide Web

A final image guides us in this coda—one not meant to "finalize" anything you have read here. Instead, dear reader, I ask that you be with me, this one last moment, in this invitation into all that is right before us, among us, and waiting for us to be with/in it. Let us continue to see sites where we are missing a pluriversal perspective.

Since I have previously imagined my work in Greensboro, North Carolina, to be a place that bore witness to Black liberation struggles in the region, reflected on through my memory work in Elsewhere Museum, I return one last time to the important work of witnessing; particularly the witnessing that brings decolonial pedagogical lessons from the pluriverse, asking us to see more.

In the summer of 2022, in my final days living in Greensboro, North Carolina, a dear friend and colleague of mine and I are making our second attempt to find the "Underground Railroad Tree" on Guilford College campus. It is a swelteringly hot and humid summer day. We are methodically following the route that she has been given by someone who knows its location, phone GPS in hand. We make many roundabout turns, probably still taking the long way there, but ultimately arrive at the sheer wonder of this ancestor. Its size marks it as in a world of its own, among a forest of other worlds. The struggle involved in finding its location seems to be teaching us about the importance

FIGURE 5.1.
Underground Railroad
Tree on Gilford campus.
Image by the author.

of hiding the magic of our worlds in plain sight—something our peoples have become quite adept at.

On the campus of Guilford College in Greensboro, North Carolina, stands a champion tulip poplar tree that is over three hundred years old (see figure 5.1) and which therefore Guilford College—through a gift of the 2016 graduating class—renamed the Underground Railroad Tree. I had heard about this tree from a colleague but had to hold out on bearing witness to it in person. By the time I learned about it, we were well into the COVID-19 pandemic, and the grounds were closed to in-person visitors. I first opted to engage in the online "tour" about how it has been storied into existence, but I really could not capture the magnitude of the tree without seeing it in person. By the time I do get to see it in person, the ritual of coming to bear witness to it also serves as a ritual of departure from this land and an opportunity to carry the lessons of its spirit with me.

According to the library website's historicization for those who engage in a self-guided tour like my friend-colleague and I did, "We cannot know if this tree served as a guide to assist enslaved runaways seeking freedom,

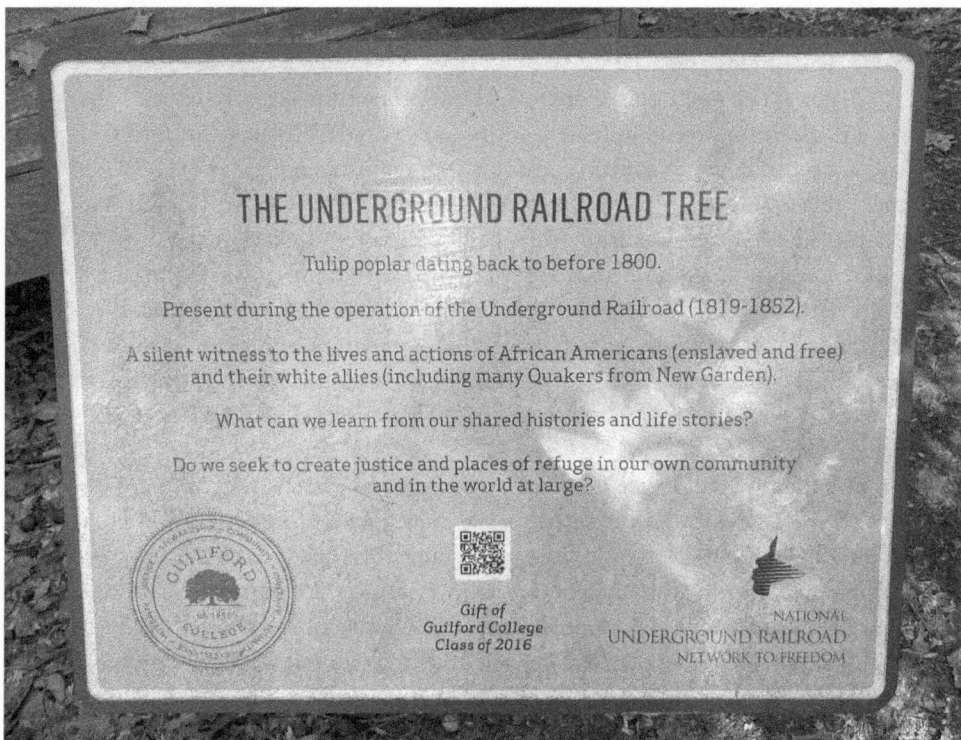

FIGURE 5.2. Plaque accompanying the Underground Railroad Tree. Image by the author.

but know it was present at that time and place. This tree was a *silent witness*" (Hege Library, 2021).[1] Furthermore, there is a plaque that accompanies the tree, at a wooden lookout near it, that also has some interesting language (see figure 5.2).

Before going any further, we must name the tree in question for the historical longevity of the lands it lives on—the occupied territory of the Keyauwee, Saura, and Saponi Peoples—further occupied by the modern/colonial police state. In this instance, it would behoove us to see this tree as both an elder and witness-bearer to Native/Indigenous peoples who might have had intimate relationships with this tree in the forest it used to stand within—people who would have stewarded this land until the Indian Removal Act of 1830. So, why is the tree only historicized as a witness-bearer and ancestor to Black people fleeing their conditions of enslavement? Especially given the

---

1. Of note: "runaways" is the term used by those who created the historicization. For the full website, see: https://library.guilford.edu/undergroundrr.

window of overlap between the Indian Removal Act of 1830 and the Fugitive Slave Acts of 1793 and 1850?

A few more open-ended rhetorical questions bear remarking on: What does it mean for a predominately white university (PWI) like Guilford College—steeped in the modern/colonial institutionalizing order of the OWW—to mark this tulip poplar tree as a witness-bearer only to Black/Afro-descendant people on colonized territory while calling freedom-seekers "runaways"? Is this a conquistador-settler move of innocence and moral posturing meant to absolve them of ancestral guilt? What about a historicization of Black/Afro-descendant people on these freedom trails, making use of the trails that were stewarded for millennia by the original peoples of this land? A pluriversal reckoning with this tree would have to, at minimum, attend to these imbricated histories.

Standing below the tremendous size of this monstrously large being, the life of this tree and the life of historical trajectories of our species become bound up with one another in the same ecology. Though this exercise in naming and historicizing this ancient tree as a witness to the underground railroad is arguably an exercise in conquistador-settler innocence to absolve historical moral dread, I leave us with the image of this tree, for our historical, political, and spiritual imaginations to picture what scientists have called the "wood wide web" (see Marshall, 2019). By this I mean that if we take as a starting point that in this instance the tree is *bearing witness to* lives of our species, we might then understand that the tree is a *being* that *perceives, feels, communicates, sees, and senses* but from its own sentient perspective—one we do not have the capacity to fully understand or sense, even if we fix our mouths to make words that we know in an attempt to locate it in an animacy hierarchy (Chen, 2012). We must be with other cosmologies that name worlds where ecological beingness does not give our species the authority to destroy and manage all other forms of sentient life, or whose worlds count in an ecological totality. We must pluralize our very notion of "a" world.

From this place, I invite us to imagine ourselves as other trees in this forest being held by the being that appears to be the eldest ancestor, this champion tulip poplar tree. Moving in this way, two possible final pedagogical lessons to close our thinking together here are as follows: (1) on a planet homogenized by the idea of a singular world, we can learn how to communicate with one another through our own kind of mycelium network by learning the ways of trees, so that we might continue to live in and reclaim the richness of our many worlds, *simultaneously*; and (2) leaning on the vantage point of the trees—which is to say, elders and ancestral guides—we can become quiet observers of the OWW's gross underrepresentation of the many worlds of our species, while continuing to craft the worlds that we want to live in, in generous relation. Through this invitation, and in this practice, we can alert one another to dangers that would impede us from becoming our fullest selves, in our worlds, like the trees that witnessed the struggle of Native/Indigenous people, Black/Afro-descendant people, and others who have only ever wanted freedom. Our goal should be to move like the trees.

Let us close this time together by imagining ourselves as trees. Our only job is to pour forth what is in our limbs during our season.[2] What if we communicated with one another from our place of striving to bring forth the greatest of our essence such that we could carry a collective intelligence, not of inclusion, but of plurality? In so doing, can we meet one another beyond the colonial wound? With respect to trees like this tulip poplar that have survived all these years, by virtue of how our ecosystem naturally works, we can imagine that this tree must have endured the material manifestation, or at least the threat of, "windstorms, ice storms, lightning strikes, wildfires, droughts, floods, a host of constantly evolving diseases, swarms of voracious insects" (Grant, 2018). May it be our example of the storms that will have to be endured ahead and how we might meet them by un/learning what has plagued us when shackled to the OWW's definitions of a life.

In all that we are up against and in trying to craft a way for ourselves as we simply try to bring forth what is within us while nature continues to take its course and present us with entirely different ecological landscapes, how do we remember the way of the trees so that we ancestrally retrieve and reactivate the resilience of the essence of the trees that live within us? I imagine the way of the trees as a tool for Black/Afro-descendant and Native/Indigenous peoples to communicate with one another while we make our worlds, bearing witness to the OWW, navigating its Human as an interface, and bringing forth all that is ours to bring forth.

•

Sedimented into our sensory perceptions exist ways of being/becoming and thinking/doing that cannot be destroyed by hegemonic constraints, legislative panic, or other forms of surveillance and policing. Unlike the popular psychological axiom to not believe everything we feel because our feelings may not hold up to a holistic reality, we can rely on other modalities of sensing our beingness as our primary sources of information. It is with this dialectic we must live. Utilizing ancestral technologies and our ecological

---

2. Here, I am paraphrasing the wisdom of my dear friend and comrade gina Breedlove.

interconnectedness enables access to worlds with other ecopoetic constellations that exist on behalf of and in the direction of *life*. These ecopoetic constellations are how we come to sense the palimpsestic fervor of ourselves and one another, in a many-world relation. We continuously become to re-exist, as beings in the fullness of our ontologies, in nonextractive relations.

What if the portal we open into the pluriverse shifts the space-time continuum of the OWW? We cohere, converge, and gather at the site where the Human has lost its way. Through embodiment and becoming, we dare to feel what else there is to be known and what was never ours to "know," exceeding what the OWW considers "knowable." We are not talking about the kind of "knowing" that works in service of classificatory logic. It is into this abyss we must give one another permission to jump, finding each other through our underground fungi webs of communication, like the trees.

May we heart-reason, m/other, break, and shoal our way into more-alive ways of being in our pluriverse. For life!

REFERENCES

Alcoff, L. (1991–1992). The Problem of Speaking for Others. *Culture Critique, 20,* 5–32.

Alexander, M. (2012). *The New Jim Crow: Mass Incarceration in the Age of Color Blindness* (Rev. ed.). The New Press. (Original work published 2010)

Alexander, M. J. (2005). *Pedagogies of Crossing: Meditations on Feminism, Sexual Politics, Memory, and the Sacred.* Duke University Press.

Alvarez, S. E., & Caldwell, K. L. (2016). Promoting Feminist Amefricanidade: Bridging Black Feminist Cultures and Politics in the Americas. *Meridians: Feminism, Race, Transnationalism, 14*(1), v–xi.

Arvin, G. (2015). Analytics of Indigeneity. In S. Nohelani Teves, A. Smith, & M. H. Raheja (Eds.), *Native Studies Keywords* (pp. 119–129). University of Arizona Press.

Bailey, M. (2021). *Misogynoir Transformed: Black Women's Digital Resistance.* New York University Press.

Barry, C.R. (2019). McLane-Ocampo Treaty (1859). *Encyclopedia of Latin American History and Culture.* https://www.encyclopedia.com/humanities/encyclopedias-almanacs-transcripts-and-maps/mclane-ocampo-treaty-1859

Blaser, M. (2012). Ontology and Indigeneity: On the Political Ontology of Heterogeneous Assemblages. *Cultural Geographies, 21*(1), 49–58.

Braithwaite, K. (1999). *ConVERSations with Nathaniel Mackey.* We Press.

Browder, C. (2021, September 3). 'I Felt Like a Tied-Up Dog': Shackled Pregnant Inmate Sues NC Prison Leaders. *WRAL News.* https://www.wral.com/i-felt-like-a-tied-up-dog-shackled-pregnant-inmate-sues-nc-prison-leaders/19857478/

Berbusse, E. J. (1985). The Origins of the McLane-Ocampo Treaty of 1859. *The Americas, 14,* 223–243.

Cardoso, C. (2014). Amefricanizando o feminismo: O pensamento de Lélia Gonzalez [Amefricanizing feminism: The thought of Lélia Gonzalez]. *Estudos Feministas Florianópolis, 22*(3): 320, 965–986.

Cardoso, C. (2019). Amefricanidade: Proposa feminista negra de organização política e transformação social [Amefricanity: A Black feminist proposal for political organization and social transformation]. *LASA Forum, 50*(3), 44–49.

Carruthers, C. (2018). *Unapologetic: A Black, Queer, and Feminist Mandate for Radical Movements*. Beacon Press.

Césaire, A. (2000). *Discourse on Colonialism* (J. Pinkham, Trans.). Monthly Review Press. (Original work published 1972)

Chafe, W. H. (1981). *Civilities and Civil Rights: Greensboro, North Carolina and the Black Struggle for Freedom*. Oxford University Press.

Chen, M. (2010). *Animacies: Biopolitics, Racial Mattering, and Queer Affect*. Duke University Press.

Cohen, S. (2015, February 2). Why the Woolworth's Sit-In Worked. *Time Magazine*. https://time.com/3691383/woolworths-sit-in-history/.

Coleman, D. B. (2019). Cuerpos y existencias cotidianas trans* como ruptura, abertura e invitación [Quotidian trans bodies and existences as rupture, opening, and invitation]. In X. Leyva Solano & R. Icaza (Eds.), *En tiempos de muerte: Cuerpos, rebeldías, resistencias* [In times of death: Bodies, rebellions, resistances] (pp. 221–238). Cooperative Editorial Retos.

Coleman, D.B. (2020, September 6). La evergadura: Ecologías Trans [Expanse: Trans Ecologies]. *Vimeo*. https://vimeo.com/455320092?embedded=true&source=vimeo_logo&owner=105934434.

Coleman, D. B. (2020). If Rigor Is Our Dream: Theorizing Black Transmasculine Futures through Ancestral Erotics. In B. LeMaster & A. Johnson (Eds.), *Gender Futurity, Intersectional Autoethnography: Embodied Theorizing from the Margins* (pp. 151–164). Routledge.

Combahee River Collective (1997). The Combahee River Collective Statement. *Black Past*. https://www.blackpast.org/african-american-history/combahee-river-collective-statement-1977/

Congreso Nacional Indígena [National Indigenous Congress]. (2021, November 16). Declaratoria 'El istmo es nuestro' ['The Isthmus Is Ours' declaration]. *Camino al andar*. https://www.caminoalandar.org/post/declaratoria-el-istmo-es-nuestro

Cooper Owens, D. (2017). *Medical Bondage: Race, Gender, and the Origins of American Gynecology*. University of Georgia Press.

Critical Resistance (n.d.). What Is the PIC? What Is Abolition? *Critical Resistance*. https://criticalresistance.org/mission-vision/not-so-common-language/

Cusicanqui, S. R. (2012). Ch'ixinakax utxiwa: A Reflection on the Practices and Discourses of Decolonization. *South Atlantic Quarterly, 111*(1), 95–109.

Day, I. (2016). *Alien Capital: Asian Racialization and the Logic of Settler Colonial Capitalism*. Duke University Press.

Day, I. (2021). Afro-Feminism before Afro-Pessimism: Meditations on Gender and Ontology. In M. Jung & J. M. Costa Vargas (Eds.), *Antiblackness* (pp. 60–81). Duke University Press.

de Certeau, M. (1984). *The Practice of Everyday Life* (S. Rendall, Trans.). University of California Press.

De la Cadena, M., & Blaser, M. (2018). Introduction. Pluriverse: Proposals for a World of Many Worlds. In M. de la Cadena & M. Blaser (Eds.), *A World of Many Worlds* (pp. 1–22). Duke University Press.

Delgado Huitrón, C. C. (2019). Haptic Tactic: Hypertenderness for the [Mexican] State and the Performances of Lia García. *TSQ: Transgender Studies Quarterly, 6*(2), 164–179.

Donald, M. (1991). *Origins of the Modern Mind: Three Stages in the Evolution of Culture and Cognition.* Harvard University Press.

Escobar, A. (2003). Mundos y conocimientos de otro modo: El programa de investigación de modernidad/colonialidad latinoamericano [Worlds and knowledges otherwise: The Abya Yala South / Améfrica Ladinan modernity/coloniality research program]. *Tabula Rasa, 1,* 51–86.

Escobar, A. (2014). Prefacio [Preface]. In Y. Espinosa Miñoso, D. Gómez Correal, and K. Ochoa Muñoz (Eds.), *Tejiendo de otro modo: Feminismo, epistemología y apuestas descoloniales en Abya Yala* [Weaving another way: Feminism, epistemology, and decolonial commitments in Abya Yala] (pp. 11–12). Editorial Universidad del Cauca.

Escobar, A. (2020). *Pluriversal Politics: The Real and the Possible.* Duke University Press.

EZLN (1994, January 1). Primera Declaración de la Selva Lacandona [First Declaration of the Lacandon Jungle]. *Enlace Zapatista.* https://enlaceZapatista.ezln.org.mx/1994/01/01/primera-declaracion-de-la-selva-Lacandona/.

Falconí Trávez, F., Castellanos, S., & Viteri, M. A. (2016). Resentir lo queer en América Latina: Diálogos desde/con el Sur [Resenting queerness in Abya Yala South / Améfrica Ladina: Dialogues from/with the South]. In D. Falconí Trávez, S. Castellanos, & M. A. Viteri (Eds.), *Resentir lo queer en América Latina: Diálogos desde/con el Sur* [Resenting queerness in Abya Yala South/Améfrica Ladina: Dialogues from/with the South] (2nd ed.) (pp. 9–20). Editorial EGALES, S. L. (Original work published 2016)

Foreman, P. G., et al. (2023, September 15). Writing about Slavery / Teaching about Slavery: This Might Help. Community-sourced document. https://docs.google.com/document/d/1A4TEdDgYslX-hlKezLodMIM71My3KTNozxRvoIQTOQs/mobilebasic

Fox, J. (2010, March 26). Mexico's Indigenous Population. *Cultural Survival Quarterly Magazine.* https://www.culturalsurvival.org/publications/cultural-survival-quarterly/mexicos-indigenous-population

Freire, P. (2011). *Pedagogy of the Oppressed* (M. Bergman Ramos, Trans.). Continuum. (Original work published 1970)

Galeano [Subcomandante Insurgente]. (2021, April 20). 421st Squadron (Zapatista Maritime Delegation). *Enlace Zapatista.* https://enlaceZapatista.ezln.org.mx/2021/04/20/421st-squadron/

Garrison Institute. (2021, March 25). *Dr. Bayo Akomolafe: Wrestling with Post-Activism and Planetary Health—Garrison Institute Fellowship* [Video]. YouTube. https://www.youtube.com/watch?v=G_L8eq-tcy8&list=PLiGEhCFloD6kp-9G1Di_ES5hSgINzX7H

Genovese, T. R. (2016). *Lento, Pero Avanzo: Indigenous Mayan Influence in Zapatista Speech and Imagery* [Unpublished MS.] Department of Anthropology, Northern Arizona University.

Gilmore, R. W. (2008). Forgotten Places and Seeds of Grassroots Planning. In C. Hale (Ed.), *Engaging Contradictions: Theory, Politics, and Methods of Activist Scholarship* (pp. 31–61). University of California Press.

Gilroy, P. (1993). *The Black Atlantic: Modernity and Double Consciousness.* Verso.

Goodwin, M. (2020). *Policing the Womb: Invisible Women and the Criminalization of Motherhood.* Cambridge University Press.

Gordon, L. (2006). *Disciplinary Decadence: Living Thought in Trying Times.* Routledge.

Grant, R. (2018, March). Do Trees Talk to Each Other? *Smithsonian Magazine.* https://www.smithsonianmag.com/science-nature/the-whispering-trees-180968084/

Green, K. M., & Ellison, T. (2014). Tranifest. *TSQ: Transgender Studies Quarterly, 1*(1–2), 222–225.

Grosfoguel, R. (2006). La descolonización de la economía política y los estudios poscoloniales: Transmodernidad, pensamiento fronterizo y colonialidad global [The decolonization of the political economy and postcolonial studies: Transmodernity, border thought, and global coloniality]. *Tabula Rasa, 4,* 17–46.

Grosz, E. (1985). Criticism, Feminism and the Institution. An Interview with Gayatri Spivak. *Thesis Eleven, 10/11*(1), pp. 175–189.

Gumbs, A. P. (2016). M/other Ourselves: A Black Queer Feminist Genealogy for Radical Mothering. In A. P. Gumbs, C. Martens, and M. Williams (Eds.), *Revolutionary Mothering: Love on the Front Lines* (pp. 19–31). PM Press.

Gumbs, A. P. (2018). *M Archive: After the End of the World.* Duke University Press.

Haddad-Fonda, K. (2017, August 8). The Asian-African (Bandung) Conference: Fact and Fiction. Black Past. https://www.blackpast.org/global-african-history/perspectives-global-african-history/asian-african-bandung-conference-fact-and-fiction/

Hall, J. D. (2005). The Long Civil Rights Movement and the Political Uses of the Past. *The Journal of American History, 91*(4), 1233–1263.

Hammer, J. (2022, February 1). Council Agrees to Settle Marcus Deon Smith Lawsuit for $2.57 Million. *Rhino Times.* https://www.rhinotimes.com/news/council-agrees-to-settle-marcus-deon-smith-lawsuit-for-2-75-million/

Hansen, T. (2002). Zapatistas: A Brief Historical Timeline. In T. Hayden (Ed.), *The Zapatista Reader* (pp. 8–15). Thunder's Mouth Press / Nation Books.

Hartman, S. (1997). *Scenes of Subjection: Terror, Slavery, and Self-Making in Nineteenth-Century America.* Oxford University Press.

Hartman, S. (2008). *Lose Your Mother: A Journey along the Atlantic Slave Route.* Farrar, Straus, and Giroux.

Hayden, T. (2002). Introduction. In T. Hayden (Ed.), *The Zapatista Reader* (pp. 1–7). Thunder's Mouth Press / Nation Books.

Hege Library and Learning Technologies (2021). Underground Railroad in Guilford College Woods. https://library.guilford.edu/undergroundrr

Henson, B. (2021). Communication Theory from Améfrica Ladina: Amefricanidade, Lélia Gonzalez, and Black Decolonial Approaches. *Review of Communication, 21*(4), 345–362.

Hernández Chávez, A. (2006). *Mexico: A Brief History.* University of California Press.

hooks, b. (2015). *Ain't I a Woman? Black Women and Feminism.* Routledge.

Hoppe, K. (2020). Responding as Composing: Towards a Post-Anthropocentric, Feminist Ethics for the Anthropocene. *Distinktion: Journal of Social Theory, 21*(2), 125–142.

Hume, A. & Osborne, G. (2018). Ecopoetics as Expanded Critical Practice: An Introduction. In A. Hume & G. Osborne (Eds.), *Ecopoetics: Essays in the Field* (pp. 1–16). University of Iowa Press.

Icaza, I., & Vásquez, R. (2013). Social Struggles as Epistemic Struggles. *Development and Change, 44*(3), 683–704.

Kaba, M. (2021). *We Do This Til' We Free Us: Abolitionist Organizing and Transforming Justice.* Haymarket Books.

Keme, E. (2018). For Abiayala [*sic*] to Live, the Americas Must Die: Toward a Transhemispheric Indigeneity (A. Coon, Trans.). *Native American and Indigenous Studies, 5*(1), 42–68.

King, T. L. (2017). Humans Involved: Lurking in the Lines of Posthumanist Flight. *Critical Ethnic Studies, 3*(1), 162–185.

King, T. L. (2019). *The Black Shoals: Offshore Formations in Black and Native Studies*. Duke University Press.

Kishwari, S. (12 January, 2023). A New Tourist Train in Mexico Will Destroy Indigenous Land and Livelihoods. *Time Magazine*. https://time.com/6245748/maya-train-tulum-yucatan-indigenous-people-land/

Kopkind, A. (2002). Opening Shots. In T. Hayden (Ed.), *The Zapatista Reader* (pp. 19–21). Thunder's Mouth Press / Nation Books. (Originally appeared as an unsigned editorial in *The Nation*, January 31, 1994)

Kowal, R. J. (2004). *Staging the Greensboro Sit-Ins*. TDR, *48*(4), 135–154.

Koyama, E. (26 July, 2001). The Transfeminist Manifesto. Retrieved from https://www.academia.edu/2754487/The_transfeminist_manifesto.

La Comisión Sexta del EZLN. (2015). *El pensamiento crítico frente a la hidra capitalista* [Critical thought in the face of the capitalist hydra]. CIDECI-Uniteirra.

Law, J. (2015). What's Wrong with a One-World World? *Distinktion: Scandinavian Journal of Social Theory, 16*(1), 126–139.

Law, R. (1992). *Oyo Empire, c. 1600–c. 1836: West African Imperialism in the Era of the Atlantic Slave Trade*. Ashgate.

Leyva Solano, X. (1999). De las cañadas a Europa: Niveles, actores, y discursos del Nuevo Movimiento Zapatista (1994–1997) [From the valleys to Europe: Layers, actors, and discourses of the New Zapatista Movement (1994–1997)]. *Desacatos: Revista de ciencias sociales, 1*(1), 56–87.

Leyva Solano, X., & Sonnleitner, W. (2000). ¿Qué es el neoZapatismo? [What is NeoZapatismo?] *Espiral, 6*(17), 163–201.

López Intzín, J. (2013). I ch'el ta muk': La trama en la construcción del *Lekil kuxlejal* (vida plena-digna-justa) [I ch' el ta muk': The storyline in the construction of *Lekil Kuxlejal* (full-dignified-just life)]. In G. Méndez Torres, J. López Intzín, S. Marcos, and C. Osorio Hernández (Eds.), *Sentir-pensar el género: Perspectivas desde los pueblos originarios* [Feel-think gender: Perspectives from original peoples] (pp. 73–106). Taller Editorial La Casa del Mago.

López Intzín, J. (2015). I ch'el ta muk': La trama en la construcción del *Lekil kuxlejal*. Hacia una hermeneusis intercultural o visibilización de saberes desde la matricialidad del sentipensar-sentisaber Tseltal [I ch' el ta muk': The storyline in the construction of *Lekil Kuxlejal*. Towards an intercultural hermeneusis or visibilization of knowledges molded from Tseltal feel-thinking and feel-knowing]. In X. Leyva Solano, C. Pascal, A. Köhler, H. Olguín Reza, and M. Velasco Contreras (Eds.), *Prácticas otras de conocimiento(s): Entre crisis, entre guerras* [Other practices of knowing(s): Between crises, between wars] (Vol. 1). (pp. 181–198). Taller Editorial La Casa del Mago.

López y Rivas, G. (2022, December 4). El corredor interoceánico y el interés nacional-popular [The interoceanic corridor and the national-popular interest]. *La Jornada*. https://www.jornada.com.mx/2022/12/04/opinion/011a2pol.

Lorde, A. (1978). *The Collected Poems of Audre Lorde*. W. W. Norton and Company.

Lorde, A. (1984). *Sister Outsider: Essays and Speeches by Audre Lorde*. Crossing Press.

Lugones, M. (2007). Heterosexualism and the Colonial/Modern Gender System. *Hypatia, 22*(1), 186–209.

Lugones, M. (2010). Toward a Decolonial Feminism. *Hypatia, 24*(4), 742–759.

Magno, M. D. (1980, June 26). América Ladina: Introdução a uma abertura [América Ladina: Introduction to an opening]. *Acesso à Lida de Fi-Menina (Seminário)* (pp. 145–165). Nova-Mente Editora.

Maldonado-Torres, N. (2007). On the coloniality of being: Contributions to the development of a concept. *Cultural Studies, 21*(2–3), 240–270.

Marcos, S. (2021a). Reflexiones sobre las luchas de las Zapatistas ¿feministas? [Reflections on the struggles of the (feminist)? Zapatista women]. *Bajo el volcán. Revisita del posgrado de sociología. BUAP, 3*(5), 395–409.

Marcos, S. (2021b, June 21). Otroa Compañeroa. La fluidez de género: Una emergencia contemporánea con raíces ancestrales [Other companion. Gender fluidity: A contemporary emergence with ancestral roots]. *Camino al andar.* https://www.caminoalandar.org/post/otroa-compa%C3%B1eroa-la-fluidez-de-g%C3%A9nero-una-emergencia-contempor%C3%A1nea-con-ra%C3%ADces-ancestrales.

Marshall, C. (2019, May 15). Wood Wide Web: Trees' Social Networks Are Mapped. *BBC News.* https://www.bbc.com/news/science-environment-48257315

Matory, J. L. (2005). *Sex and the Empire That Is No More: Gender and the Politics of Metaphor in Oyo Yoruba Religion.* Berghahn Books.

Mbembe, A. (2012). Necropolítica: Una revisión crítica [Necropolitics: A Critical Revision]. In E. Chávez McGregor (Ed.), *Estética y violencia: Necropolítica, militarización y vidas lloradas* [Aesthetics and violence: Necropolitics, militarization, and mourned Lives] (pp. 131–137). Museo Universitario de Arte Contemporáneo.

McKittrick, K. (2015). Yours in the Intellectual Struggle: Sylvia Wynter and the Realization of the Living. In K. McKittrick (Ed.). *Sylvia Wynter: On Being Human as Praxis* (pp. 1–8). Duke University Press.

McDowell, I. (2021, February 18). Seven of the Eight GPD Police Officers Who Hogtied Marcus Smith Received Merit Raises. *Yes! Weekly.* https://www.yesweekly.com/news/seven-of-the-eight-gpd-officers-who-hogtied-marcus-smith-received-merit-raises/article_f7af18ac-713a-11eb-aee2-27a895c7be60.html

Mendoza, B. (2014). La epistemología del sur, la colonialidad de género y el feminism latinoamericano [The Epistemology of the south, the coloniality of gender and Latin American feminism]. In Y. Espinosa Miñoso, D. Gómez Correal, and K. Ochoa Muñoz (Eds.). *Tejiendo de otro modo: Feminismo, epistemología y apuestas descoloniales en Abya Yala* [Weaving another way: Feminism, epistemology, and decolonial commitments in Abya Yala] (pp. 91–104). Editorial Universidad del Cauca.

Mignolo, W. (2000). *Local Histories / Global Designs: Coloniality, Subaltern Knowledges, and Border Thinking.* Princeton University Press.

Mignolo, W. (2008). Revisando las reglas del juego: Conversación con Pablo Iglesias Turrion, Jesus Espadín López, e Iñigo Errejón Galván [Revising the rules of the game: A conversation with Pablo Iglesias Turrion, Jesus Espadín López, and Iñigo Errejón Galván]. *Tabula Rasa, 8,* 321–334.

Mignolo, W. (2011). Epistemic Disobedience and the Decolonial Option: A Manifesto. *Transmodernity: Journal of Peripheral Cultural Production of the Luso-Hispanic World, 1*(2), 44–66.

Mignolo, W., & Walsh, C. (2018). *On Decoloniality: Concepts, Analytics, Praxis.* Duke University Press.

Mitchell, M. (2022, November 29). Building Resilient Organizations: Toward Joy and Durable Power in a Time of Crisis. *Non-Profit Quarterly.* https://nonprofitquarterly.org/building-resilient-organizations-toward-joy-and-durable-power-in-a-time-of-crisis/

Mora, M. (2018). *Política Kuxlejal: Autonomía Indígena, el estado racial e investigación descolonizante en comunidades Zapatistas* [Kuxlejal politics: Indigenous autonomy, the racial state, and decolonizing research in Zapatista communities]. CIESAS.

Nash, J. (2021). Birth Geographies: Race, Reproductive Justice, and the Politics of the Hospital. *Harvard Journal of Law and Gender, 44*(2), 299–38.

Navarro, L. H. (1999, March). The San Andrés Accords: Indians and the Soul. *Cultural Survival Quarterly Magazine.* https://www.culturalsurvival.org/publications/cultural-survival-quarterly/san-andres-accords-indians-and-soul

Noé, I. (2009). Site Particular. In S. R. Riley & L. Hunter (Eds.), *Mapping Landscapes for Performance as Research: Scholarly Acts and Creative Cartographies* (pp. 149–150). Palgrave MacMillan.

Now This News. (2018, April 5). *Sistersong on North Carolina's Ban on Shackling Pregnant Inmates* [Video]. YouTube. https://www.youtube.com/watch?v=gLg3-nRXS2o

Oropeza, D. (2021a, May 6). Squadron 421: Zapatistas Sail Against the Grain of History. *Schools for Chiapas.* https://schoolsforChiapas.org/squadron-421-Zapatistas-sail-against-the-grain-of-history/

Oropeza, D. (2021b, August 18). Zapatistas, Women, and Gender Dissidents: On the Encounter in Notre Dame des Landes. *Pie de Página.* https://piedepagina.mx/Zapatistas-women-and-gender-dissidents-on-the-encounter-in-notre-dame-des-landes/

Oyěwùmí, O. (1997). *The Invention of Women: Making an African Sense of Western Gender Discourses.* University of Minnesota Press.

Packer, T. (2021). Guns, Torches, and Badges: The 1979 Greensboro Massacre, the Charlottesville Unite the Right Rally, and the Last Impacts of Racial Violence on Black and Anti-Racist Communities. *Souls: A Critical Journal of Black Politics, Culture and Society, 22*(2–4), 141–159.

Page, C., & Woodland, E. (2023). *Healing Justice Lineages: Dreaming at the Crossroads of Liberation, Collective Care, and Safety.* North Atlantic Books.

Quashie, K. (2012). *The Sovereignty of Quiet: Beyond Resistance in Black Culture.* Rutgers University Press.

Quijano, A. (1992). Colonialidad y modernidad/racionalidad. *Peru Indig, 13*(29), 11–20.

Quijano, A. (2007). Coloniality and Modernity/Rationality (S. Therborn, Trans.). *Cultural Studies, 21*(2–3), 168–178.

Rauch, N. F., & Schachtel, E. L. (2020). Zapatismo, una identidad en constante movimiento [Zapatismo, an identity in constant movement]. *Revista electrónica de psicología política, 18*(4), 17–41.

Rios, F. (2019). Améfrica Ladina: The Conceptual Legacy of Lélia Gonzalez (1935–1994). *LASA Forum, 50*(3), 75–79.

Ríos-Quiroz, D., Castillo-Santiago, M. A., Guízar-Vásquez Jr., F. G., & Medina-Sansón, M. L. (2021). Historias y cambios en el paisaje en dos ejidos de la Selva Lacandona, Chiapas [History and landscape changes in two "ejidos" of the Lacandona Rainforest, Chiapas]. *Cuadernos geográficos, 60*(2), 236–254.

Roberts, D. (2017). *Killing the Black Body: Race, Reproduction, and the Meaning of Liberty.* Vintage Books. (Original work published 1997).

Rodríguez Aguilar, M. Y. (2021). Grieving geographies, mourning waters: Life, death, and environmental gendered racialized struggles in Mexico. *Feminist Anthropology.* https://doi.org/10.1002/fea2.12060

Ross, L. J. (2017). Reproductive Justice as Intersectional Feminist Activism. *Souls, 19*(3), 286–314.

Sharpe, C. (2016). *In the Wake: On Blackness and Being.* Duke University Press.

Sherman, S., Scheer, G., Boyette, J., & Howe, P. (2013). *The Elsewhere Storybook*. Elsewhere Museum. https://static1.squarespace.com/static/5ef1e060a980b2706df431b2/t/5f91c7368c5194 7af4b7dcbd/1603389253097/Elsewhere_TheStorybook.pdf.

Shotwell, A. (2016). *Against Purity: Living Ethically in Compromised Times*. University of Minnesota Press.

Simpson, A. (2014). *Mohawk Interruptus: Political Life across the Borders of Settler States*. Duke University Press.

Sirenio, K. (2021, September 5). 'Compañeroa es una palabra que te incluye como eres': Marijose [Compañeroa is a word that includes you as you are: Marijose]. *Pie de página*. https:// piedepagina.mx/companeroa-es-una-palabra-que-te-incluye-como-eres-marijose/

SisterSong Women of Color Reproductive Justice Collective. (2021). *Advocates Secure an End to the Shackling of People in Labor in NC* [Press Release] https://myemail.constantcontact.com/ PRESS-RELEASE--NC-Prison-Officials-Agree-to-End-the-Shackling-of-People-in-Labor-. html?soid=1102470515351&aid=qmI3MIAUaBQ

Sojourner Truth Memorial Committee. (27 February, 2022). Sojourner Truth's Famous Speech: Ar'n't I A Woman? Ain't I A Woman. *Sojourner in the News*. https:// sojournertruthmemorial.org/sojourner-truths-famous-speech-arnt-i-a-woman-aint-i-a- woman/#:~:text=The%20accuracy%20of%20this%20account%20has%20been%20challenged, language%2C%20and%20some%20clear%20errors%20about%20Sojourner%E2%80%99s%20 life

Snorton, C. R. (2017). *Black on Both Sides: A Racial History of Trans Identity*. University of Minnesota Press.

Spillers, H. (1987). Mama's Baby, Papa's Maybe: An American Grammar Book. *Diacritics, 17*(2), 64–81.

Stanley, E. (2011). Near Life, Queer Death: Overkill and Ontological Capture. *Social Text, 29*(2[107]), 1–20.

Sweat, C. (2018, March 26). State Prisons Announce New Action on Shackling Pregnant Inmates. *WRAL News*. https://www.wral.com/state-prisons-announce-new-action-on-shackling- pregnant-inmates-/17444938/

Taylor, D. (2016). *Performance* (A. Levine, Trans.). Duke University Press.

Taylor, D. (2020). *¡Presente! The Politics of Presence*. Duke University Press.

Taylor, F. (2019, September 8). Marcus Deon Smith Was Killed 1 Year Ago by Police. His Life Still Matters. *Truthout*. https://truthout.org/articles/marcus-deon-smith-was-killed-1-year-ago- by-police-his-life-still-matters/

Tinsley, N. O. (2008). Black Atlantic, Queer Atlantic: Queer Imaginings of the Middle Passage. *GLQ, 14*(2–3), 191–215.

Toledo, V. M. (2015). *Ecocidio en México: La batalla final es por la vida* [Ecocide in Mexico: The final battle is for life]. Grijalbo.

UCPA (União dos Coletivos Pan-Africanistas). (2018). *Primavera para as Rosas Negras: Lélia Gonzalez* [Spring for the Black Roses: Lélia Gonzalez]. Editora Filhas da África.

Valencia, S. (2018). *Gore Capitalism* (J. Pluecker, Trans.). Cambridge University Press.

Valencia, S. (2019). Necropolitics, Postmortem/Transmortem Politics, and Transfeminisms in the Sexual Economies of Death. *Transgender Studies Quarterly, 6*(2), 180–193.

Walcott, R. (2020). Diaspora, Transnationalism, and the Decolonial Project. In King, T. L., Navarro, J., & Smith, A. (Eds.), *Otherwise Worlds: Against Settler Colonialism and Anti- Blackness* (pp. 343–361). Duke University Press.

Walsh, C. (2013). Introducción: Lo pedagógico y lo decolonial, entretejiendo caminos [Introduction: The pedagogical and the decolonial, interweaving paths]. In C. Walsh (Ed.), *Pedagogías decoloniales: Prácticas insurgents de resistir, (re)existir, y (re)vivir* [Decolonial pedagogies: Insurgent practices for resisting, (re)existing, and (re)living] (Vol. 1) (pp. 23–68). Ediciones Abya-Yala.

Walsh, C. (2014). Pedagogical Notes from the Decolonial Cracks. *E-misférica, 11*(1). https://hemisphericinstitute.org/en/emisferica-11-1-decolonial-gesture/11-1-dossier/pedagogical-notes-from-the-decolonial-cracks.html

Walsh, C. (2017). Gritos, grietas y siembras de vida: Entretejeres de lo pedagógico y lo decolonial [Screams, cracks, and sowings of life: Interweavings of the pedagogical and the decolonial]. In C. Walsh (Ed.), *Pedagogías decoloniales: Prácticas insurgents de resistir, (re)existir, y (re)vivir* [Decolonial Pedagogies: Insurgent Practices for Resisting, (Re)existing, and (Re)living] (Vol. 2) (pp. 17–45). Ediciones Abya-Yala.

Walsh, C. (2023). *Rising Up, Living On: Re-Existences, Sowings, and Decolonial Cracks.* Duke University Press.

Warren, C. L. (2018). *Ontological Terror: Blackness, Nihilism, and Emancipation.* Duke University Press.

Wilderson III, F., & King. T. L. (2020). In King, T. L., Navarro, J., & Smith, A. (Eds.) *Otherwise Worlds: Against Settler Colonialism and Anti-Blackness* (pp. 52–76). Duke University Press.

Willets, S. (2020, May 8). Black Mama's Bail Out and the Abolition of Cash Bail. *Ms.* https://msmagazine.com/2020/05/08/held-for-ransom-dismantling-the-unjust-cash-bail-system/

Williams, S. and Coleman, D. (2021). Elsewhere. In T. Loud & Z. Charlton (Eds.), *Out of Place: Artists, Pedagogy, and Purpose* (pp. 254–263). Punctum Books.

Wynter, S. (1995). 1492: A New World View. In V. Lawrence Hyatt & R. Nettleford (Eds.), *Race, Discourse, and the Origin of the Americas: A New World View* (pp. 5–57). Smithsonian Institution Press.

Wynter, S. (2003). Unsettling the Coloniality of Being/Power/Truth/Freedom: Towards the Human, after Man, Its Overrepresentation—An Argument. *CR: The New Centennial Review, 3*(3), 257–337.

Yusoff, K. (2018). *A Billion Black Anthropocenes or None.* University of Minnesota Press.

Zapatista Women. (2018, March 26). Words of the Zapatista Women at the Closing Ceremony of the First International Gathering of Politics, Art, Sport, and Culture for Women in Struggle in the Zapatista Caracol of the Tzotz Choj Zone. *Enlace Zapatista.* https://enlaceZapatista.ezln.org.mx/2018/03/26/words-of-the-Zapatista-women-at-the-closing-ceremony-of-the-first-international-gathering-of-politics-art-sport-and-culture-for-women-in-struggle-in-the-Zapatista-caracol-of-the-tzotz-choj-zone/

Zapatista Women. (2019, February 13). Letter from Zapatista Women to Women in Struggle Around the World. *Enlace Zapatista.* http://enlaceZapatista.ezln.org.mx/2019/02/13/letter-from-the-Zapatista-women-to-women-in-struggle-around-the-world/?fbclid=IwAR1Di7Eoy4sqqN4hYFWOThM5lviexxG1tw5kiHuiySl9GOrykfKCf7kL72s

INDEX

Page numbers in italic indicate figures.

www.ingramcontent.com/pod-product-compliance
Lightning Source LLC
Chambersburg PA
CBHW020705270326
41928CB00005B/274